Realms of the Self

THE GOTHAM LIBRARY
OF THE NEW YORK UNIVERSITY PRESS

The Gotham Library is a series of original works and critical studies published in paperback primarily for student use. The Gotham hardcover edition is primarily for use by libraries and the general reader. Devoted to significant works and major authors and to literary topics of enduring importance, Gotham Library texts offer the best in literature and criticism.

Comparative and Foreign Language Literature:
Robert J. Clements, Editor

Comparative and English Language Literature:
James W. Tuttleton, Editor

Realms of The Self

Variations on a Theme in Modern Drama

Arthur Ganz

New York University Press · New York *and* London

Copyright © 1980 by New York University

Library of Congress Cataloging in Publication Data

Ganz, Arthur F   1928-
   Realms of the self.

   (The Gotham library of the New York University Press)

Bibliography: p.
   Includes index.
   1. Drama—20th century—History and criticism.
2. Drama—19th century—History and criticism.
3. Self in literature. I. Title.
PN1851.G23   809.2′9353   80-16755
ISBN 0-8147-2979-7
ISBN 0-8147-2980-0 (pbk.)

Manufactured in the United States of America

Parts of these chapters have appeared previously in different form. The essays on Wilde, Synge, and Shaw derive from material published in *Modern Drama,* those on Chekhov and Miller from articles in *Drama Survey.* Earlier discussions of Giraudoux and Williams were published in *PMLA* and *The American Scholar* respectively. The study of Pinter is based on essays in the *Educational Theatre Journal* and in PINTER: A Collection of Critical Essays © 1972, Prentice-Hall, Inc., Englewood Cliffs, N.J. The author extends his thanks to the editors who have kindly granted permission to draw on these sources.

For
MARGARET
Who gave me her undivided attention.

Acknowledgments

This book, written over a number of years in the intervals between teaching duties, undoubtedly owes much to friends and students whose thoughts I have unconsciously appropriated. If I
cannot truly express contrition, I can at least offer my thanks. I
would also like to express my gratitude to the American Philosophical Society for a grant that helped further my work on Shaw. My
colleague Arthur Golden was consistently encouraging. To my
teacher Eric Bentley I owe a special debt, for his work demonstrated to me what the study of the drama should be. Ruby Cohn
kindly read the manuscript of this book in an early form, offering
thoughtful comment and generous support. My wife's contributions to this book are acknowledged in the dedication, but they
remain quite beyond measure, consisting of time (taken from her
work), insights, and much forbearance.

Contents

Introduction

If asked to choose a date for the beginning of the modern drama, few of us would immediately select 1866. But since it marks the year in which Henrik Ibsen, by publishing the vast, heroic verse drama *Brand,* began the process that turned him from an unsuccessful provincial playwright into a figure of consequence in European literature, that date is at least a candidate for the honor. *Brand,* however, is more than an arbitrary starting point. Although its extravagant scope and exalted diction are alien to the dominant theatrical forms of our time, something of its hero's relentless aspiration toward self-fulfillment pervades a surprising number of significant plays in this century. As Brand, by an effort of will attempts to transform the imperfect world about him into a realm where the self may live out its dreams unimpeded, he is anticipating an action often to be repeated in the history of the modern theater. Brand is the least amiable of heroes, but he would have understood the impulse, voiced again after almost a hundred years of drama by the kindly Bérenger of Ionesco's *The Killer,* to recapture the moment when he had recognized himself as "a smiling being in a smiling world."

But in our theatre this impulse is seldom realized, and then only through the exercise of a special kind of imagination. If later heroes tend not to be swept away in the grandeur of an avalanche—Willy Loman's automobile "accident" is a more typical catastrophe—they have at least engaged in a similar effort to reshape a world. Figures like Brand, demonic moralists demanding an exalted spiritual commitment beyond ordinary affections and limitations, may be out of fashion in both contemporary life and theatre, but the dream of total fulfillment—of the achievement of a self intimately known, boundlessly loved, wholly expressed, and at peace in a world attuned to its desires—continues to haunt our culture and our drama. In that sense, Brand, a tragic hero for Ibsen, is an archetypal presence for the modern theater, the first in a long line extending from such figures as Hedda Gabler, through Barbara Undershaft and Henry IV, to Sartre's Orestes and the hero of Sam Shepard's *La Turista*, all of whom run up against the circumstances of society and the restrictions of the human temperament in their search for a world where the self may be at rest.

Our dream of reshaping or finding this world and realizing the self within its sheltering borders is, as this study suggests, part of our romantic [1] inheritance. That to some degree we all share it is the sign of its post-romantic modernity. The Faustian Brand is extraordinary in the intensity of his aspiration, but unlike Marlowe's Renaissance Faustus, Brand sets himself before his world as a messianic leader demanding that all men be as he is. Few of us have not heard at least echoes of that demand, have not felt that the world should so arrange itself as to make the fulfillment of our ideal selves possible, even as the surprise at its failure to do so has steadily decreased. For if we have inherited the romantic ideal of the self and its capacity for realization, we have also inherited its inevitable counterpart, the skepticism about the trustworthiness of the instincts, the nobility of the savage, the profundity of the child. In modern drama the search for self-fulfillment is marked by a consistently qualified confidence in its overt achievement; the realm of the self tends more and more to be conceived in visionary, private, inner terms.

Since this book is directly concerned with remarkable thematic similarities and only incidentally with the common romantic sources of these congruences, the nature of a playwright's ancestral allegiance will be suggested only from time to time. The emphasis will always be on the individual plays and on their relationship to each other and to the work of the other playwrights. Each writer is here considered in an individual section; the writers most closely related are grouped in chapters; and the book as a whole comprises two parallel units. In one way or another, the playwrights in the first part of this book all preserve the dream of an ideal world and of a self worthy to inhabit it. Through some strategy of transcendence they try to create in the realm of art a world in which the self can flower. Oscar Wilde and John M. Synge would seem to have little in common except their roots in that Anglo-Irish Protestant class that has shaped so much of modern literature, but in fact the artistic strategies they evolve for escaping the restrictions the real world imposes on the self are astonishingly similar. In the work of both the world is reshaped into a realm of art where the limitations of life can be surpassed and perfection achieved through beauty. By making self-realization an essentially aesthetic process Wilde escapes the moral restraints of Victorian society and Synge his pervasive sense of inevitable mortality.

But for the more complex writers dealt with in Chapter 2 so comparatively simple a transformation of reality is not adequate. In his special way each of these finds some method of transcending the boundaries of the real world without denying its nature. In Chekhov self-fullment is postponed to some future far beyond the lifetimes of his characters; in Shaw it is found in a "heaven," real or metaphoric, to which certain characters ascend; in Giraudoux a supramortal world summons his heroes to forsake the human one. Each of these playwrights, though he has shaped a world that admits of total fulfillment, nevertheless retains an allegiance to the real one where work is done, as in Chekhov and Shaw, or where life has its own graces, as in Giraudoux. Moreover, the consciousness in all five of these dramatists that they are juxtaposing, often incongruously, the limited world of reality and their ideal helps make each of them a major comic artist.

Although laughter comes at moments to all of the writers in the second part of this book, it comes less often and less amiably. For these playwrights, most of them more nearly contemporary, find some deep division or chasm between the self and the surrounding world that frustrates an even more intense desire for self-fulfillment. And when their characters descend into the inner world to battle with monsters there, they often find that their private refuge has become a prison.

Despite notable differences in temperament and apparent subject matter, the two American playwrights included here, Tennessee Williams and Arthur Miller, share, as Wilde and Synge did, a central vision and, in tune with those earlier writers, retain at least a dream of the self as innocent and thus as capable of a happy fulfillment. In the private passional world of Tennessee Williams the self struggles to maintain a belief in its innocence against the encroachments of a judgment of guilt. Although Arthur Miller has looked outward on the politics and economics of our times, his most striking utterances are voiced from within a personal family world of a father, mother, and two rival brothers that recurs throughout his work. In this world the self attempts to assert its innocence, not through love, as in Williams, but through knowledge—through a cleansing recognition of its own nature.

Once again, as it did in the first half of this book, the work of three playwrights of greater weight and power embodies the full complexity of the theme of self and world. Set in the outer world of bourgeois life and even of Norwegian politics, Ibsen's plays nevertheless deal centrally with a conflict within the self between an impulse toward fulfillment through gratification and an opposing tendency toward stern self-exaltation. But whereas the internal struggle in Ibsen is between conflicting impulses as the self confronts the outer world, in Pirandello the barrier between the realm of external actions and presences and the inner one of self-perception is the central source of torment. For Harold Pinter, as for Ibsen, one aspect of the self seeks power and aggrandizement while another opposes this impulse. Yet so fearful have been the discoveries in the inner world that Pirandello began to explore (it is, we sense, the true setting of Pinter's plays) that the aggrandizing impulse can be dealt with only by lethargy and withdrawal, by an imperative denial of the vital instincts. With Pinter, we have come to the ultimate retreat from those forces of aspiration in which so much trust had once been placed.

To convey adequately—through the close study of a group of playwrights, major and lesser—how central the theme of the self questing for a world of fulfillment is in the modern drama, writers from the "classic" period around the turn of the century as well as more recent figures had to be included. But since the familiar procession of major playwrights would not have suggested the range inherent in this material, some selection was essential to find room for those crucial figures of limited but intriguing achievement whose variety gives our theatre much of its special flavor, and to allow a demonstration of the pervasiveness of a theme not only down the length of the modern drama but dominating the significant work of specific dramatists.

Aside from considerations of space, other reasons would have made the inclusion of certain widely admired figures problematic. The work of Strindberg and Brecht, for example, is certainly relevant to the theme of this book. The desperate battles for power in Strindberg's earlier plays and the images of aspiration (e.g., the flowering castle of *A Dream Play*), in the later ones suggest a self torn between impulses of aggrandizement and abnegation. The macabre world of capitalist exploitation through which so many of Brecht's heroes move is, at least arguably, a symbolic projection for an inner world in which the self struggles for dominance. But to discuss the works of these playwrights at length would, for this writer, have entailed in both cases a downward revaluation of their present stature, an argument deeply distracting from the purposes of this book. No such reassessment is called for in the case of Samuel Beckett, whose contributions to the theatre have been equalled only by those of the great playwrights from the turn of the century. Yet the theme of the self in retreat from its own claims to power, so central to Beckett's drama and this book, is in Beckett part of a larger metaphysic, whereas in the work of his disciple Harold Pinter it is treated with the greater clarity and concentration that a writer of narrower range sometimes offers. Not only is Pinter's work more immediately helpful to the aims of this volume, but a further benefit accrues from focusing on him rather than on his mentor. If, as a critic has despairingly observed, Beckett is beginning to overtake Napoleon, Wagner, and Jesus as an object of discourse, perhaps there is some virtue in forgoing, at least for the moment, the addition of one more grain to that "impossible heap" (to lift a phrase from *Endgame*) of criticism that the devout must contemplate with mixed feelings: reverence, fatigue, and terror.

The pattern of this book's arrangement, suggesting significant relations of playwrights to each other and breaking through conventional categories of chronology and style, is best able to illumine crucial connections of theme and substance. The very conjunctions and congruences suggested earlier (the creation of an aesthetic refuge in the theater of Wilde and Synge; the conception of a transcendent realm energizing the work of Chekhov, Shaw, and Giraudoux; the affirmation of essential innocence in the plays of Williams and Miller; the struggle of the self against inner divisions in Ibsen, isolation in Pirandello, and lethargy in Pinter) reveal the plays here discussed not only as products of particular temperaments but as elements of a coherent body of literature. Both these inevitable temperamental differences and the continuing tension between realistic and nonrealistic modes have tended to mask the modern drama's unity, which resides in its persistent obsession with the quest for self-fulfullment, a quest made steadily more dubious by the vicissitudes of modern life and the treacherous perplexities of the modern consciousness.

Part I:

Excursions

1.
Wilde and Synge

Oscar Wilde: The Realm of the Dandy

In Act II of *The Importance of Being Earnest* Jack returns to his country house and announces the death of his supposed brother, the profligate Ernest:

> DR. CHASUBLE. Was the cause of death mentioned?
> JACK. A severe chill, it seems.
> MISS PRISM. As a man sows, so shall he reap.
> DR. CHASUBLE. (Raising his hand) Charity, dear Miss Prism, charity! None of us is perfect. I am myself peculiarly susceptible to draughts.[1]

When we laugh at Miss Prism's excessive moralizing and at Dr. Chasuble's suavely foolish evasion of it, we know that we are reacting to something other than a delightful joke and that our laughter is uneasy. After all, a clergyman who cannot distinguish between a moral and a physical failing should strike us as a somewhat disquieting figure, and yet in the world in which Dr. Chasuble exists his attitude seems entirely reasonable. We have come to realize that *The Importance of Being Earnest* is not, as Arthur Symons called it, "a sort of sublime farce, meaningless and delightful," or, in William Archer's words, "nothing but an absolutely willful expression of an irrepressibly witty personality," [2] but rather a richly brilliant comedy, full of force and substance. But, although the presence of that substance has been recognized, its nature remains elusive.

Otto Reinert has suggested that it is satiric, that Wilde is exposing "the ludicrous and sinister realities behind the fashionable façade of an overcivilized society," that the behavior of Gwendolen and Cecily, for example, reveals a "cynical realism" [3] usually ignored by Victorian prudery. One need not deny the existence of a satirical element in Wilde to argue that in making satire the central aim of *The Importance* one ignores something crucial in the play's tone and meaning, and one alters the real direction in which its criticism moves.

Even when Wilde is at his most critical, he retains for his social world an ambiguous admiration (quite different from the truly satiric attitude of W. S. Gilbert, whose heroines are at least as ferociously realistic as Gwendolen and Cecily but whose puppet world is always ultimately ludicrous and mechanical).[4] The provincial Irish boy who came down from Oxford to conquer London never stopped desiring the approbation of the grand social world nor believing that to be part of it was an achievement. And when the mature comic writer chose to depict London society, it was an idealized portrait of wit, luxury, and elegance that he drew. Thus, what seems to be, and to some extent is, a barbed critique of the hypocrisies of mourning in Algernon's celebrated comment on a recently widowed lady—"I hear her hair has turned quite gold from grief"—has about it something not altogether conventionally critical. Our suspicions are at least aroused when we remember that Algernon's witticism was composed by the author of Dumby's quip in *Lady Windermere's Fan:* "The youth of the present day are quite monstrous. They have absolutely no respect for dyed hair." We need not suppose that Wilde's work has total verbal consistency to believe that Dumby's remark casts a special light on Algernon's. If in Wildean terms dyed hair is a value to be respected, then it is not too fanciful to see the widowed lady as more than a woman overly hasty in her cosmetic efforts. She has freed herself from the sentimental morality of the age and re-created herself as a kind of artwork ("I never saw a woman so altered; she looks quite twenty years younger"). It is the approval, or at any rate the lack of absolute disapproval, in the tone of these words as uttered by Lady Bracknell—as curiously amoral a dowager as the Reverend Dr. Chasuble is a clergyman—which suggests that behind the conventional satiric criticism of Algernon's line there lurks a mischievous hint that the artificial, the antifamilial, the antisocial may not only be accepted but idealized.

The whole world of *The Importance,* finally, is an idealized one. To create it the Victorian society that Wilde knew is not so much criticized as transmuted into a realm of grace and wit in which the Wildean self—and all of the characters are in one way or another extensions of that self—can exist in freedom and fulfillment. However, the homeland of the Wildean self is by no means a fantasy world of vapid charm; in fact, it is like the biblical world of Wilde's *Salome,* both beautiful and sinister—the two elements being equally parts of its attraction. In place of the bejeweled costumes of Herod's court we see the exquisite dress of the London dandy; in place of the open perversity of the Princess Salome is the ambiguous morality of Dr. Chasuble and the hint that dyed hair may be superior to natural.

We find an intriguing contrast here with the work of Flaubert, whose fictional worlds embrace the gorgeous evils of *Salammbô* and the contemporary actualities that finally destroy Emma Bovary. But whereas the French realist could take his exotic dreams and suggest how absurdly they fared in the tawdriness of a Bovary world, Wilde had to gratify his need by converting London society into something more bearable, a realm of art not only unassailable by vulgarities and corruption but safe from social and sexual censure. For, however much the world of Victorian society was attractive to Wilde, however much he desired to be accepted by it, that world remained always dangerous for the secret homosexual and, in some measure, repugnant to the aesthetic critic. In *The Importance of Being Earnest,* where the worlds of art and of society become one, the elegant dandies onto whom Wilde has projected his self can find a universe as ornate and amoral as that of Wilde's biblical imaginings, a universe in which they can flourish without fear and without restraint.

To understand this world in which the self can know freedom and fulfillment we must look more closely at his society comedies, those plays where Philistine [5] Victorian society, instead of being transformed into an exquisite if sinister realm of perfect form, is dealt with in comparatively conventional terms, both intellectually and theatrically. Compounded of the well-made intrigues of the nineteenth-century theatre [6] and, more significantly, from the sentimental morality of Victorian Philistinism, these plays, though vastly inferior to *The Importance,* tell us something crucial about it: what Wilde left out of his masterpiece, what he had to leave out to create its special aesthetic realm.

All the society comedies repeat a similar pattern of action: the central character, someone who has in his past a secret sin, now yearns to be forgiven by the social world. Mrs. Erlynne, who has alienated herself from good society by running away from her husband, fills that role in *Lady Windermere's Fan,* a play whose motive force is the outcast's desire for social absolution. She knows the weaknesses of Philistine society, but Mrs. Erlynne has suffered from her ostracism and warns her daughter against a similar fate.

> MRS. ERLYNNE. You don't know what it is to fall into the pit, to be despised, mocked, abandoned, sneered at—to be an outcast! To find the door shut against one, to have to creep in by hideous by-ways, afraid every moment lest the mask should be stripped from one's face, and all the while to hear the laughter, the horrible laughter of the world, a thing more tragic than all the tears the world has ever shed. You don't know what it is. One pays for one's sin, and then one pays again, and all one's life one pays. You must never know that.

This speech is of course a piece of nineteenth-century stage rhetoric, which if it stood alone in Wilde's work could tactfully be ignored. But in every play there are passages, if not always as unfortunate in their phraseology, at any rate comparable in their content, that suggest the desire of a repentant outcast to to be released from social condemnation.

Although Mrs. Erlynne is easily recognizable as that stock figure, the woman-with-a-past, one of the innumerable descendants of Marguerite Gautier, the lady of the camellias, Wilde uses this figure for his own purposes. Played off against Mrs. Erlynne is a cold and unforgiving moralist, her daughter, Lady Windermere, whose education is the real action of the play. She learns that no one is irreproachable, that a single act is not a final indicator of character, that a sinner may be a very noble person indeed. When at the end of the play Lord Windermere tells Lord Augustus, about to marry Mrs. Erlynne, that he is getting a very clever woman, Lady Windermere, who now knows better, says: "Ah . . . you're marrying a very good woman."

The pattern is somewhat different in *A Woman of No Importance*, but the essential point remains the same. Mrs. Arbuthnot, the character who parallels Mrs. Erlynne, has, like her predecessor, a secret sin in her past, in this case an illegitimate union that has produced a son. Although Mrs. Erlynne has led a life of pleasure and wickedness and Mrs. Arbuthnot has devoted herself to good works, each is depicted as a sinner who has remained pure in heart and therefore, according to Wilde, deserves to be pardoned. As Mrs. Erlynne was opposed by the inflexible Lady Windermere, so Mrs. Arbuthnot is by the young puritan, Hester Worsley, whose conversion is no less complete: at the end of the play, when Mrs. Arbuthnot says that she and her son are outcasts and that such is God's law, Hester rebukes her, claiming that "God's law is only love." The pattern of the sinner proved noble at heart and the puritan converted is again fulfilled.

In *An Ideal Husband*, it suits Wilde's convenience to make the woman-with-a-past, in the person of Mrs. Cheveley, the villainess. Here the sinner who must be pardoned is Sir Robert Chiltern, and the puritan who must be converted is his wife. When Chiltern, who helped establish his personal fortune and thus his political career by selling a state secret, is blackmailed, he fears not only the ruin of his career but the loss of his wife, who has always idealized him. Above all, he desires her pardon and her love. "It is not the perfect, but the imperfect who have need of love," he says; "all sins, except a sin against itself, Love should forgive." Even after the threat of blackmail has been removed, Lady Chiltern demands that her husband retire from public life, but she finally relents and comes to realize that, as Lord Goring says, "women are not meant to judge us, but to forgive us when we need forgiveness. Pardon, not punishment is their mission."

It is easy to see the concealed sin and the plea for acceptance and forgiveness as a reflection of the situation forced upon Wilde by his homosexuality. In his *Journal* (26 June 1913) André Gide hints at a concealed meaning in Wilde's plays, presumably along these lines. Robert Merle in his excellent study of Wilde is more specific.[7] He suggests not only that Wilde, in demanding pardon for his sinners, is demanding pardon for himself but that Wilde makes this demand most strongly for Mrs. Arbuthnot because her sin, like his, is sexual.[8]

What Merle says is true, but to see in Wilde's plays, or even in the Philistine sections of them, only a reflection of his sexual inversion is to limit them unnecessarily. For example, Wilde's treatment of the woman-with-a-past (Chiltern is a male variant on this figure; the golden-hearted prostitute is a plebian descendant) goes beyond being merely a hidden rationalization of his sexual conduct. When we trace this figure back to perhaps its most significant source, the heroine of Rousseau's *La Nouvelle Héloïse,* we recognize at once that in Wilde the meaning of this figure is far closer to Rousseau's conception than to that of Dumas *fils.* Whereas in Dumas the figure is the vehicle of a critique, however modest, of the social and sexual standards of the bourgeoisie, in Wilde it is a means for asserting both the radical innocence of the self and a closely related motif, the idea of redemption through love. When, because she has loved her daughter, Mrs. Erlynne's transgressions are washed away and she is certified as "a very good woman," Wilde is partaking in a crucial nineteenth-century religious transformation in which the capacity to love supplants grace and pardon as the means of recovering a state of purity. Thus, however debased their artistic mode, Mrs. Erlynne and Mrs. Arbuthnot and Sir Robert Chiltern bring to mind other, far grander presences in nineteenth-century culture: the Ancient Mariner, for example, delivered when he blessed the water snakes "unawares," or Tannhaüser, the knight of song, who, though he had lain in the arms of Venus, could demand his release from her enslavement ("O Königin, Göttin lass mich ziehen") and ultimately be redeemed through love.

Yet, as we distinguish the psychological and even religious themes that Wilde touches on, we must be careful not to deny the plays' more directly social concerns. The figure of the woman-with-a-past also embodies a concern with social estrangement, but here too we must avoid unduly circumscribing its meaning. Wilde's sexual exile from English society was part of a broader dissociation from a culture that had come more and more to reserve its greatest admiration for scientific and mercantile rather than aesthetic achievements. Nevertheless, Wilde's social feelings always remained ambiguous. Whatever his reservations about his culture, he could never accept the role of the exile until it was forced upon him by the disaster of his personal life. Thus, in the fantasy world of his society comedies the exile always repents, always desires forgiveness, and always receives it. In these divided feelings Wilde shared something of the impulses of the great exile artists of his day, even if he lacked some of their gifts and their steadiness of purpose. Although Ibsen took the small Norwegian town of his youth and, turning it into a microcosm of the bourgeois universe, revealed its weaknesses and hypocrisies to the world, he was drawn back to his native country to spend his old age and to die there. If Ibsen's admirer, James Joyce, lived out his exile to the death, he remained even more obsessed with the minutiae of the life of his birthplace and, in a sense, left Dublin only to live there eternally. Ibsen, offending all of Europe and yet coveting public honors, and Joyce, forever re-creating in art the world he had fled, are only the most obvious exemplars (obvious by the scope of their achievements and the simple, geographical nature of their removal) of the exile artist's ambivalent attitude toward the middle-class world. Long before he was thrust out of respectable society Wilde, too, was an exile artist, and like others of the kind he never finally freed himself of the desire to come home.

The Philistine aspects of his plays invariably brought out the worst in Wilde as a stylist, but because his language rings false we cannot assume the emotion that produces it is untrue. Behind the mechanical facades of their well-made plots the society comedies are deeply expressive of the isolation of an artist and an individual man. Their Philistine aspects reveal that the dandiacal stance in Wilde was not a casual pose nor the easy expression of an impulse to amuse but the product of an emotional and intellectual conflict visible in the division of his plays into opposing parts. For even as the sentimental melodrama of the society comedies suggests a profound commitment to Philistine values, the dandiacal sections of these plays and—more significant still—the whole of *The Importance of Being Earnest* indicate a simultaneous commitment to a radically contradictory vision of life. When Wilde rejected the coarseness, the pitiless morality, and the incomprehension of beauty in his society, this most extreme of aesthetic critics, in search of a new basis for life, turned to the only part of experience in which he had faith—to art, whose secret for him lay in the achievement of perfect form. It is the pursuit of form turned into a mode of life (aesthetics replacing ethics) that he introduced into his plays cloaked with the elegance and wit of nineteenth-century dandyism.

Wilde must have seen himself as a follower of such men as Brummell; Byron; d'Orsay; and, probably above all others, Disraeli, like himself an artist, a man apart from the crass bourgeoisie, whose wit and extraordinary dress were instruments with which he had achieved a position of power.[9] With Disraeli in mind, a remark by Lord Illingworth in *A Woman of No Importance,* "a man who can dominate a London dinner table can dominate the world," is a little less bizarre than it at first seems.

Disraeli, however, was only an example; Barbey d'Aurevilly and Baudelaire were the theorists of dandyism as a philosophy of life and art. In *Du Dandyisme et de Georges Brummell,* Barbey, still a figure of some note when Wilde frequented Parisian literary circles, had presented the most elaborate nineteenth-century disquisition on dandyism. Barbey never saw dandyism as a mere matter of elegance in dress but as a philosophy, as a "manner of living composed entirely of nuance, as always happens in societies at once very ancient and very civilized." His insistence on dandyism as a rule of conduct for a society past its prime must have impressed the decadents of the 1890s, but the element that would most have appealed to Wilde was Barbey's view of the dandy as individualist, as "the element of caprice in a stratified and symmetrical society." The dandy demonstrates his individualism and superiority with his wit, by shocking without being shocked. He is one of those "who wish to produce surprise while remaining impassive."

If Wilde did not adopt the theory of dandyism from Barbey, he probably became familiar with it, or at any rate reinforced it, through Baudelaire's essay "Le Dandy." Like Barbey, Baudelaire insisted that "dandyism is not, as many unreflecting persons seem to think, an immoderate taste for dress and material elegance. These things are for the perfect dandy only a symbol of the aristocratic superiority of his spirit." Dandyism is individualism, "the ardent need to produce something original . . . it is a kind of cult of the self . . . it is the pleasure of astonishing and the proud satisfaction of never being astonished." But it is also the compulsion to distinguish himself from the ordinary in an effete, unworthy era. "Dandyism," wrote Baudelaire, "is the last burst of heroism in a decadent age." Wilde called dandyism a philosophy; Baudelaire went even further: "in fact," he wrote, "I would not be entirely wrong in considering dandyism as a sort of religion." [10]

In Wilde's plays, where the religion of dandyism is translated into art, we see what he took from his sources and what he added to them. To Wilde, as to Barbey and Baudelaire, dandyism was not an affectation of dress but an attitude toward the world, and specifically toward the world of Victorian Philistinism with its materialism and its code of puritanical morality. The French theorists reinforced in Wilde the idea of the dandy as committed to "the cult of the self," a heroic individualist who, like Disraeli as Wilde saw him, used his grace and wit to oppose and dominate the crass world about him. In the society comedies, where the Philistine world has equal status with the dandiacal, the conflict between them is clear and open. The Philistine may insist that his heart has remained pure, but he admits that he has sinned and asks society for pardon. The dandy, however, instead of acknowledging his sin, denies that sin exists and creates a set of dandiacal standards by which he indicts society itself. The Philistine is humble, the dandy belligerent; the Philistine's defense is sentimental rhetoric, whereas the dandy's weapon is wit. In *The Importance of Being Earnest,* however, their relationship is more subtle. Here, where *everyone* is ultimately a dandy, the Philistine world is present only indirectly, in such elements as the solemnity of Jack, the supposed girlish innocence of Cecily, the overbearing respectability of Lady Bracknell. Although ridiculed by the dandy, these continual reminders of conventionality offer him a measure of his own excesses, a reassurance that he has been as much playful as destructive. And yet, for all such ambiguity of feeling, the dandy is ultimately serious; for all his grace and wit, he is not a clown but a critic.

Dandiacal criticism, however, should be distinguished from satire, for when the dandy is satirical at all, he is so only incidentally. Wilde can satirize such behavior as the methodical husband hunting of fashionable society, when Lady Bracknell tells Jack that he is not down on her list of eligible young men, "although," she says, "I have the same list as the dear Duchess of Bolton has. We work together, in fact." In this case, Wilde agrees with the ostensible opinion of society, that arranged, mercenary marriages are evil. This agreement, rare in Wilde, is essential to the traditional satirist, who recognizes a social norm and criticizes deviations from it, but the dandy is himself a deviationist and critic of the norms of mundane society. The Wildean dandy, however, is not a satirical reformer but a visionary creator of his own realm of existence, and, in relation to the real world, he is a subversive.

Indeed, however graceful or seemingly innocuous his presence, the dandy is often recognized by the conventional world as wicked. "Dear Lord Darlington," exclaims the Duchess of Berwick in *Lady Windermere's Fan*, "how thoroughly depraved you are"; Lord Illingworth, the chief dandy of *A Woman of No Importance,* is introduced in much the same way, as Lady Stutfield observes, "The world says that Lord Illingworth is very, very wicked." (Even the likable Lord Goring of *An Ideal Husband* is prepared to accept his role and boasts playfully of his bad qualities. "When I think of them at night," he impishly remarks, "I go to sleep at once.") [11]

Although Wilde could allow a worldly intriguer to play with the idea of sinfulness as a soporific or introduce full-blown the familiar figure of the wicked nobleman, the Gilbertian "bad bart.," it was quite a different matter to cast a sinister light on the sort of character who appears in *The Importance of Being Earnest.* To call such a dandy as the charming and witty Algernon wicked or subversive may seem at first unduly harsh. Algernon, one might say, is only trivial. But triviality is the dandy's disguise. It is in fact the traditional clown's mask, from the concealment of which he can say what he wishes without fear of retaliation. In Wilde's other plays the dandies are often openly villainous, but here, through the unreality of the situations and the delicacy of the language, Wilde has thrown a cloak of seeming innocence over a very sinister personage. Algernon's statements, then, may be flippant in tone, but they are not innocuous in content. Whereas the satirist makes fun of the abuses of marriage, the dandy denigrates the institution itself; his aim, as we have seen, is not reform but destruction. Those institutions that sustain the Philistine world and trammel the self are to be undermined, elegantly but ruthlessly. When the manservant Lane observes that in married households the champagne is rarely of the highest quality, Algernon transposes taste and morality at the expense of the latter by exclaiming "Good Heavens! Is marriage so demoralizing as that?" His attempt to avoid not just Lady Bracknell's dinner party but the proximity of Mary Farquar, "who always flirts with her own husband across the dinner table. That is not very pleasant. Indeed, it is not even decent," transcends satire to become a subtle critique of conjugality itself. Lady Bracknell, though she seems an arch-Philistine, often assumes the dandiacal voice and shares Algernon's point of view. In the third act she makes her attitude clear, remarking of Jack's father that he was eccentric, "but only in later years. And that was the result of the Indian climate, and marriage, and indigestion, and other things of that kind." Like that of Dr. Chasuble, the refusal to distinguish between the physical and the spiritual, here between an ailment and a sacrament of the church, subverts all conventional values.

Lady Bracknell and Dr. Chasuble are not alone in being dandies by indirection, concealing their dandyism beneath a Philistine exterior. Jack's seeming virtue and respectability mask a similar belligerence toward the world of bourgeois prudery in which the dandiacal self cannot flourish and whose values it must destroy. Never losing his air of high-minded solemnity, Jack all but obliterates the conventional Victorian view of truth by speaking of it in terms usually reserved for depravity: truth "isn't quite the sort of thing one tells to a nice, sweet, refined girl"; to be truthful is to be "reduced to . . . a painful position," to find oneself "quite inexperienced in doing anything of the kind"; one must ultimately beg forgiveness for "speaking nothing but the truth" all through one's life, "a terrible thing." For the seemingly ingenuous Cecily, seriousness is a sign of ill health, philanthropy "so forward," opinions she shares with Lady Bracknell who greets the news that Bunbury has been quite "exploded" with her own version of the term: "Exploded! Was he the victim of a revolutionary outrage? I was not aware that Mr. Bunbury was interested in social legislation. If so, he is well punished for his morbidity." It is in fact Lady Bracknell who, when speaking in her dandiacal voice, most openly defies the Philistine standards, equating the respectable with the repugnant:

> LADY BRACKNELL. Is this Miss Prism a female of repellent aspect, remotely connected with education?
> DR. CHASUBLE. (Somewhat indignantly) She is the most cultivated of ladies, and the very picture of respectability.
> LADY BRACKNELL. It is obviously the same person.

Whenever ordinary morality appears, it becomes entangled with ugliness and is made to seem ridiculous. That Miss Prism, greeting the news of the carefree Ernest's death, should unconsciously justify dandiacal mockery of moral pronouncements with "What a lesson for him! I trust he will profit by it" arouses a complex laughter. We mock Miss Prism's obtuseness in supposing that Ernest's character can be elevated after his death, but also and by a very slight extension we are led to deride the notion that any sort of moral reform is possible or even desirable. Suddenly our laughter has become the laughter of the triumphant Ernest as he slips away from the constraints of Philistinism into a realm of dandiacal freedom.

Only here can the dandy direct his attention to what truly absorbs him—himself. An intense individualism—a concentration on the self and an insistence that it be able to flourish without bounds—are among the central tenets of Wildean dandyism. So committed is the dandiacal individualist to the contemplation and cultivation of his own self that he seems at times reluctant to admit the existence of others, or at least to react to their feelings. Even Miss Prism, the most decorous of Philistines, has her flirtation with dandyism, presenting us at one moment with a comic version of this self-infatuation. When at the play's climax Jack rushes in with the crucial handbag and begs Miss Prism to establish his parentage by identifying it, her careful and lengthy examination culminates in a reply of stunning irrelevance to Jack's concerns:

MISS PRISM. . . . And here on the lock are my initials. I had forgotten that in an extravagant mood I had had them placed there. The bag is undoubtedly mine. I am delighted to have it so unexpectedly restored to me. It has been a great inconvenience being without it all these years.

Although the laughable incongruity of her remark conceals its inhumanity, there is in Miss Prism's foolish preoccupation with her handbag something similar to the icy self-sufficiency of Gwendolen and Cecily, both of whom happily choose to center their affections on the name Ernest before they come to know its possessor. Cecily, in fact, manages to conduct an elaborate courtship in the absence of her beloved. As for Lady Bracknell, she is an individualist not only in her self-sufficiency but in what she implies about keeping the personality inviolate. When Jack hurries upstairs to hunt frantically for the handbag, she remarks, "This noise is extremely unpleasant. It sounds as if he was having an argument. I dislike arguments of any kind. They are always vulgar and often convincing." A Wildean dandy, in fact, desires to be not individual but unique. When Lord Augustus of *Lady Windermere's Fan* ventures to accept one of Cecil Graham's remarks, the latter answers, "Sorry to hear it, Tuppy; whenever people agree with me I feel I must be wrong." Beneath these jokes is Wilde's genuine reluctance to let any exterior force affect his personality, for he was engrossed in what Baudelaire called "the cult of the self." Even in prison Wilde wrote (in *De Profundis*): "I am far more of an individualist than I ever was. Nothing seems to me of the smallest value except what one gets out of oneself. My nature is seeking a fresh mode of self-realization. That is all I am concerned with."

However much this particular comment, considering the circumstances under which Wilde wrote it, reflects the desperate rationalizing of a man whose life had collapsed, it stems directly from the code of dandiacal individualism that Wilde had previously shaped. That code was useful to Wilde precisely because it already contained an element of defensiveness and of social belligerence. By taking the limits of his own personality as the boundaries of admissible reality, the dandy can—as Wilde to some degree was able to—protect himself against the strictures of society. If all values come from the self, then the moral standards of others are irrelevant to him; he may abuse or disregard them as he pleases. For him, other persons have little existence; they are only the medium through which sensations, pleasant or otherwise, are conveyed to him. But the sensations themselves are important, for it is through them that the dandy creates the self: the more exquisite the sensations he can experience, the richer will be the self he is trying to realize (Wilde here proves almost too devoted a student of Pater, his master at Oxford, whose famous conclusion to *The Renaissance* emphasized "not the fruit of experience, but experience itself").

In *A Woman of No Importance* Mrs. Allonby says that life "is simply a *mauvais quart d'heure* made up of exquisite moments." It is this desire to savor the pleasures of such a moment that makes Algernon when returning Jack's cigarette case and asking his friend to explain why he is Ernest in town and Jack in the country, say, as he hands Jack the case, "Here it is. Now produce your explanation, and pray make it improbable." However, the characters most given to relishing novel sensations are Cecily and Gwendolen. While awaiting the entrance of the reprobate Ernest, impersonated by Algernon, Cecily remarks, "I have never met any really wicked person before. I feel rather frightened. I am so afraid he will look just like everyone else." And when Algernon enters "very gay and debonair," she sighs in disappointment, "he does!" Cecily does not fear Ernest's wickedness; she fears that if he does not *seem* wicked, he will fail to give her the *nouveau frisson* she seeks. Since, in the world of dandiacal individualism, rich sensations are crucial to the growth of the self, the dandy comes very close to equating self-gratification with self-development. Thus, it is not the loss of a friend but the loss of a sensation that Cecily fears when she calls "even a momentary separation from anyone to whom one has just been introduced" almost unbearable; in the same spirit she deplores the absence, not of the appropriate nature, but of the appropriately exciting name in the man to whom she has engaged herself. Perhaps the clearest illustration of the dandy's self-centered relishing of emotion is Gwendolen's "The suspense is terrible, I hope it will last." The continuation of her pleasurable sensation is dependent upon the continuation of Jack's distressful hunting for the handbag, but such a consideration cannot affect her. Bounded by the confines of his individual self, the dandy rejects human entanglements to feed forever upon a succession of novelties.

But though the dandy sustains himself by relishing his own sensations and defends himself from the encroachments of the Philistine world by the belligerence, direct or indirect, of his wit, his own world—that in which the self is not threatened—is the world of art. That the Wildean dandy's ultimate faith lies in the superiority of aesthetic form is suggested by Gwendolen's comment: "In matters of grave importance, style not sincerity is the vital thing." Baudelaire also stressed the superiority of the artificial to the natural and admired the conscious artifice of the dandy's toilette; however, he emphasized the dandy's revulsion from the moral standards of his age and connected him with aesthetics only by implication. For Wilde, in contrast, the dandy embodied above all his theories of art; only through the triumph of aesthetics could Wilde negate the power of Philistine ethics, both in the external world and within the self. Sometimes the negation of ethics is subtle and apparently playful, as in the moment referred to at the beginning of this chapter when Dr. Chasuble, in telling us that he is "peculiarly susceptible to draughts," obliterates any question of moral failings. At other times, protected by the shield of dandiacal wit, Wilde allows himself to be astonishingly open and direct. "My dear Windermere, manners before morals," says Mrs. Erlynne in *Lady Windermere's Fan.* In the same play Lord Darlington maintains: "It is absurd to divide people into good and bad. People are either charming or tedious." (Wilde had used almost exactly these words in the Preface to *The Picture of Dorian Gray:* "A work of art is neither moral nor immoral, only well or poorly written.") When Wilde wrote that Phipps, the dandiacal butler of *An Ideal Husband,* "represents the dominance of form," he made the dandy the incarnation of aesthetic form, which for Wilde, as he explained in "The Critic as Artist," was the basis of all art:

> For the real artist is he who proceeds, not from feeling to form, but from form to thought and passion . . . realizing the beauty of the sonnet-scheme, he conceives certain modes of music and methods of rhyme, and the mere form suggests what is to fill it and make it intellectually and emotionally complete. . . . Yes, Form is everything. It is the secret of life.

It is this element, this absolute faith in pure aestheticism, that makes the Wildean dandy unique, and because it is dominated by him *The Importance of Being Earnest* is a unique play. It stands alone among English comedies, not only because of the quality of its wit, but because no other writer has approached the theatre with theories and attitudes comparable to Wilde's. It stands alone among Wilde's plays because the dandiacal element in *The Importance,* unlike that in the society comedies, is not in open conflict with a Philistine element and limited to its own sections of the play but appears everywhere and makes of the entire work a kind of dandiacal utopia, a world of perfect form.[12] "For the canons of good society," Wilde wrote in *Dorian Gray,* "are, or should be, the same as the canons of art. Form is absolutely essential to it."

Form for Wilde is found only in art, never in nature. It is in speaking of nature that the dandy's preference for the artificial is most clearly revealed. In *Lady Windermere's Fan* Dumby mentions that young Mr. Hopper has bad manners. "Hopper is one of nature's gentlemen," replies Cecil Graham, "the worst type of gentleman I know." During the interview scene in Act I, Lady Bracknell expresses her disapproval of Jack's house in the country. "A country house!" she exclaims, ". . . You have a town house, I hope? A girl with a simple, unspoiled nature, like Gwendolen, could hardly be expected to reside in the country." The opening pages of "The Decay of Lying" offer a particularly clear gloss on this speech. "My own experience," says Vivian, the elegant purveyor of dandiacal opinions, "is that the more we study Art, the less we care for Nature. What Art really reveals to us is Nature's lack of design, her curious crudities . . . her absolutely unfinished condition. . . . Art is our spirited protest, our gallant attempt to teach Nature her proper place."

It is always perfection of form that the dandy seeks; content is irrelevant to him. After one of Algernon's more outrageous sallies, Jack exclaims in exasperation, "Is that clever?" Algernon replies, "It is perfectly phrased! and quite as true as any observation in civilized life should be." Even Algernon's servant, Lane, is revealed as a dandy: when Algernon remarks, "Lane, you're a perfect pessimist," the manservant replies, "I do my best to give satisfaction, sir." For the dandy, to be recognized as having achieved perfection in anything is a notable tribute; to be praised for distinction in a field of endeavor that the Philistine world deplores is the highest accolade.

That this insistence on perfect aesthetic form has many disguises is revealed in Gwendolen's request: "Cecily, mama, whose views on education are remarkably strict, has brought me up to be extremely short-sighted; it is part of her system; so do you mind my looking at you through my glasses?" A mother with "strict" views on education, constituting in fact a "system," might be expected to advocate such Philistine ideals as diligence and high intellectual attainment; but instead the product of her educational labors is merely a fashion—shortsightedness—that is trivial and yet deliberately chosen. Indeed it is precisely the achievement of shortsightedness—negating whatever natural qualities of vision Gwendolen may be presumed to have had—that constitutes the assertion of the aesthetic will. Gwendolen, as Lady Bracknell has brought her up, is a conscious artistic creation and must obey the rules of form.

Often, however, the dandy speaks without any disguise, and no one is more open than the seemingly innocent Cecily. When Algernon says that he has pretended to be Ernest in order to meet her, she asks Gwendolen's opinion of this excuse:

> CECILY. (To Gwendolen) That certainly seems a satisfactory explanation, does it not?
> GWENDOLEN. Yes, dear, if you can believe him.
> CECILY. I don't. But that does not affect the wonderful beauty of his answer.

The dandy, with his code of artistic form, is indifferent to both Philistine truth and Philistine morality. When Cecily displays a trinket that she has given herself on Algernon's behalf, she remarks, "Yes, you've wonderfully good taste, Ernest. It's the excuse I've always given for your leading such a bad life." This obliteration of conventional morality is nowhere so apparent as in Cecily's first words to the disguised Algernon:

> CECILY. You, I see from your card, are Uncle Jack's brother, my cousin Ernest, my wicked cousin Ernest.
> ALGERNON. Oh! I am not really wicked at all, cousin Cecily. You mustn't think that I am wicked.

CECILY. If you are not, then you have certainly been deceiving us all in a very inexcusable manner. I hope you have not been leading a double life, pretending to be wicked and being really good all the time. That would be hypocrisy.

The obsessive presence of moral terminology points up the entire absence of moral substance in the dandiacal system where form (the shape of one's role in life) takes precedence over content (goodness or evil). As Algernon, misguidedly assuming that he is assuaging girlish timidity, insists that he is "not really wicked," Cecily whisks away ethical considerations. Never deviating from the language of Wilde's earlier mode of sentimental melodrama ("I hope you have not been leading a double life"), Cecily, announcing that it is "inexcusable" not to have been wicked, "hypocrisy" to have been good, becomes a kind of triumphant Dorian Gray, remaining demure and beautiful while advocating, if not enacting, on aesthetic grounds, an immoral life.

In one form or another dandyism dominates *The Importance of Being Earnest,* even the pun in its title concealing a dandiacal meaning. As the various couples embrace at the end of the play, Lady Bracknell rebukes her newfound relative:

LADY BRACKNELL. My nephew, you seem to be displaying signs of triviality.
JACK. On the contrary, Aunt Augusta, I've now realized for the first time in my life the vital Importance of Being Earnest.

When Lady Bracknell accuses Jack of being trivial, he replies that he realizes the importance of being earnest, or sincere and moral, but lurking beneath the reassuring, Philistine earnest is the dandiacal Ernest, for the name is after all the beautiful form that the self-centered, dandiacal heroines love while remaining indifferent to its content, the character of its bearer. To realize the importance of being Ernest is to understand the dominance of form; it is to be a Wildean dandy. The graceful pun that seems to set a tone of careless humor epitomizes in itself the meaning that can be found in the dandiacal sections of the society comedies and on almost every page of Wilde's masterpiece.

The code of dandyism, however—the assertion that the rules of art are the rules of life, that perfection of form is the only virtue, that the self must flower untrammeled—was not only obviously and tragically impossible for Wilde to realize in life but remained elusive in art as well. Only once was he able to shape his vision into an absolutely coherent work. But fully to recognize the nature of this arcadia of dandyism that is *The Importance of Being Earnest* we must understand its precariousness even as we revel in its charm. That *The Importance* becomes more pastoral as it becomes more improbable is perhaps an accident of the plot, but it remains nonetheless suggestive of its character and its relation to the wider reality around it. The play begins in a "luxuriously and artistically" furnished flat in Mayfair with two young men about to spend a night out in London; though their suggested diversions—dinner, the Club, a theatre—are innocuous enough, the shadow of Dorian Gray falls, however faintly, over this scene. But though the dialogue continues to insinuate the dandiacal vision, exquisite and sinister, the action veers away to the innocence of the countryside where these Victorian nymphs and shepherds play out their games of love.

Here, too, in the perfect aesthetic world of *The Importance* where all the characters are dandies and the self is free there must be safeguards. For the work itself is to be exhibited before a Philistine audience that might understand too much of what the lines say to it. But the sweetness of the setting and the implausibility of the plot with its reminiscences of classical romance constitute, if not the open plea for pardon that we find in the society comedies, at least an assertion of innocence. Even as line after line of wit obliterates bourgeois morality and substitutes dandiacal aesthetics, the play itself assures us that an action patently unreal set in a garden full of laughter and elegance cannot be so disquieting as, to the attentive ear, it sometimes seems to be.

In the society comedies, on the other hand, any disquieting elements appear to be quite visible. Unlike *The Importance,* where all the characters seem innocent but are guilty (of the crime of art), the society comedies offer us characters whose guilt seems beyond question: the woman-with-a-past, the man with a secret sin. Moreover, their emotions and behavior are all that any Philistine could ask: an admission of guilt, a sense of exile, an act of repentance and sacrifice, a longing for pardon and acceptance. And yet, even in those parts of the society comedies that seem safely committed to the Philistine vision, all is not well. For the sinner—having deserted husband and family, sold a state secret, produced an illegitimate child—has nonetheless contrived to remain innocent. The best and wisest characters in the plays know that Mrs. Erlynne is a good woman; that Mrs. Arbuthnot has lived by God's law—love; that Sir Robert need not resign his post; that, in fact, the sinner has always been pure in heart. By a curious legerdemain (also characteristic, as we will see, of the work of Tennessee Williams) Wilde has been able, even in these flawed comedies, to present the self as both the sinner who has known guilt and the innocent who has remained uncorrupted. And in the dandiacal parts of these plays, as in the whole of *The Importance of Being Earnest,* there is, ostensibly at least, no guilt. Here the self knows no moral imperatives, only the rules of form.

To create a special world, however fragile, is no trivial act. That Wilde could do it only once, with the perfect grace of *The Importance,* reveals that his achievement was limited in scope but not in nature. Wilde, one must remember, was not only a writer but—to exaggerate only slightly—the prophet of a new religion. Living at a time when the old Judeo-Christian faith seemed to be losing its validity, he saw new systems rising and attempting to take its place (the religion of science, for example, with Huxley and Zola as literary prophets). Wilde's belief in the efficacy of aesthetic form— it was the state religion of the realm of dandyism—could not withstand the rigors of its contact with punitive Victorian moralism. But the quest for a sustaining world for the self not only survives the collapse of Wilde's efforts but is clearly manifested in the work of John M. Synge, a contemporary and fellow Irishman, whose particular vision links him most closely to Wilde.

John M. Synge: The Refuge of Art

The newspaper attacks that greeted Synge's first play, *In the Shadow of the Glen,* and the famous riots at the opening performance of *The Playboy of the Western World* took as their theme the notion that Synge was a traducer of Irish womanhood and a corrupter of the Irish nation.[13] Although these charges seem at this date, certainly outside Ireland, to be rather whimsical and although Synge's admirers may by now be excused from defending him against them, an unfortunate side effect of the controversies they evoked was to focus attention on the specifically national elements of Synge's work.[14] To argue that this emphasis was unfortunate because it has obscured the central character of the plays is not to deny that the language and atmosphere of western Ireland were the essential materials that Synge used. But though the journeys that he made to the Aran Islands undoubtedly liberated Synge's creative impulses, the results of that liberation were not quite what had been anticipated.

When Yeats met the youthful Synge in Paris, where he had drifted while searching for a career in the arts, and told him to go to Aran to "express a life that has never found expression," [15] he was asking Synge to perform an action that was as much political as literary. By dignifying Irish peasant life and creating a national literature Irish writers hoped to demonstrate the reality of a special ethnic identity and thus the right to independence. (Beyond these considerations was an obeisance to the deeper nineteenth-century idea of a mystic unity and virtue inherent in *das Volk*.) But Yeats himself did not follow this advice—his Irish plays, even the propagandistic ones, tend to deal with a dream Ireland of the mythic past—and ultimately Synge did not either.

What Synge found in Aran was not so much a noble peasantry that deserved to be separated from England but, as he felt, a people, who were living in a romantic unity with nature, already separated from the crass ugliness of modern bourgeois society. Moreover, and more important, he found the materials with which he could forge a world of beauty that would stand against the sense of the absoluteness of death that rarely seems to have been far from his mind. Although there is no doubt that Synge observed the mode of life of Aran closely and drew elements of action and expression directly from it, the simple re-creation of that life on stage was never part of his achievement. Rather, Synge used what he had drawn from the life of Aran and of western Ireland to create a visionary world in which the dramatic struggle was always between the destructive effects of life and time and the vivifying hope of a dream of beauty. Even in *The Aran Islands,* a largely descriptive account of Synge's visits there, we see the aestheticizing of Aran, the transformation of the place's manner of life into something to be contemplated and relished by the fine eye and delicate sensibility of the artist:

> The kitchen itself, where I will spend most of my time, is full of beauty and distinction. The red dresses of the women who cluster round the fire on their stools give a glow of almost Eastern richness, and the walls have been toned by the turf-smoke to a soft brown that blends with the grey earth-colour of the floor. . . .
> Every article on these islands has an almost personal character, which gives this simple life, where all art is unknown, something of the artistic beauty of mediaeval life. The curaghs and spinning-wheels, the tiny wooden barrels that are still much used in the place of earthenware, the home-made cradles, churns, and baskets, are all full of individuality, and being made from materials that are common here, yet to some extent peculiar to the island, they seem to exist as a natural link between the people and the world that is about them.[16]

When Synge speaks of "the artistic beauty of medieval life," we recognize that he is applying to Aran some of the characteristic nineteenth-century idealizing of the Gothic by the Pre-Raphaelites and others; when he tells us that the domestic implements are "full of individuality," we hear the echo of Ruskin's contempt for the ugly, depersonalized products of factory labor; and, most significantly, when he suggests that there is a "natural link" between the people and their world, we glimpse through Synge's eyes a wished-for realm in which, despite poverty and ultimate mortality, the self might live at ease.

The absence of factories, and of the modern industrialized world that they exemplify, is crucial to Syge's appreciation of Aran, for it is this absence that gives the artist the opportunity that elsewhere is lost:

> In Ireland for a few years more, we have a popular imagination that is fiery and magnificent, and tender; so that those of us who wish to write start with a chance that is not given to

writers in places where the springtime of local life has been forgotten, and the harvest is memory only, and the straw has been turned into bricks.

Not only has Synge let slip the truth (in this sentence from the Preface to *The Playboy of the Western World*) that Irish life is not so much valuable for itself but because it is material for "those of us who wish to write," but he has also recognized that this life will last only "for a few years more." The elegiac cadences at the end of this sentence evoke a note to be heard most openly in *Riders to the Sea* but nonetheless persistently through all of Synge's plays. It is the sense that only in a world of beauty, usually one created precariously through language, can the artist's self be fulfilled and that such a world is always on the point of dissolution. Synge's subject is not the nation of Ireland but the realm of art, and the central character is always a projection of the artist's self.

Even in Synge's first play, *In the Shadow of the Glen,* a short and deceptively simple piece, the whole range of his themes and attitudes—the painful sensitivity of the artist, the alienation of his self from the ordinary world, the destruction of beauty by the forces of life and time, and its paradoxical survival through the alienated artist himself—appears complete. Curiously, it is one of the limitations of the play, the fact that it is too slender to carry the load of meaning that the author has worked into the text, that makes it so convenient an introduction to Synge's writings. Here Synge must present almost explicitly what in his later masterpieces is more subtly developed.

Nevertheless, *In the Shadow of the Glen* is not without its own subtlety. Its most suggestively developed character, for example, appears only in references made to him by others, but in these speeches he takes on some of the strength and keenness of heroes of legend. Although Patch Darcy is only a local shepherd who has gone mad from loneliness and died on the back hills, the Tramp, who is Synge's ultimate spokesman, refers to him with reverence. "That was a great man, young fellow," he tells Michael Dara, "a great man I'm telling you. There was never a lamb from his own ewes he wouldn't know before it was marked, and he'ld run from this to the city of Dublin and never catch for his breath." Nora too had admired Darcy and greets this tribute to his memory with pleasure. "He was a great man surely, stranger." Well before they leave together at the end of the play, Nora and the Tramp are united by their admiration for the solitary herdsman who, despite his skill and his identification with the creatures of nature, has succumbed to the loneliness of life. They recognize in themselves both the sensitivity and the feeling of alienation of which Darcy is the symbol.

It is in Nora, however, that these attributes are most fully developed. Sensitive to the loneliness of the solitary glen with the shadow of death upon it, she comes to see in the empty countryside something of the emptiness of existence in the ordinary, meaningless, mortal world. "For what good is a bit of a farm with cows on it, and sheep on the back hills," she asks, "when you do be sitting looking out from a door the like of that door, and seeing nothing but the mists rolling down the bog, and the mists again, and they rolling up the bog, and hearing nothing but the wind crying out in the bits of broken trees were left from the great storm, and the streams roaring with the rain." In this vast solitude of wind and mist, this universe of emptiness, there is only the endless passing of life and the destruction of beauty. Looking ahead, Nora sees the specter that she will become: "Peggy Cavanaugh . . . walking round on the roads, or sitting in a dirty old house, with no teeth in her mouth, and no sense and no more hair than you'd see on a bit of a hill and they after burning the furze from it." Obsessed with these images of hopeless wandering, or inevitable ugliness and decay, she finds meaningless both the personal attractions of her young lover, Michael Dara, and the peasant prosperity of her coarse, greedy husband.

In return, Dan Burke hates his wife not only because he fears she will betray him but because he senses that she rejects the money values that he represents. Indeed, his hatred extends beyond Nora to include the Tramp, and it centers on their tendency to talk about their feelings. As Dan orders his wife out of the house, he exclaims, "there'll be an end now of your fine times, and all the talk you have of young men and old men, and of the mist coming up or going down." The contempt for language (and the unconscious fear that language can create worlds for the self that are a seductive alternative to his own) is shown in Dan's ironic echoing of Nora's words and culminates when he orders the Tramp out of the house along with her. "Let her walk out of the door, and let you go along with her, stranger . . . for it's too much talk you have surely."

Nora, however, sensitive to the lure of language, accepts the Tramp as her escort with the words, "but you've a fine bit of talk, stranger, and it's with yourself I'll go," while the Tramp recoils from Dan's suggestion that he has a bad wife, saying, "is it herself, master of the house, and she a grand woman to talk?" It is not surprising that Nora's talent for expression should so attract a mere tramp, for Synge has a profound identification with this figure. The homeless wanderer of the roads, despised but free, living in semi-exile from ordinary society, becomes symbolic of the artist, whose longing for a world of beauty also separates him from bourgeois society, and in Synge's mind the two coalesce. This passage on tramps from his essay "The Vagrants of Wicklow" makes a suggestive gloss for this play (and for *Playboy* and the other works that deal with the figures of vagrants):

> Their abundance has often been regretted; yet in one sense it is an interesting sign, for wherever the labourer of a country has preserved his vitality, and begets an occasional temperament of distinction, a certain number of vagrants are to be looked for. In the middle classes the gifted son of a family is always the poorest—usually a writer or artist with no sense of speculation—and in a family of peasants, where the average comfort is just over penury, the gifted son sinks also, and is soon a tramp on the roadside.

Because he is an artist and not simply a vagrant, the Tramp offers Nora, along with his companionship, a kind of Wordsworthian prose poem on the beauties of nature and the consolations of a life immersed in them. Not so much by what it says as by its artfulness of rhythm and richness of imagery the speech attempts to evoke an adequate alternative to the coarse, commonplace world of Dan and Michael:

> TRAMP. Come along with me now, lady of the house, and it's not my blather you'll be hearing only, but you'll be hearing the herons crying out over the black lakes, and you'll be

hearing the grouse and the owls with them, and the larks
and the big thrushes when the days are warm, and it's not
from the like of them you'll be hearing a talk of getting old
like Peggy Cavanagh, and losing the hair off you, and the
light of your eyes, but it's fine songs you'll be hearing when
the sun goes up, and there'll be no old fellow wheezing, the
like of a sick sheep, close to your ear.

Unfortunately, the actual life of a vagrant, with its hardships
and exile, is not really an adequate realization of the world suggested by the Tramp's words. Even Nora herself, who accepts that
life, has her reservations. "I'm thinking it's myself will be wheezing
that time," she says, "with lying down under the Heavens when
the night is cold." The world that is evoked by the Tramp's speech
is not, like the natural world of Wordsworth, irradiated by "something far more deeply interfused"; indeed it is sustained only by
picturesque images of herons and black lakes; it is in fact a world
of language, a world of art. When Nora and the Tramp walk out of
the cottage, leaving behind them the blind acquisitiveness of Dan
and Michael, they cannot in reality walk out into a realm of
beauty where age and decay are obliterated by fine songs and the
rising sun—the world that has been envisioned by the Tramp.
They can only walk onto the roads of Ireland where beauty, as
Nora seems to recognize, is as much subject to destruction as it is in
the cottage. Finally, the ending of the play is delicately poised
between a triumphant rejection of the coarse world of reality and a
brooding commitment to the precarious world of art.

Yet this conclusion, apparently so indecisive, is obviously deeply
meaningful for Synge. Although he wrote six plays in his short
career, Synge found only two endings for them. One is the acceptance of death; the other is the rejection of the ordinary settled
existence for the life of a wanderer tramping the roads. That the
latter ending, despite its sense of loss and exile, is the relatively
optimistic one tells us much about the essential sadness lying beneath even the brightest of Synge's plays. This ending is the one
that Synge can use for his comedies, but it remains always ambiguous. The artist figure may turn away from his two enemies, the
coarseness of common life and the destruction of beauty by time,
to a world of natural loveliness created by language; but because

that world is always dependent on the power of art, it is always threatened by the power of reality. At some level of consciousness the wanderer figure shares the Keatsian recognition of the melancholy that "dwells with Beauty—Beauty that must die."

This sad awareness initially seems absent from *The Tinker's Wedding*, the most nearly farcical of Synge's comedies. After all, the wanderers of this play are not a tramp and an outcast or a blind beggar and his wife, as in *The Well of the Saints*,[17] but a cheerful and reasonably contented family of tinkers. Far from seeking a vision of idyllic freedom, they themselves embody it. But when Sarah Casey, the beautiful young tinker woman, insists on breaking the customs of her people and actually marrying Michael Byrne, the man she lives with, a sense of danger enters the play. For she is attempting to forsake not merely a tradition of tinker life but what Synge conceives of as a self-contained world, the realm of charm and beauty that the tinkers inhabit. Moreover, she risks losing her world for the vulgar legitimacy of the commonplace society represented by the Priest. Although this material is presented farcically in what is the most consistently lighthearted of Synge's plays, even here the theme of the decay of beauty appears. Sarah begins to realize her error only when Michael's mother, Mary, "an old, flagrant heathen" who knows "it's a little short while only till you die," makes her see that the marriage she has innocently set such store by will not mitigate any of the inevitable effects of time. "Is it putting that ring on your finger," she asks Sarah, "will keep you from getting an aged woman and losing the fine face you have?" Amid the farcical uproars of the play's ending this somber note modulates to one of resigned melancholy as old Mary, turning away from the Priest, speaks a last reminder of the passing of beauty. "And it's little need we ever had of the like of you to get us our bit to eat, and our bit to drink, and our time to love when we were young men and women, and were fine to look at." Once again Synge has, in the life of the tinkers, suggested an image of beauty and hinted at its isolation and destruction.

In *The Playboy of the Western World,* Synge's masterpiece and the most richly developed of the wanderer plays, a world of great deeds is created through the power of language and destroyed by the reassertion of reality. Moreover, the creator of that world, the artist whose speech has power to enchant, becomes again the central figure of the play, and the development of his nature along with his ultimate isolation from the community about him become its central actions. Even before Christy Mahon appears, dirty, shivering, and alone, at Michael Flaherty's public house and tells the story that through the magic of art transforms a squalid scuffle into a heroic murder and Christy himself into the playboy, we see that Pegeen and the other characters, with the exception of the timid Shawn Keogh, are prepared to disdain the commonplace and to admire rebellious strength and the power of rhetoric to transform the ordinary world into a place of wonder. When Pegeen laments the lack of worthy men in the district, she shows herself ready to applaud just the qualities that Christy, as he becomes the artist, will be thought to possess. "Where now will you meet the like of Daneen Sullivan," she asks, "knocked the eye from a peeler, or Marcus Quin, God rest him, got six months for maiming ewes, and he a great warrant to tell stories of holy Ireland till he'd have the old women shedding down tears about their feet." After Christy has told his story, Pegeen not only praises him but recognizes him as the poet that in embryo he is: "I've heard all times it's the poets are your like, fine fiery fellows with great rages when their temper's roused." Several times during the play, in fact, Christy is specifically designated a poet. After he has won at all the games and sports, Pegeen says that he has "such poet's talking and such bravery of heart." The Widow Quin applauds his praises of Pegeen as "poetry talk," and even Christy himself finally recognizes his identity, saying that he has spoken "words would raise the topknot on a poet in a merchant's town." [18]

However, the most striking illustration of Christy's status as poet is provided by the prizes that he receives for his victories in the village games. Although he has won at leaping and racing, his trophies—"A bagpipes! A fiddle was played by a poet in the years gone by! A flat and three-thorned blackthorn would lick the scholars out of Dublin town"—suggest consecration as a bard rather than triumph as an athlete. There is no reason to suppose that Christy can play the musical instruments, but they are symbols of his status. Even the blackthorn, since it is specifically for combating pedantry, is perhaps a comic surrogate for Apollo's staff as well as a support for the wandering poet.

Nor is it surprising that Christy should receive the bard's implements from the villagers. Throughout, their attitude has been notable, not only because of their lack of moral feeling about the supposed crime (this much Synge took from his source—see *The Aran Islands,* pp. 369-70), but because they see Christy primarily in aesthetic terms. He is at once the hero and the poet who immortalizes the hero. Thus, their admiration of Christy is boundless as long as he is mainly a storyteller. The villagers, however, are essentially a kind of bourgeois audience, appreciative but timid. Confronted, as they suppose, by the reality of Christy's act as an intrusion into the safety of their lives, they retreat into conventional attitudes. Because they are children of the western world (far from the modern urban life of Dublin), they still have a taste for fantasy; but because they are in the play the representatives of commonplace life, they cannot tolerate the hero-poet's daring to realize that fantasy, to become the substance of his tale, and they retreat from him in fear. The realm of art and the poet's self cannot finally coexist with the world of ordinary life.

The Playboy of the Western World, then, presents the story of a young poet who enters a fresh and, as he supposes, sympathetic world. Finding himself accepted and admired, he flowers out into a self-realization strong enough to allow him ultimately to withstand the betrayal of the society that fears his fully developed powers. This rather grim tale lies only partly concealed beneath a surface texture that, however comic, adds its own suggestion of acerbity to the total play. The kind of grotesque humorous dialogue that Synge hinted at in *The Tinker's Wedding* is in certain ways different from the lush, poetic speech that Ronald Peacock called Synge's central achievement [19] but that other critics such as Corkery and Bourgeois have found to be, on occasion, too static and literary.[20] (The speech of the Tramp from *In the Shadow of the Glen,* quoted earlier, is a convenient example of such highly wrought language.)

In *Playboy* the richness and melodiousness of the dialogue contrast ironically, even grotesquely, with an element of the commonplace that gives the language here a cutting edge lacking in the other plays. When, for example, Christy agrees to stay on at Michael James's public house, thus quelling Pegeen's fear at being left alone, Jimmy Farrell greets this decision with a burst of enthusiastic rhetoric: "Now by the Grace of God, herself will be safe this night, with a man killed his father holding danger from the door, and let you come on, Michael James, or they'll have the best stuff drunk at the wake." The pious ejaculation, the emphasis on Pegeen's safety, the heroic vision—reinforced by rhythm and alliteration—of Christy physically defending the door against a personified danger all contrast bizarrely with the reminder that Christy is supposedly a murderer and with the sudden descent into the coarseness of Jimmy's greed at the end of the speech. In the same way, Christy's image of his splendid state on the day of his hanging is undercut by the very words in which he presents it: "And won't there be crying out in Mayo the day I'm stretched upon the rope with the ladies in their silks and satins snivelling in their lacy kerchiefs." The connotations of "snivelling" shift the tone of this speech to the mock-heroic. Even in the celebrated love scene between Pegeen and Christy, the most lyrical passage in the play, there is an ironic undercurrent of comedy:

> CHRISTY. It's little you'll think if my love's a poacher's or an earl's itself, when you'll feel my two hands stretched around you, and I squeezing kisses on your puckered lips, till I'd feel a kind of pity for the Lord God is all ages sitting lonesome in his golden chair.

To keep the emotion of the scene within bounds (passion is not to be fulfilled in this play), Synge combines in one speech the genuinely lyrical with the element of the grotesque suggested by the squeezed kisses, the puckered lips, and the image of the Almighty overcome by ennui.

These are random examples, which could easily be multiplied, of a type of incongruity that is basic to this play. It produces the copious stream of laughter that leads to the apparent gaiety of the ending when the playboy announces that he is off to go "romancing through a romping lifetime." But underneath this comic ending there lies, as we have seen, a bitter one centering on the image of the alienated poet. If Christy is not to go back to grubbing on his father's farm, he has only one future: to become a tramp, an exile bard wandering the roads. The comedy of this play, ironically undercutting the characters' attitudes, has darkened our view of them and led us toward this ending also.

In *The Playboy of the Western World* the sense of loss, which for

Synge is always the loss of an image of beauty, is built into the action: it is Christy's loss of a place of refuge, of a community's admiration, of a woman's love, of a world he has created with words; Pegeen's loss of the playboy himself and of the fantasy he seemed to have realized in his speech and actions. However, in Synge's two tragedies, *Riders to the Sea* and *Deirdre of the Sorrows,* the idea of loss is not only central to the action but a theme for discourse as well. *Riders,* in fact, is so concentrated a lament as to be almost less a play than a kind of dramatic elegy. In this characteristic passage, for example, which occurs when the two girls discover that the clothes they are examining belonged to their dead brother, the echoing phrases, the intensity of the images, and the balanced rhythm all produce the effect of formal lamentation:

> CATHLEEN. Ah, Nora, isn't it a bitter thing to think of him floating that way to the far north, and no one to keen him but the black hags that do be flying on the sea?
> NORA. And isn't it a pitiful thing when there is nothing left of a man who was a great rower and fisher, but a bit of an old shirt and a plain stocking?

The destructive power of the great sea of life and time, which is as above continually present in the imagery of the play, is reinforced by the suggestions of mystery that appear in the text. When, for example, Maurya announces her sinister vision of Michael following Bartley to the sea, she says, "I've seen the fearfullest thing any person has seen, since the day Bride Dara seen the dead man with the child in his arms." What is perhaps a half memory of Goethe's *Erlkönig* with its picture of the desperate father and the child lured to its death by remorseless spirits, intensifies the mood of despair.

But more striking even than the mysterious power of the force that destroys youth and the strength and beauty that Synge nearly always associates with it is Maurya's almost eager acceptance of the total desolation that the sea has finally brought her. "It isn't that I haven't said prayers in the dark night till you wouldn't know what I'ld be saying; but it's a great rest I'll have now, and it's time surely. It's a great rest I'll have now, and great sleeping in the long nights." This startling sigh of relief at being released from involvement with the pain of existence which we find here in one of

Synge's earliest works is a remarkable anticipation of the sense of
ease with which in his last play Deirdre suicidally decides to return
to Ireland "where there'll be a rest for ever, or a place for forget-
ting."

Both Synge's tragedies center on the destruction of youth and
beauty, but *Deirdre,* though it lacks the concentrated force of *Riders,*
develops this theme more fully and links it more explicitly with the
theme of art. We do not find in *Deirdre,* as we have in others of
Synge's plays, the figure of the artist taking part in the action but
rather a consciousness in many of the characters that they are
themselves immutable parts of a work of art. The prophecies that
surround Deirdre suggest an atmosphere of determinism, but more
significantly, she and those about her seem from the first conscious
of being no more than elements in an already conceived legend.
"It's more than Conchubor'll be sick and sorry, I'm thinking,"
Lavarcham says early in the play, "before this story is told to the
end." Deirdre looks forward to the time when she will have "a little
grave by herself, and a story will be told forever." She says she has
no power "to change the story of Conchubor and Naisi and the
things old men foretold." Just before her suicide at the end of the
play, when Naisi is dead and Conchubor's kingdom is in ruins,
Deirdre exaltedly envisions "the way there will be a story told of a
ruined city and a raving king and a woman will be young for
ever."

At this point Deirdre echoes her own words of a few moments
earlier spoken over the body of Naisi "who is young for ever." The
youth and beauty of Deirdre and Naisi will survive through their
perpetuation in art; the "story will be told for ever." "It is not a
small thing," as Deirdre says, "to be rid of grey hairs and the
loosening of the teeth." The eternity of love and beauty that she
and Naisi envision is not to be found "on the ridge of the world"
but in a quite different realm—the unchanging perfection of their
legend. To assure the perfection that can transcend the limitations
of the human condition, Deirdre accepts and even insists on the
return to Ireland, knowing that death awaits her there. One of the
weaknesses of the play lies in the fact that although human limitations have in fact been transcended Synge still needs but cannot
find a psychologically credible reason for Deirdre's decision, her
fear that Naisi may one day perhaps cease to love her being sin-

gularly inadequate. But since her essential motives are aesthetic rather than psychological, perhaps it is not surprising that Deirdre's conduct should seem perverse. The elderly gentleman who departed for Byzantium in order to be turned into a golden bird must have appeared a little odd to those left behind on the shore.

Synge may never have fully realized the depth of his affinity to his friend and codirector of the Abbey Theatre, but throughout his work there is a consciousness of the power of art as a response to the pain and transience of ordinary life that is reminiscent of the Yeats who celebrated the eternal city of Byzantium. Although Synge's pastoral vision of rural Ireland is far from Yeats's dream of the hieratic grandeur of the drowsy Emperor's court, they are both attempts to step out of time and create through language a world in which the artist's self can stand free of mortality. And just as Yeats's poem chronicles a leave-taking from that country which is not for old men, the land of endless fecundity, so Synge's plays are essentially dramas of departure. In the wanderer plays the central characters from Nora Burke through Christy Mahon always conclude by leaving behind them a life of respectability and assured status or settled comfort for an unending journey out onto the roads of Ireland. By leaving that life the wanderer wishes to escape not only the greed and coarseness of commonplace existence but the ugliness, age, and decay that inevitably attend on mortality. And from the beginning of Synge's work the literal discomforts and insecurities of the life of a beggar or tramp become symbols of the painful spiritual exile of the artist, separated from the bourgeois world, seeking a realm of permanence and beauty. For the wanderer here is always a projection of the artist's self, and their quests are one.

In the two tragedies, *Riders to the Sea* and *Deirdre of the Sorrows,* the departures are from life into a world of death. Moreover, they are departures that are willed or anticipated with relief, even with gratitude. As old Maurya accepts the deaths of her last two sons and her own death-in-life, she in some measure triumphs over her ancient enemy the sea, which, sweeping inevitably through time, has destroyed her men. The triumph over time becomes even more explicit in *Deirdre,* where death is willed so that the lovers may live eternally fulfilled in the world of beauty that is their legend.

Heroic Ireland, as Synge envisioned it, and contemporary fashionable London, as Oscar Wilde re-created it in his plays, are, for all their obvious differences, both ultimately aesthetic realms. Synge's loquacious tramps and Wilde's witty exquisites are both exiles from bourgeois society and its values, monetary and moral; both attempt to create through the power of language worlds of beauty in which the self can live at ease. The dandy and the tramp would hardly recognize each other if they met, but like Algernon and Ernest they are brothers.

They have, moreover, a wide family of relations, not only in the Aesthetic Movement, but within the modern drama in general. For if their commitment to beauty as a response to the demands of existence links Wilde and Synge to such figures as Pater, Swinburne, and even to Poe and Gautier, their desire to create special worlds for the self reveals an affinity with other playwrights in the theatre of their age and ours. The drama of their fellow Anglo-Irishman Bernard Shaw reveals a surprisingly similar impulse—to withdraw the hero from the world of action to one of stasis. Jean Giraudoux is preoccupied with a vision of a symbolic, supramortal realm at once alluring and frightening. And Anton Chekhov, like Synge ill and dying through most of his creative life, takes—as Synge did—the journey to another realm (in Chekhov a journey through time) as the central metaphoric action of his plays. The creation of a world of art is the special characteristic of the drama of Wilde and Synge, but the creation of a visionary realm of the self is one of the characteristic marks of the modern theatre.

2.

Chekhov, Shaw, Giraudoux

Anton Chekhov: Arrivals and Departures

That a special distinguishing quality of Chekhov's art, and one that links him thematically with much of the modern drama, should have gone largely unremarked is less surprising than it might initially seem. Although the evocation of a visionary realm in which the longing of the self may be satisifed occurs in all four of the final plays, it does so by suggestion, through symbols woven into the complex texture of the Chekhovian drama. Moreover, before the presence of this symbolic world could be recognized, before its connections with the arrivals and departures that frame Chekhov's actions could be grasped, certain problems often raised regarding his dramaturgy had to be dealt with.

The plays, after all, contain little dramatic action but much rambling, pseudo-philosophical speechmaking, and they dwell with gloomy persistence on a world characterized by lassitude and defeat. In the face of such criticisms Chekhov's advocates have set out, sometimes with nearly overwhelming energy, to prove that

37

contrary to first appearances he is both a competent playwright and an optimistic thinker. That he is a skilled and careful craftsman is, by now, hardly open to question. The dialogue that once seemed so aimless has upon examination revealed itself as succinct and controlled. David Magarschack, for example, has shown how many of the apparently irrelevant intrusions that seem to break the flow of conversation in Chekhov's plays are in fact ironic commentaries integral to the total meaning of the passages in which they occur.[1] Eric Bentley's trenchant analysis of the changes Chekhov made in developing *Uncle Vanya* out of his earlier play called *The Wood Demon* reveals with particular clarity the precision and technical control he had developed by the final period of his career.[2]

But if Chekhov's competence as a playwright has been established, questions about the tone of his works and the nature of his vision of life are far from settled. Certainly the image of the mournful, elegiac Chekhov has been profoundly modified; in fact, for some, it has been abolished. Magarschack tells us that Chekhov's last plays, far from being dominated by a mood of frustration, constitute "a drama of courage and hope."[3] Determined to show us Chekhov's comic side, he goes on to maintain, after quoting Chekhov's description of Mme Ranevsky, the owner of the cherry orchard, "These are all the outward expressions of a woman who . . . 'has lost her life,' or in other words has thrown it away on trifles, and it is this that forms the ludicrous or comic essence of her character."[4] One need not deny that *The Cherry Orchard* has a large admixture of humor, even at times of farce, but one may wonder if the spectacle of a gracious and intelligent woman ruining her life is quite as amusing as Magarschack suggests. Here, at any rate, the attempt to show Chekhov as more humorous than at first he seems succeeds only in portraying him as less humane than he actually is. Nevertheless, so widespread has been the idea that Chekhov must be rescued from his reputation as a gloomy playwright that in 1958, for example, no less than three critical articles appeared stressing the essentially comic nature of *The Cherry Orchard*.[5]

Ultimately, however, the question of the comic versus the pathetic Chekhov has tended to be self-defeating as a device for achieving a better understanding of Chekhov's art. However valuable as a corrective, the emphasis on humor has encouraged an unproductive focusing on details of character or situation. Thus, the admirers of the comic Chekhov, for instance, are likely to find in Treplev, the young writer of *The Seagull,* a hysterical, attitudinizing would-be Hamlet, whereas the advocates of the sensitive, melancholy playwright will see a frustrated artist finally driven to suicide. But the structural pattern of action of the play as a whole suggests that these two readings are simply not relevant and that the significant point about Treplev is neither that he is ridiculous nor that he is pathetic but that he is a man who cannot learn what he must know to survive.

This pattern of action in these last plays of Chekhov involves, as so often in the work of Synge, a symbolic journey. And just as Synge's characters wander not only onto the roads of Ireland but into a dubious future, so those of Chekhov often find themselves at the ends of the plays confronted not only by the vastness of the Russian countryside but by a journey into a future where glimmers of happiness have become immeasurably distant. Chekhov's dramatic world, however, encompasses both the initial bustle of arrival as well as the melancholy of departure. It is in fact an irony of Chekhov's that his plays, on the surface so static, should be concerned with arrivals and departures that always delineate the limits of the action. The comings and goings of Arkadina and Trigorin serve this function in *The Sea Gull,* as do those of Yelena and Serebryakov in *Uncle Vanya.* In *The Three Sisters* the longed-for trip to Moscow as well as the arrival of Vershinin and the final departure of the battalion carry on the journey motif, which in *The Cherry Orchard* is expressed by Mme Ranevsky's trip from Paris and her return to it.

In itself, however, the journey motif seems to do little to clarify Chekhov's meaning. Robert Corrigan simply notes its presence in passing; [6] Magarshack suggest only that it provides convenient occasions for introducing physical action on the stage.[7] But when this motif is considered in relation to the kinds of persons who make the journeys, the reactions that their arrivals and departures evoke, and the lives of those in whom these reactions are aroused, it offers a key to the structure and meaning of the Chekhovian drama. Briefly, then, in each of Chekhov's last plays the action is initiated by the arrival of a character or group of characters in what we come to recognize as a Chekhovian setting, a house in the country or in a small town, isolated in space and even in time, a miniature world. The characters who impinge upon this world tend, with certain exceptions, to be comparatively unmoved by their encounter with it. Since their function is to evoke reactions while remaining for the most part unchanged themselves, we may refer to them as catalyst characters. At the heart of each play stand its central figures, those whose feelings—invariably of longing—are most profoundly aroused by the encounter with the catalyst group. The meeting with the catalyst group regularly engenders in the central characters a yearning for a new state of being in a world beyond the life of pettiness, drudgery, and disappointment to which their selves are confined.

Though in Chekhov this sense of longing is usually associated with love, few of the love relationships are consummated and none is happy. However, the romantic yearning that permeates these plays and helps give them their special flavor extends beyond the various affairs of the heart with which the major characters are so much occupied. Of the secondary figures grouped around the central ones, many share this yearning, though love is not necessarily what evokes it. Moreover, the emphasis on vast stretches of time that appears over and over again in Chekhov's dialogue extends the emotions of the characters beyond their individual lifetimes to remoter realms of experience. But most notably, there is in each play a major symbol—the sea gull, Astrov's forests in *Uncle Vanya*, Moscow in *The Three Sisters*, and in Chekhov's final play the cherry orchard itself—which to the reader or observer becomes a central point of coherence for the sense of romantic longing. As the symbol (significantly, in the last three plays a *place)* unifies the yearnings of the different characters, it also expands them beyond the range that any single character's emotions could encompass.

So far the pattern we have discerned reinforces the image of the melancholy Chekhov of tradition, but another element fits into this pattern, altering its character. Although, as we have previously observed, too much emphasis on the comic Chekhov can lead to oversimplification, an understanding of the function of the pervasive element of comedy in his plays is essential to a full appreciation of their art. At times the comic approach is basically tolerant of faults or limitations; the characters who provoke it (e.g., Telyegin) are, like Mr. Pickwick or the early Chaplin, the objects of an indulgent affection. Since it keeps us satisfied with the characters as they are, what we can call Chekhov's humor acts as a counter-balance to the longing for change so passionately expressed by the characters themselves. On the other hand, Chekhov's comic view can be more openly critical, making the characters and their yearnings objects of satire. Tusenbach and Vershinin, for all their sensitivity and goodwill, are given to philosophizing so extravagantly about the future as to make both themselves and their noble yearnings upon occasion merely ridiculous.

In addition, the sense of romantic longing in Chekhov is qualified not only by his comedy in both its tolerant and satiric aspects but by the ways in which the characters themselves react to their inability to translate aspiration into reality. Their dreams have been stimulated or brought into being by the advent of the catalyst figures, but when they depart the central characters are faced with the failure of their desires. However, instead of falling into despair, they invariably turn to the idea of work as an answer to the emptiness of their lives. Putting aside any thought of happiness for themselves, they accept a lifetime of labor, the results of which will be gathered, if at all, by others far in the future. What is significant in their actions is not the message, "work for others" (that in fact is often embodied in speeches that are awkward and obviously meant to be, at least in part, amusing), but the painful acceptance of a quiet and mature resignation. Nevertheless, although the transition from a state of eager yearning, which Chekhov presents through the theme of love, to one of patient endurance, which he associates with work, is the central psychological action of his plays, the romantic vision of progress to a happy world in the future is never abandoned. Even in the darkest plays, there is at least a suggestion that the dream can ultimately be realized.

Thus, in the basic pattern of action a catalyst group lifts the central inhabitants of the Chekhov world to a state of romantic longing associated with love, which when their dream is found to be unrealizable they will have to exchange for patient resignation. As the catalyst characters depart, the central figures commit themselves to an existence of selfless labor and a faint hope of happiness in a future beyond their lifetimes. Any such paradigm, however it may clarify a play's structure, can of course never yield its total meaning, which we apprehend by experiencing the work and by examining closely the details of its texture. Moreover, since we may presume that Chekhov wrote to satisfy the demands of his art rather than the preferences of his critics, we need not be surprised to find that, although no play deviates greatly from the basic pattern, none follows it absolutely.

The Sea Gull, for example, poses a special problem in regard to its central symbol. Apparently the gull is to be related directly to Nina. Almost as soon as she enters, she says, "but I feel pulled to this place, to this lake, as if I were a sea gull." Even in her final interview with Treplev her mind, haunted by memories of the past, keeps wandering uneasily back to that identification. "I'm a sea gull. No, that's not it," she repeats over and over. Meanwhile, Chekhov has clearly—even it would seem a little heavy-handedly—drawn a parallel between them in the action of the play. Treplev, jealous at Nina's obvious admiration for Trigorin, has shot the gull and presented it to her. Seeing Nina with the dead bird, Trigorin is struck by an idea for a story. "A young girl, like you," he muses, "has lived in a house on the shore of a lake like a sea gull, and she's as free and happy as a sea gull. Then a man comes along, sees her, and having nothing better to do, destroys her, like this sea gull here." Artfully placed just before the second act curtain, the speech foreshadows Trigorin's seduction and subsequent desertion of Nina. When at the end of the play she bitterly recalls her lover's words—"a subject for a short story"—the inference seems clear enough. Nina is the beautiful, helpless sea gull, carelessly destroyed by Trigorin. The only thing wrong with this interpretation is that it is entirely at variance with the events of the play and the feelings of its characters. Nina is not destroyed; neither is Trigorin casual in his relations with her. The charming but nonetheless silly, stage-struck girl whom we meet in Act I is at the end of the play an actress of talent and a woman of character. She has been scarred by what she has endured, but she is ready to cope with her life. Trigorin, who in his relationship with Nina describes himself as possessed by "a love that's young and beautiful, a love that's poetic, a love that carries you off into a world of dreams," may be deceiving himself but is hardly passing the time having "nothing better to do."

Although Trigorin's idea for a short story functions by foreshadowing the injury he will do to Nina, Chekhov does not allow it to limit the play's major symbol. Treplev, for instance, obviously sees the gull in relation to himself as well as to Nina. When he presents her with the dead bird, he clearly wishes her to take it as a symbol of their love, which she has destroyed, and of himself, for he tells Nina that he intends to commit suicide. Moreover, the gull is connected, as Nina has already suggested, with the lake beside which Treplev's play was presented. "You know," Arkadina recalls, "ten or fifteen years ago you could hear music and singing almost every night. There are six estates on the lake. Oh, and I remember such laughter, and noise, and there were shootings too—and the love affairs, love affairs all the time." By now the gull is associated not only with Nina and the destruction of her dream but with Treplev and his love as well as with the beauty and romance of the first act setting. It has, in fact, connections with all the characters who dream of a world of beauty and happiness and with their ultimate disappointment in not realizing that dream.

But the gull is more than a widely diffused symbol of romantic longing. In the fourth act the gull returns. It has been stuffed at the request of Trigorin, but when Shamraev shows it to him he does not remember it. That Trigorin should no longer recall the incident of the gull is hardly surprising, but, curiously, Treplev, too, seems to have forgotten it. When he tells Dorn that Nina seemed a little unbalanced because she always signed her letters "Sea Gull," he offers in explanation, not the incident of the gull, but a literary parallel from Pushkin's *The River Nymph* in which a miller calls himself a raven. Trigorin and Treplev are dissociated from the gull, but Nina remembers it. And like Nina, the gull has undergone a change. The life has been drained out of it, but in its new form it survives and even keeps a kind of permanence. Nina, too, though injured, has evaded destruction, and in the world of her art, even as an actress, we may believe that she achieves something of the timelessness that pertains to all beauty.

At the end of the play Chekhov focuses the symbol of the sea gull, comparatively diffused earlier, on Nina, because she is the only one of his characters who completes the full cycle of feeling already described. Stimulated by the catalyst characters, Trigorin and Arkadina, she dreams of love and fame but finds instead a life of labor in the practice of her art and the courage to accept it. "What matters most," she tells Treplev in words that, with variations, will be echoed at the end of each of Chekhov's final plays, "is knowing how to endure, knowing how to bear your cross and still have faith. I have faith now and I can stand my suffering [and] when I think of my calling, I'm not afraid of life." Usually Chekhov associates the theme of work with that of time, envisioning a long period of labor that must precede any possibility of human happiness. But since Nina cannot, in character, philosophize about the future of humanity, Chekhov, with wonderful subtlety, introduces the ideas of time and change—and of a world transformed by their workings—in her recollection of the speech from Treplev's play. Purged of the excrescences that made Arkadina think it "right out of the decadent school of the symbolists," it evokes a realm of desolate beauty, though we remember that in the original there was also a sense of ultimate triumph:

> Men, lions, eagles, and partridges, horned deer, geese, spiders, and the silent fish of the deep, starfish and creatures which cannot be seen by the eye—all living things, all living things, all living things having completed their cycle of sorrow, are now extinct. For thousands of years the earth has given birth to no living thing, and this poor moon now lights its lamp in vain. In the meadows, the cranes no longer waken with a cry, and the sound of the May beetles, humming in the lime groves, can no longer be heard.

The sea gull, then, at first the symbol of a romantic yearning for beauty and happiness, comes as the play progresses to represent the typically Chekhovian reaction of pain, courage, and acceptance of disappointment, and to be connected if indirectly with a transcending vision of a special universe.

Yet he who initially evoked that universe cannot attain the kind of strength Nina ultimately achieves. Weakly dependent on Arkadina (like Trigorin) and frustrated in his love for Nina, Treplev is unable to find in his art a reason for existence. His style, Trigorin tells us, is vague and his characters lifeless. "I'm still floating in a maze of dreams and images," he admits, "without knowing what it is I am to do." Although Chekhov's central characters can live without love or happiness, they must know what they are to do.

For those lesser personages whose function is largely to reflect, with diminished intensity, the feelings and dilemmas of the central characters, such knowledge is not so necessary. Sorin, for example, functions throughout the play merely as a comic restatement of the theme of frustrated aspiration. All his longings, to get married, to be a writer, had come to nothing. Even a momentary impulse to sing ends in failure. In Act I he begins to sing "The Two Grenadiers," then stops and turns to Nina and Treplev. "Once I started singing this," he tells them, "and the Assistant County Attorney said to me: 'Your Excellency, you certainly have a powerful voice.' Then he thought for a minute and said 'and a bad one, too!' " It is typical of the subtle irony of Chekhov's touch that the song that Sorin starts, Schumann's setting of Heine's *Die Beide Grenadiere,* should be one of the great romantic evocations of the power of the will (here a will that vows to seize upon its object even from beyond the grave), precisely the quality that Sorin lacks. Masha, Medvedenko, and Polina are clearly part of the chain of frustrated lovers; Dorn seems at first to have escaped the distresses that overbear the others, yet even he confesses that on his trip abroad he liked Genoa best because in that place there was always a crowd in which he could obliterate his own identity. Only by dissociation does he evade the frustrations of his friends' unrealized yearnings. Shamraev alone is truly exempt from pain, for he is so dominated by his comic obsessions as to be totally insensitive. Here, too, we see one of Chekhov's persistent patterns. The characters who escape suffering are regularly those on the lowest level of sensibility, and hence those who whose aspirations to transform their lives are minimal or nonexistent.

In *Uncle Vanya,* for instance, only Marina, the old nurse, and Marya Vassilyevna, Vanya's mother, remain unaffected by the emotional upheavals of the play, upheavals centrally concerned with loss, longing, and change. For the simple nurse the resumption of the ordinary domestic routine will put everything right again. The attempted murder of the Professor and Vanya's suicidal state are trivialities to her. "It is a long time," she sighs in the midst of these distresses, "since I, poor sinner, have eaten noodles." Her counterpart, less winning, more intellectual but no less dissociated, is Marya Vassilyevna, who hardly interrupts the annotating of her pamphlets to notice the human agonies around her.

Curiously, in Chekhov's dramatic scheme these persons of low sensibility who are least involved in the action bear some similarities to the catalyst figures, in this case Serebryakov and Yelena, who are always at its center. Although the old Professor touchingly mourns the loss of his academic dignities and realizes that he is a burden on the family, his irascibility and egoism, culminating in the selfishness of his scheme to sell the estate, show that he resembles Marya Vassilyevna in a certain lack of human feeling as well as in his pedantry. Because of the limitations of his nature and of his mind, his labors are meaningless for the future, and his final words of condescending advice to Astrov, the most active person in the play, "do something, my friend! Work! You must work!" are a notable instance of Chekhovian irony.

The case of Yelena, the other catalyst character, is at once more complicated and more interesting. A woman of intelligence and goodwill, she, like Trigorin before her, shares the yearning of the central figures to escape from the drabness of their lives into a world of greater color and beauty. In words that anticipate those of Major Barbara, she says, "Oh, to be free as a bird, to fly away from all those drowsy faces and their monotonous mumblings and forget that they have existed to all! Oh, to forget oneself and what one is." Moreover, she understands something of the evil that the people about her do, destroying one another just as they destroy Astrov's forests. "You are all possessed by a devil of destructiveness," she tells Vanya, "you have no feeling, no, not even pity, for either the woods or the birds or women, or for one another." What she does not understand is that she is herself that devil of destructiveness. She is the dream of unattainable beauty that lures man into lassitude and morbid self-absorption. At the beginning of the play Vanya has observed that since her arrival he has no longer worked, and as early as Act II Astrov offers a hint about Yelena's nature: "She is very beautiful, there's no denying it, but, after all, all she does is eat, sleep, go for walks, fascinate us by her beauty and nothing more." Near the end of the play, in a moment of illumination, he speaks even more openly:

> The moment you and your husband arrived here, everyone
> whom you found busy and engaged in active, creative work
> felt compelled to drop it and give himself up to you and your
> husband's gout for the entire summer. You and your husband
> have infected all of us with your idleness. I became infatuated

with you and I have done nothing for a whole month, and in the meantime people have been ill and the peasantry have been grazing their herds in my newly planted woods . . . so that wherever you and your husband go, you bring destruction everywhere. I am joking, of course, and yet I am strangely convinced that if you had remained here, we should have been overtaken by the most terrible desolation and destruction.

More than anyone else Astrov is sensitive to the significance of Yelena and Serebryakov, for despite his weakness he is throughout at once the most idealistic and the most clear-headed of all the characters. It is his idealism that gives the play its major symbol, the forests that he tends and plants and that, like the sea gull, come to represent a realm of beauty and happiness. With an enthusiasm generated by her love for Astrov, Sonya presents his program of reforestation in its most optimistic light. In places where the climate has been tempered by forests, she says, "less energy is wasted on the struggle with nature and that is why man there is more gentle and loving; the people there are beautiful, supple, and sensitive, their speech is refined and their movements graceful. Art and learning flourish among them, their philosophy is not so depressing, and they treat women with refinement and nobility." (We sense the delicate Chekhovian irony in Sonya's placing the treatment of women as a climax to the development of art, learning, and philosophy.) Astrov himself modifies Sonya's words by placing the happiness associated with the forests far in the future, where, in Chekhov, it must inevitably be. "But when I cross those peasant forests which I have saved from the axe," he tells his listeners, "or hear the rustling of the young trees, which I have set out with my own hands, I feel as if I had had some small share in improving the climate, and that if mankind is happy a thousand years from now I shall have been partly responsible in my small way for their happiness." Although these words, too, are qualified by a hint of irony—as he finishes his speech, Astrov gulps down a glass of vodka—suggestions of the forest, beautiful and remote, and of the climate, literal and moral, that it will hereafter make possible rest behind, and contrast with, the tragi-comic confusions and distresses of the characters.

Despite the fact that the visionary Astrov is the most nearly heroic person in the play, when Chekhov completed his work he changed its title from *The Wood Demon,* Astrov's nickname in the earlier version, to *Uncle Vanya.* The shift is particularly striking, since Chekhov seems at first to have diminished the significance of Vanya's role. In the earlier version he had killed himself; here he merely shoots at the Professor and misses. Nevertheless, not only does his act remain the climax on which the play turns, but his course of development, unlike Astrov's, follows the essential Chekhovian pattern. For Vanya, although he may be less intriguing than Astrov as a character, is more significant as an exemplar. Long before the action of the play begins Astrov has felt the full weight of a hard and loveless life. Setting his goal beyond the confines of his own existence, he is laboring with courage and dignity to make a future world joyful for others. He has, in other words, already arrived at the position that most central figures in Chekhov reach only after they have passed through their crises. Though momentarily distracted by Yelena's beauty, he returns, after a brief excursion, only to the point he had previously occupied. Vanya, however, had believed that his devotion to and support of Serebryakov constituted at least a vicarious fulfillment of his own self. The frantic intensity of his frustrated longing for Yelena shows the depth of his distress at finding himself deceived. Only when the catalyst characters, having done their work, depart, does Vanya complete the full Chekhovian cycle from innocence through romantic longings to resolution. Vanya is necessarily the focal character in the play, for no one else realizes so suddenly and so strongly the nature of his frustration, and no one yearns so desperately to transcend it.

After Vanya has brought the play to its climax by his attempted murder of Serebryakov, it is appropriately his niece, Sonya, who leads him to accept the life of patient labor that is regularly the ultimate destiny of Chekhov's central figures. She, too, has followed a similar path, though in a far quieter way. (One critic has suggested that Vanya, Astrov, and Sonya are different aspects of a single "individual" who is the protagonist of the play, but his idea, though ingenious, blurs the distinctions that Chekhov is at pains to make).[8] Although her love for Astrov is not the product of an illumination produced by the catalyst figures, its frustration is the result of Yelena's meddling. But in spite of her own grief, she induces Vanya to return to Astrov the bottle of morphine he had stolen, intending to commit suicide, and in the elaborate and beautiful speech that closes the play establishes a mood of patience and limited hope. The speech's religiosity is part of Sonya's character, but the irony and pathos evoked by her finding a world of happiness only in death derive from Chekhov's vision. It is the human elements of courage, endurance, and faith that he wishes to suggest through the pathetic figure of Sonya just as he has already done through the humorous one of Telyegin. For Sonya's gentle godfather is designed to do more than provide comic relief. An early one-act play, *On the Highroad,* had already embodied the material of Telyegin's life, a husband deserted by his wife on their wedding day and then impoverished, in a sentimental melodrama, but here in the pathetic dignity with which Telyegin bears his sufferings Chekhov anticipates comically and in miniature the disappointing destinies of his major characters.

These destinies, however, are not entirely determined by the characters themselves. Their fates are worked upon by an external force, which though absent from *The Sea Gull* and only peripheral in *Uncle Vanya,* comes to occupy a crucial position in *The Three Sisters.* The heavy, grinding weight of ordinary, day-to-day life in the world of provincial Russia is, as it appears in Chekhov, partly a product of his acute observation of the prerevolutionary Russian scene and partly a symbolic projection of his own recognition of the power of time to wear away that sense of vital enthusiasm with which life is commonly begun. *Uncle Vanya* opens with Astrov commenting on the "senseless, dirty, stupid" life that finally "swallows you up," and in the last act he refers to it again as he and Vanya confront their empty futures:

> Yes, my friend, in this entire community there were only two decent and intelligent men, you and I. Ten years or so of this life of ours, this wretched life of the commonplace and the trivial, have sucked us under and poisoned us with their destructive vapors, and we have become as contemptible, as petty, and as despicable as the others.

In *Uncle Vanya* this life is only referred, to, but in *The Three Sisters* it comes onstage in the person of Natalya Ivanovna, Andrey's fiancée and later his wife. Behind her stand unseen her powerful lover,

Protopopov, and the inhabitants of the entire provincial town in which the Prozorovs live. In her pettiness, her vulgarity, her acquisitiveness, and her hunger for power, Natalya is the visible embodiment of that life of coarseness and greed that is the opposite of the free, gracious, longed-for existence the Prozorov sisters always associate with the Moscow of their youth and yearn to recapture by returning there in the future.

This central opposition, between the real life of the town and the nostalgic and visionary life of Moscow, is symbolized by the contrast between its two catalyst characters. Even as Natalya thrusts herself into the lives of the central figures at the climax of the first act, Colonel Vershinin, the new commander of the battalion, also arrives in the opening act, not unexpectedly bringing associations with Moscow, for the sisters remember that he had frequented their house. And just as Natalya is totally obsessed with the petty life of the present, so Vershinin is always envisioning the glorious world of the future. Over and over again he bursts forth with speeches of praise for the life man will one day lead: "Why, in two or three hundred years life on this earth will be wonderfully beautiful. Man longs for a life like that, and if he doesn't have it right now, he must imagine it, wait for it, dream about it." The total failure of his life in the present, a typical Chekhovian irony, does not detract from our sympathetic apprehension of what he says, for that failure contrasts most favorably with the total success of Natalya's unpleasant machinations. Their opposition, however, is intensified by the love affair each conducts. Natalya's coarse and placid liaison with Protopopov brings the Prozorovs, with whom our sympathy is always bound, only misery, whereas Vershinin's love for Masha brings her the only happiness she will ever know. And finally, Vershinin's departure at the end of the play, as is usually the case with a catalyst figure, marks the characters' acceptance of a harsher reality. Natalya's actions, in a sense, have the same effect. However, instead of herself leaving, she forces the departure of the sisters, expelling them from the house that is a last tenuous connection with their memories and hopes of happiness.

Between these two extremes, the vulgar realities of Natalya and the insubstantial dreams of Vershinin, the three Prozorov sisters, the central characters of the play, find themselves trapped. Olga, the eldest, enunciates her longing to escape almost as soon as the curtain rises on the first act. "I wanted so much to go home again. Go home to Moscow," she says. Ironically, however, Moscow, at once a remembrance of the past and a dream of a happy life in the future, is furthest from her reach. Already she has "aged and grown a lot thinner." Soon she will be headmistress of the local girls' school and irrevocably committed to the life of the town. Masha, though married to a local schoolteacher, is yet capable of attempting to escape from the life. Still attractive, she tries in her affair with Vershinin to satisfy her longings for happiness. For Irina, the youngest, the dream of Moscow seems genuinely possible, but slowly the heavy weight of reality begins to settle upon her. By the end of the third act she observes, like Olga, that she is "getting thinner and uglier and older." Ultimately, even her attempt to accept a limited happiness with Tusenbach is frustrated, and she joins her sisters in the play's final words, an autumnal threnody in which, as always with Chekhov, a life of labor leads only to the hope that happiness will be achieved by others far in a future that might perhaps illumine the meaning of present suffering.

The painful effect of a stultifying reality is most starkly revealed in Andrey, who becomes deeply submerged in the life of the town, leaving the work of enlightenment, which was to have been his, to his sisters. In Irina's two suitors Chekhov has arranged a careful contrast. Tusenbach, a kind of practical Vershinin, is devoted to work and new life, whereas the egocentric, Byronic Solyony cannot get the odor of the grave off his hands. If Kulygin, a variation on the theme of well-meaning futility, reminds us of Medvedenko and Telyegin and if Anfisa, in her delight at being provided for, suggests the old nurse of *Uncle Vanya*, Cherbutykin is an extraordinary and original creation. Once a physician and a man of feeling who had loved the mother of the sisters, he has become so coarsened and dehumanized that his own solipsistic doubts—"perhaps I'm not even a man at all, but just imagine that I've got hands and feet and a head. Perhaps I don't exist at all"—seem by the last act, which he spends in a state of cheerful tranquillity even though the fiancé of his favorite, Irina, is being killed, to have become a terrible truth. In all of Chekhov he is the most pitiful and frightening example of the destructive effects of an existence without meaning because without yearning.

Although nothing in *The Cherry Orchard* approaches in painfulness this portrait of the total annihilation of the self that Chekhov has drawn in *The Three Sisters,* the two plays are bound together by a basic structural similarity. Just as Natalya and Vershinin had embodied the contrast between coarse reality and insubstantial dream, so in *The Cherry Orchard* the two catalyst figures represent irreconcilable opposites between which the central character finds himself indecisively poised. As always in Chekhov, these two figures are a man and a woman, for the contrast in sexes adds powerfully to their range of suggestion. When Lyubov Ranevsky arrives at the beginning of Act I, she brings with her the whole pattern of feeling that is, over the course of the play, associated with the cherry orchard. Not only is the orchard beautiful in itself, but it derives dignity from being part of a great estate and of a grand, aristocratic life of the past. Yet also connected with the orchard is a strong sense of guilt for the injustices that sustained it. As Trofimov reminds Anya, "Your grandfather and your great-grandfather, and all your ancestors were serf owners—they owned living souls. Don't you see human beings staring at you from every tree in the orchard, from every leaf and every trunk?" Even the guilty life of the past, however, has by now been drained out of it. Old Feers remembers the preserved cherries that once were shipped to Moscow and Kharkov. "And the dried cherries used to be soft, juicy, sweet, and very good. . . . They knew how to do it then . . . they had a way of cooking them." But when Lyubov asks where the recipe is, he can only reply, "They've forgotten it. Nobody can remember it." Even in Lyubov personally the orchard evokes mixed feelings, since it carries memories of her happy girlhood and of the drowning of her son. The orchard, then, becomes a rich symbol bearing associations, not only of youthful innocence, beauty, and dignity, but of guilt, decay, and death.

Lyubov's efforts to save the orchard are inevitably futile (the money that she obtains is ridiculously insufficient), yet she is totally committed to the life of the past that it represents. To her Lopahin's scheme is meaningless since it would destroy her conception of the gracious and beautiful world she once knew, a conception more poignant for being only partly true. But if she is obsessed with a longing for the past, the other catalyst figure is equally absorbed in a vision of the future. Petya Trofimov, the former tutor of her lost son, also arrives at the beginning of the play. For him, the only thing of significance is the paradisical future that he envisions at the end of mankind's great struggle. "Humanity," he declares, "is continually advancing, is continually seeking to perfect its powers." Yet though he preaches the doctrine of work as the remedy for the lassitude and squalor of the actuality about him, he does no work himself but remains an eternal graduate student rhapsodizing ecstatically about the road to a future world:

> To free ourselves of all that's petty and ephemeral, all that prevents us from being free and happy, that's the whole aim and meaning of our life. Forward! We march forward irresistibly towards that bright star shining there in the distance! Forward!

The opposition of Lyubov, obsessed with the past, and Trofimov, who believes only in the future, is a variation of Chekhov's usual dramatic pattern. Although the two catalyst figures always establish a symbolic contrast, here they also express that sense of romantic yearning usually reserved for the central characters. Nevertheless, since they spend the play longing for objectives that are beyond their powers to achieve, they remain only catalyst figures, unchanged by what they undergo. At the end of the play Lyubov merely returns to her lover in Paris and Trofimov to his classes in Moscow. Moreover, in the climactic third act Chekhov presents the confrontation in which each reveals the faults of the other. Lyubov, too weakly human, is infatuated with a man who has swindled her; Trofimov, too ethereal, boasts that he is above love when he is only timid and prudish.

Poised between these two extremes stands Lopahin, whose role Chekhov himself characterized as central to the play in a letter recommending it to Stanislasvsky.[9] When Lopahin announces in Act III that he has bought the cherry orchard, he makes an unalterable break with that past that throughout the play he has attempted sympathetically but blunderingly to sustain. Up to this point Lopahin, the son of a peasant but now a prosperous bourgeois (the similarity to Chekhov's background cannot be overlooked), has hesitated between the antithetical worlds of past and future. His peasant reverence for the aristocracy and his genuine affection for Lyubov engendered by her kindness have led him to align himself with the past and try to save the estate for her. But he fails to realize not only that his scheme would destroy with the orchard the life of the past that it symbolizes but that it constitutes an inherent commitment to the life of the future. Speaking of the people who use the kind of summer cottages he proposes for the estate, he says, "Right now, all they do is sit on the porch and drink tea, but later on they might begin to grow a few things, and then your cherry orchard would be full of life again . . . rich and prosperous." Later, he reveals his unconscious aspirations even more explicitly. In reply to Trofimov's comments on the lassitude of the intelligentsia, Lopahin says that, though he works hard, "you have only to start doing something to realize how few honest, decent people there are. Sometimes, when I can't sleep, I start thinking about it. God's given us immense forests, and wide-open fields, and unlimited horizons—living in such a world we ought to be giants!"

For all his attempts to aid Lyubov, Lopahin is in reality committed, not to the past, but to the work of the present and ultimately to the world of the future, as his purchase of the estate finally confirms. When in the last act he and Trofimov say good-bye, the companionship of the two visionaries, one practical and the other ethereal, becomes apparent. "You know," Trofimov says to his friend (after rebuking him, with unconscious irony, for his schemes for the future of the estate), "in spite of everything I like you. You've got beautiful delicate fingers, like an artist's, you've a fine sensitive soul." Lopahin affirms their friendship with appropriate practicality, offering to lend Trofimov money. Finally, after the student earnestly reasserts his position in the avant-grade of humanity's march toward "the greatest happiness," Lopahin accepts the unending labor that is finally what gives meaning to the lives of Chekhov's heroes "When I work all day long, without resting," he tells Trofimov, "I'm happier and sometimes I even think I know why I exist."

Despite the closeness with which the various subsidiary figures echo the themes associated with the central characters, only one other person shares something of Lopahin's courageous resignation. Not surprisingly, it is Anya, Trofimov's other admirer, whose farewell to her mother contains, in a brighter tone, those suggestions of work and the passing of time that have appeared earlier in the final words of Nina, Sonya, and the three sisters. "You'll come back soon, Mama . . . won't you? I'll study and pass my exams [presumably for a teacher's certificate] and then I'll work and help you. We'll read together, Mama . . . all sorts of things . . . won't we? We'll read during the long autumn evenings. We'll read lots of books and a new wonderful world will open up before us." In her housekeeping practicality, Varya seems, like Lopahin, committed to the idea of labor, and she, too, has idealistic longings; but her work is not animated by a transcending vision, and her idealism does not progress much beyond a vague longing for the life of a religious pilgrim. She remains, finally, suspended between the worlds of past and future.

The claims of a past world are presented in such comic, pathetic, and farcical figures as Gaev, Feers, and Pishchik. In Gaev and Feers, Chekhov portrays the ultimate decadence of the relationship between the irresponsible master and the mindlessly devoted servant, while Pishchik's frantic borrowings constitute a farcical version of Lyubov's attempts to save her cherry orchard. Moreover, Dunyasha's infatuation with Yasha, one of those typical Chekhovian figures of coarse sensibilities who remain unmoved by the catastrophes occurring about them, is a comic vulgarization of, and thus a comment on, Lyubov's affair with her Parisian lover.

Chekhov brings this parody love affair before us because Lyubov's sexual life is a significant element in the play. (Her allure may finally help account for Lopahin's continued bachelorhood; we have seen already in the involvement of Treplev with Arkadina how much Chekhov had sensed about the dynamics of the oedipal relationship.) In this regard, in fact, Lyubov is typical of the female catalyst figures, most of whom are women of great charm and all of whom are sexually vital—that is, they are either engaged in love affairs or are the objects of men's sexual interest. In particular, however, Lyubov reminds us of Arkadina (though they are opposites in money matters) in her vivacity, frivolity, and manipulative charm. Indeed, Lyubov's third act scene with Trofimov, when she cajoles him back into good humor after rebuking him for his prudishness, evokes, however faintly, another echo of Arkadina's tempestuous relationship with her son. Quite different sexual characteristics are suggested by the other two catalyst women, ranging from the greedy possessiveness of Natalya, who swallows up Andrey and luxuriates in her affair with Protopopov, to the exquisite lassitude of Yelena, who—like an ondine of Giraudoux—becomes the beguiling dream of transcendent beauty.

When we consider the men of the catalyst group, however, we find something very different. Even when they are involved in love relationships, none of these men is very active. Trigorin, despite his brief arousal by Nina, is dominated by Arkadina's energy; Serebryakov is nursed rather than loved by his wife; Vershinin "philosophized" before his affair with Masha and will do so after it has ended; Trofimov says that he and Anya are "above love." Indeed, we hardly perceive any of these man in the role of lovers. A perpetual graduate student, a verbalizer of unrealized dreams, an elderly scholar hiding from his empty pedantry, a writer self-compelled to produce repeatedly the same limited work—all of them are in some way feeble, insubstantial, living on the fringes of things: resigned, irascible, at best nursing vague aspirations.

The extraordinary, continuing opposition between the male and female catalyst figures suggests that Chekhov's artistic instincts have made them more than what we have already perceived them to be, the agents that stimulate the central characters to wish for a world of happiness beyond what they have known. The entire movement of these plays is evoked by the very nature of the catalyst group. In the beauty, the charm, the simple libidinal energy of these women, Chekhov suggests the roots of the impulse to find the transcendent world. But in the men whom they draw with them we see the fatigue, the weakness, the ephemeral dreams that are its end. Deeply buried in Chekhov's plays there is one of the ultimate romantic images, that of the fatal enchantress and the knight whom she holds in thrall. It is these figures who arrive at the beginnings of Chekhov's plays, who rouse the central characters to long for a world in which the self may know happiness, who preside over the courageous recognition that such a world belongs to the infinite future, and who—unaltered—depart, embodying in themselves the impulse to life and beauty as well as its end in death.

Bernard Shaw: The Ascent to Heaven

It is the peculiar nature of Shaw's plays that from the beginning they simultaneously embody romantic optimism and romantic disillusion. William Archer's account of first seeing Shaw in the British Museum alternately studying the French translation of *Das Kapital* and the score of *Tristan und Isolde* is suggestive here. Characteristically, Shaw was to be attracted not only by optimism, progress, and social action but by the opposing qualities of passivity, withdrawal, and fulfillment in death.

The continuing dramatic tension in Shaw's work is generated, at least in part, by a conflicting vision of the world—as a place where the self can be perfected; where continuing reform and improvement are possible; or as the abode of vulgarity, greed, and brute stupidity in which man retains his distasteful and irredeemable self. The optimistic vision is by far the more conscious one. It is the vision of the man of ideas, the social reformer, the satirist determined to laugh men into a recognition of their follies. Ostensibly, it is the vision that underlies the theory of Creative Evolution, that notable manifestation of romantic optimism, with its commitment to eternal progress and unlimited possibilities. But in fact that curious theory is an aspect of the negative, pessimistic vision, for the ultimate end of Creative Evolution is a withdrawal from the failures and limitations of the human condition into a world of pure, self-contemplating intellect. Shaw the activist projects a faith in progress and perfectibility, but Shaw the negativist embodies with equal force a sense of disillusion and its attendant impulse toward withdrawal and rejection.

The preachments of the optimistic Shaw are easily enough recognizable, but the presence of the other is sometimes harder to perceive. It appears most strikingly in a pattern of dramatic action that we may characterize as an ascent to heaven, sometimes a literal ascent, often a figurative one. At the end of some process of education or discovery the central character in a Shavian play will usually withdraw from the world of action, of commitment, of life in fact, to a different one, sometimes conceived of as a world of pure intellectual contemplation, always remote from the ordinary human world, supposedly superior to it. Although this intellectual "heaven" has many different forms in the plays, it is always, finally, the realm where the self takes refuge when it comes to know the failures and imperfections of existence.

When Shaw is most aware of these failures and distressed by these imperfections, the act of withdrawal from the human world is depicted as the necessary act, a deliberate, unqualified response to the limitations of life. But Shaw's vision is not always so dark: in many plays the heaven to which one withdraws is comparatively near the ordinary world; the ascent to it is not immutable. Some counterbalancing commitment to life and social action is made, mitigating the absoluteness of the withdrawal. Much of the interest in following the progress of Shaw's work lies in tracing the variety and complexity of the balances he contrives between his conflicting impulses. Since the optimistic Shaw is a public personage but the despairing Shaw a private one, his commitments to life and action can be made openly and directly, but his impulse to withdraw must be expressed through such extended metaphors as the one this study develops: the ascent to heaven.

Only at its harshest and most remote is this strange heaven directly recognizable. Edmund Wilson, for example, speaks of the "lunar horror" of *Back to Methuselah,* in which the Ancients of the final play aspire to ascend from the flesh and become pure intelligences.[10] Earlier Ludwig Lewisohn had described this "bleak parable" as "the monument of a great despair." [11] Lewisohn implies that this despairing position is one that Shaw arrived at only in old age and after contemplating the horrors of World War I. But such a conception of Shaw's mind or its development is not adequate, for throughout Shaw's career when his plays are at their richest and most brilliant, other heavens and other ascents appear, more interesting for being less obvious.[12]

Of these one of the most intriguing is found at the end of Shaw's third play, *Mrs. Warren's Profession.* Not only is this play, at least arguably, Shaw's first of general theatrical and artistic significance, but it establishes most strikingly the pattern with which we are concerned. Ostensibly, the play is occupied with an immediate social issue, the exploitation of female labor as the economic basis of prostitution. In the climactic confrontation at the end of Act II, Mrs. Warren makes her daughter recognize that for a poor girl prostitution is the only escape from the degradation of poverty. "It's far better than any other employment open to her," Mrs. Warren explains.[13] The scene works dramatically because of the psychological force of Mrs. Warren's attack on Vivie and the whimsical ingenuity with which Shaw makes Mrs. Warren reverse the clichés of conventional morality ("if there's a thing I hate in a woman, it's want of character. . . . It's not work that any woman would do for pleasure, goodness knows. . . . Of course it's worth while to a poor girl, if she can resist temptation.") Nevertheless, the economics of this passage are dated; most working girls need not turn to prostitution in order to survive. But in the next act there is a scene in which the economics remain more nearly valid. When Crofts explains to Vivie that the income he derives as an investor in Mrs. Warren's business is not different in kind from the income others obtain from investment in industries that exploit workers, he is unconsciously offering a general criticism of laissez-faire capitalism.[14] "If you're going to pick and choose your acquaintance on moral principles, you'd better clear out of this country," he says forcefully, "unless you want to cut yourself out of all decent society."

But even this more striking point—that everyone in a society participates in its economic immoralities—is confined to a comparatively brief scene. Most of the play, in fact, is taken up with other matters; Vivie, not her mother, is its central personage, and Vivie's education through the sequence of persons whom she encounters its central concern. Praed, for example, is absolutely essential to Shaw's purposes in this respect, but the thread by which he is connected to the action is, to put it mildly, fragile. Apparently, he has not known Mrs. Warren sexually, or even known what her business is, much less invested in it (perhaps because Shaw is pardonably reluctant to say that art, too, supports and is supported by the brothel); he is Mrs. Warren's "friend," though what the cultivated aesthete and the hearty, vulgar madam have to say to each other is not easy to conceive. But however unlikely his presence, he must appear onstage to sing the beauties of Italian art, to ask Vivie, "Are you to have no romance, no beauty in your life?" and to receive her answer, "I don't care for either, I assure you."

Just as Praed embodies the claims of the sentimental romantic artist,[15] as Shaw conceives of him, foolishly dedicated to beauty as an end in itself, so Frank Gardner is present in order to represent the claims of romantic love. Since Shaw wants such claims rejected even more forcefully than Praed's, he is at considerable pains to make Frank an ostentatiously undesirable young man. Although charming and intelligent, Frank is weak, shiftless, self-indulgent, and entirely irresponsible. Moreover, he may very well be Vivie's half brother. Shaw introduces the incest motif in part to get a grand climax at the end of Act III but more importantly to get a strong emotional prohibition against Frank's and Vivie's relationship. When, immediately after Crofts's revelation, Frank invites Vivie into his arms, she replies "[*with a cry of disgust*], Ah, not that, not that. You make all my flesh creep." Yet having got his prohibition, Shaw is not prepared to deal with it—that is, with the subject of frustrated incestuous passion—and by the beginning of the fourth act Vivie and Frank both protest that in the first place they do not believe Crofts's revelation and in the second they are indifferent to it. But in rejecting the incest theme Shaw also rejects the ostensible basis for Vivie's refusal of Frank and leaves her sexual repugnance without objective justification.

"After all, what is troubling Vivie," Eric Bentley notes, "does go beyond the rationally established causes." [16] Moreover, precisely the same is true of Vivie's relation to her mother. Nearly as powerful as the scene in which Mrs. Warren exposes the truth about her life to Vivie in Act II is their last confrontation, in which Vivie finally and absolutely rejects her mother. It is distinguished by its extraordinary emotional power and its equally extraordinary lack of intellectual coherence. Earlier in this last act Vivie has been so revolted by the knowledge that her mother is continuing to manage the brothels that she cannot bear to speak of the matter to Praed and Frank but must write instead. She begins by rejecting her mother on this basis. However, as soon as Mrs. Warren defends herself ("I must have work and excitement or I should go melancholy mad. And what else is there for me to do?"), nothing more is heard of the matter, but Vivie is as adamant as ever. "You ask me to give you the peace and quietness of my whole life," Vivie says to her mother. Yet no such thing has been asked; Mrs. Warren does not wish to live with Vivie but only to see her from time to time and to live vicariously through the elegant life she proposes for her.

Ultimately, Vivie is reduced to offering her mother's failures of perception as a reason for their separation. "If I had been you, mother," she says, "I might have done as you did: but I should not have lived one life and believed in another. You are a conventional woman at heart. That is why I am bidding you good-bye now." But Vivie's claim is quite unconvincing. If Mrs. Warren has believed in conventional "respectability," she has always known that she could achieve it only through unconventional means. Moreover, the notion that Vivie cannot have any relations whatever with a conventional person is itself rather strange.

It seems less so, however, by the end of the play, as Vivie removes herself to a realm in which she will have few relations of any sort. (At this point Vivie's impulse to separate herself from life is very different from the enthusiastic desire for a business career and the boredom with art that she displays in Act I.) Among the devious rationalizations for breaking with her mother, one statement seems more direct: "Now once for all, mother, you want a daughter and Frank wants a wife. I don't want a mother and I don't want a husband." In its brutal directness this absolute denial carries much of the true emotional force of the scene, which, if intellectually evasive, is powerful and moving. It is so in part because Shaw identifies both with Mrs. Warren in her demands for affection and her rage and grief at its denial and with Vivie in the icy strength with which, sensing them as dangerous, she protects herself from those demands. (Shaw's accounts of his Dublin childhood with its social and emotional strains are valuable here.) But though his feelings are divided, Shaw ultimately focuses on Vivie and her reaction to the education she receives during the play; her rejection of art, of society, of love as equally tainted; and her withdrawal to that curious "heaven," the isolated chambers of Fraser and Warren, a realm of pure numerical calculations where the self may find refuge from the demands of life. As precisely as anything in Shaw's earlier work, this world anticipates the vortex of pure intellect to which the Ancients of *Back to Methuselah* come at the end of mankind's education.

Before Shaw arrived at that late version of his central pattern, however, he worked and reworked it many times, playing variations on it, yet never straying far from his basic theme. Within the confines of this chapter only certain representative examples of this

Shavian vision can be considered. Although strikingly varied in temper and subject matter, each projects an image of the self divided between the impulse to find fulfillment in the real world of human action and the longing to ascend to its own heaven of contemplation.

That heaven tends to appear, not surprisingly, at the conclusions of Shaw's plays, as in *Mrs. Warren's Profession* and in another of his significant early works, *Candida,* whose heroine's charm and maternal warmth contrast so strongly with the cool self-sufficiency of Vivie Warren. But behind Candida's charm we sense the presence of the destructive, emasculating, "Strindbergian" woman whose candid truth must inevitably destroy her husband's self-respect, though in the play Shaw avoids confronting that fact. "Outside the play," as Eric Bentley shrewdly observes, "Shaw is against Candida. Inside it, he is both for her and against her, but he is for her effectually and against her ineffectually." Bentley suggests that although "Shaw's intellect is against Candida, his emotions are for her," [17] but there is in fact a strong emotional pull in both directions. On the one hand, there is the optimistic vision in which Candida is the protecting and loving helpmeet and Morell is happily committed to the world of domestic bliss and political action. (His opinions are Shaw's; like Shaw, he is a great speechmaker.) But as the play progresses, this vision becomes less alluring. The possibility is raised that the dream of reform and progress is an illusion, that the great and serious speechmaker is a mere entertainer whose message no one will take seriously, that domestic happiness means childish dependence on a dominant—perhaps even cruel—woman.

It is this negative vision, especially in regard to the emotive life, that Marchbanks comes to see more and more clearly. From the first he considers Morell's ideas mere verbiage, and he dreams of withdrawing to a "poetic" fantasy world of love:

> MARCHBANKS. . . .—a tiny shallop to sail away in, far from the world, where the marble floors are washed by the rain and dried by the sun, where the south wind dusts the beautiful green and purple carpets. Or a chariot—to carry us up into the sky, where the lamps are stars, and don't need to be filled with paraffin oil every day.

MORELL [*harshly*]. And where there is nothing to do but to be idle, selfish and useless.

. . . .

MARCHBANKS [*firing up*]. Yes, to be idle, selfish and useless: that is to be beautiful and free and happy. . . .

The divided nature of Shaw's own feeling (he is, after all, the activist Morell as well as the poet Marchbanks) is shown in the evenness of the debate and in the fact that, though he allows Marchbanks to triumph here, he cannot find for the poet a convincing diction and must lapse into Swinburnian clichés. When at the end of the play Marchbanks sees what love—exemplified by Candida and Morell—is, he exclaims, "[*rising with a fierce gesture of disgust*]. Ah, never. Out, then, into night with me!" No longer desiring happiness—"life is nobler than that"—he goes out into the night that is awaiting him. Shaw suggested to James Huneker that this night was "Tristan's holy night" and that Marchbanks was "a god going back to his heaven, proud, unspeakably contemptuous of the 'happiness' he envied in the days of his blindness, clearly seeing that he has higher business on hand than Candida." [18] If he is, like so many other Shavian heroes, ascending to heaven, the "higher business" can have little to do with human life. Tristan's holy night enfolds a love that leads only to death.

A man who in a later play quite literally chooses death also finds himself engaged in a kind of combat with a clergyman and romantically involved with the clergyman's wife. But despite the gallantry of its hero, Dick Dudgeon, *The Devil's Disciple,* though lively and attractive, and sustained theatrically by the very melodramatic elements that it parodies, is a far less coherent work than *Candida.* At first it appears to be contrasting the natural, as Shaw would say "vital" morality of Dick Dudgeon with the joyless, systematic, artificial morality of his puritan family. Such indeed is the subject of the first act, but most of the characters of that act, and its subject with them, disappear after it is over. Its place, however, is taken by a second subject: the opposing claims of vital morality and romantic love. After Dick has allowed himself to be arrested in place of Anderson, Judith, distressed at her husband's failure to return the sacrifice, comes to suppose that Dick is sacrificing himself for love of her. But though Judith is willing to play Lucy

Manette, Dick refuses the role of Sidney Carton. Unlike Marchbanks, he seems to have known from the first the illusions of love;
he explains to Judith that he was rather following the law of his
own nature in taking another's place. When she can only reply,
"you mean that you do not love me," he answers "[*revolted—with
fierce contempt*]. Is that all it means to you?"

But this subject, too, is dropped shortly, and near the end of the
play another appears: the reversal of roles, as Anderson discovers
that he is not a clergyman but a soldier and Dick that he is not the
Devil's Disciple but a saint. Shaw seems to have supposed that this
subject was the ultimate one, since he gives Anderson a very explicit speech defining it:

> ANDERSON. Sir, it is in the hour of trial that a man finds his
> true profession. This foolish young man boasted himself the
> Devil's Disciple; but when the hour of trial came to him, he
> found that it was his destiny to suffer and be faithful to the
> death. I thought myself a decent minister of the gospel of
> peace; but when the hour of trial came to me, I found that
> it was my destiny to be a man of action, and that my place
> was amid the thunder of the captains and the shouting.

Yet this speech is curiously misleading and the subject essentially
false. In actuality Anderson changes comparatively little. The step
from the vigorous, sensible, successful parson to the active soldier is
not such a large one. As Anderson in both his roles is essentially
involved in, and committed to, the world, so Dick both as Devil's
Disciple and as saint lives apart from the world, committed to the
higher law of his own self. If he is to be a clergyman, as the play
whimsically asks us to believe, he is hardly likely to be the kind
Anderson was.

What, then, is the real subject? There is another significant figure in the play, usually taken to be a kind of wonderful excres-
cence, but it is no accident that Burgoyne has all the best lines.
Shaw himself seems not to have been aware of what he was doing
with Burgoyne, for he wrote to Ellen Terry, "Burgoyne is a gentleman; and that is the whole meaning of that part of the play. It is
not enough, for the instruction of this generation, that Richard
should be superior to religion & morality as typified by Judith. He

must also be superior to gentility—that is, to the whole idea of modern society." [19] But this explanation notably fails to account for the sense of grace, of perception, of decisiveness and power that radiates through Burgoyne's wit. Especially it does not account for the obvious sympathy between him and Dick. Burgoyne is a first sketch for a character who will embody some of Dick's moral perception but will combine it with a sense of power. If Anderson is committed to the world and its illusions and if Dick can do no more than suffer and withdraw into martyrdom, Burgoyne can both act and know. He is both in the world and, by the power of his wit and perception, beyond it. He prefigures Caesar, the first Shavian superman.

If one is to understand this figure, one must know his origins. It is important, then, to see Burgoyne, not as a whimsical comic addition to *The Devil's Disciple,* but as a significant synthesis of Dick and Anderson. One thus recognizes that in creating the Shavian superman, the figure of the hero-saint to which he so often reverts, Shaw is attempting to symbolize in art a resolution for the dilemma inherent in his vision. He is creating in his work an image of the fulfilled self immersed in the world of action but free of its stupidities and vulgarities, still committed to the world of inner contemplation but not bound by its morbidity and passivity.[20]

In Caesar these contrary aspects of the self exist in nearly perfect balance. He seems at first preeminently the man of action raised to the highest power. Forceful, competent, without illusions, he controls the world about him with quiet grace. (In fact, Caesar's practicality comes very near to latent socialism. Theodotus, in grief at the burning of the library of Alexandria, cries wildly, "Will you destroy the past?" Caesar answers, suggestively, "Ay, and build the future with its ruins.") But the active, committed, optimistic Caesar is balanced by a remote, contemplative Caesar, who finds his image in the sphinx—whom he addresses at the beginning of Act I:

Hail, Sphinx! salutation from Julius Caesar! I have wandered in many lands, seeking the lost region from which my birth into this world exiled me, and the company of creatures such as I myself. I have found flocks and pastures, men and cities, but no other Caesar, no air native to me, no man kindred to me. . . . Sphinx, you and I, strangers to the race of men, are no strangers to one another. . . . My way hither was the way of destiny; for I am he of whose genius you are the symbol: part brute, part woman, and part god—nothing of man in me at all.

This remarkable confession of essential remoteness, one of Shaw's more nearly successful attempts at a "poetic" prose, with its revulsion from the world ("Rome is a madman's dream") and its longing for solitary contemplation ("an image of the constant and immortal part of my life, silent, full of thoughts, alone in the silver desert"), tells us that Caesar's power derives as much from his separation from the world as from his understanding of it. Cleopatra suggests the quality of this self-sustaining alienation in the fourth act when Pothinus asks if Caesar loves her:

CLEOPATRA. Love me! Pothinus: Caesar loves no one. Who are those we love? Only those whom we do not hate: all people are strangers and enemies to us except those we love. But it is not so with Caesar. He has no hatred in him: he makes friends with everyone as he does with dogs and children.

In this moment of sad illumination that Shaw extends to her Cleopatra sees in the human world universal hatred relieved only by occasions of love and in Caesar's world, as free of hatred as it is empty of love, an infinite benevolence stemming from an absolute separation, for she knows that to Caesar men are utlimately no more than "dogs and children."

It is commonly observed that in the course of the play Caesar educates Cleopatra, but it is less obvious that in doing so he is attempting, symbolically, to educate mankind. For Cleopatra—passionate, willful, loving and hating without restraint—embodies just those emotions she describes as characteristically human. Indeed, after she had had Pothinus killed in "just" revenge, all agree that she was right, except Caesar:

CAESAR. If one man in all the world can be found, now or forever, to *know* that you did wrong, that man will have either to conquer the world as I have, or be crucified by it. . . . And so to the end of history, murder shall breed murder, always in the name of right and honor and peace, until the gods are tired of blood and create a race that can understand.

Although Caesar relents and places Cleopatra on the throne, he knows that his experiment in education is a failure, that mankind can manipulate power but not itself, that the gods have not created a race that can understand. He willingly withdraws from Cleopatra's human world of Egypt to his ultimate destination (through Rome) in the realm of death.

Don Juan's withdrawal from the hell of love and beauty in Act III of *Man and Superman* seems, at first glance, to bear little resemblance to Caesar's withdrawal from Egypt, but there is a striking verbal link between these two characters suggesting that their actions are analogous. As Don Juan leaves, the Devil warns Dona Ana and the Commander against the gospel of the "Life Worshippers":

> THE DEVIL. . . . Beware of the pursuit of the Superhuman: it leads to indiscriminate contempt for the Human. To a man, horses and dogs and cats are mere species, outside the moral world. Well, to the Superman, men and women are a mere species too, also outside the moral world. This Don Juan was kind to women and courteous to men as your daughter here was kind to her pet cats and dogs; but such kindness is a denial of the exclusively human character of the soul.

Shaw desires, consciously at least, that we see the Devil as a shabby sentimentalist whose arguments are not to be trusted, but no such qualification vitiates Cleopatra's admiration for that Caesar who "makes friends with everyone as he does with dogs and children." Something of the same remoteness from flesh and blood—"those two greasy commonplaces" as Don Juan describes them—pervades both characters and suggests that Caesar's return from Egypt is indeed an anticipation of Don Juan's ascent to heaven.

But though *Man and Superman* echoes *Caesar and Cleopatra* in the nature of its most significant personage, it goes back to earlier works for its general psychological pattern. In the contrast between Tanner, whom we meet in Acts I, II, and IV, and Don Juan, who dominates the philosophical conversation of Act III, is a reminiscence of the central figures of *Candida* and even of *The Devil's Disciple.* Just as Morell had embodied the necessity of a commitment to the real human world, that is, to marriage and social action, whereas Marchbanks had represented a rejection of that world and a withdrawal to a higher one (the pattern followed by Parson Anderson and Dick Dudgeon), so John Tanner—speechmaker, committed reformer, and clown—must remain in the world to marry Ann and try to make it better while his alter ego, Don Juan Tenorio, is free to follow Eugene Marchbanks and so many other Shavian heroes to a quite different realm.

Because the essential point of the play lies in the contrast between its parts, because it ultimately expresses a divided commitment, it is a mistake to consider either part in isolation from the other. (In performance, too, an audience should and will happily sit through all four acts when they are properly done.) Both parts are necessary to project in dramatic terms the conflict between the differing aspects of the Shavian self, the confident activist and the despairing thinker, each of which needs its own area of fulfillment.[21]

Once this relationship between its parts becomes clear, certain difficulties inherent in the play disappear or, at least, are greatly minimized. For example, with the prefatory letter to A. B. Walkley announcing themes of the highest significance, the philosophical dialogue of the third act, and the full text of *The Revolutionist's Handbook, Man and Superman,* seems a most weighty and portentous work indeed. Most of it, however, is taken up by what Shaw himself called "a trumpery story of modern London life," a farce in which a clever girl entraps a reluctant young man. But if Don Juan's ascent is to have its proper emotional force (and the hell of love and beauty that he leaves is only the ordinary world with its wishes fulfilled), then the human world must be a place of clownish triviality to justify its rejection in favor of the "reality" of heaven. For the same reason the "tragic" theme announced by Shaw in his prefatory letter, the conflict between the woman and the man of genius, the philosopher-artist, cannot be allowed to materialize in the play. Again, Shaw cannot allow the politics of his characters—Tanner the revolutionary, Ramsden the old-fashioned liberal, Straker the educated workman, Mendoza and his crew the radical theoreticians, Malone, Sr., the capitalist entrepreneur—so much scope that they contradict his hidden sense of the folly and futility of the world. If the final point of the play is to be the necessity—in such a world—of breeding the superman, of creating what Caesar called "a race that can understand," then the possibility of effective political action before that eugenic triumph is achieved must be discounted.

Even though the theme of love and marriage enters into both parts of the play and leads one to expect a parallel development, the difference in treatment is so great that the effect is one of contrast. Tanner grandiloquently talks of woman as propagator, of "the whole purpose of Nature embodied in a woman," but most of what he says to Tavy is no more than the advice of one young bachelor to another: "It is a woman's business to get married as soon as possible, and a man's to keep unmarried as long as he can." It is the supposed rake Don Juan and not Tanner who speaks seriously of "the great central purpose of breeding the race" beyond the limitations of mankind as it is. Tanner the conventional bachelor runs from Ann, but it is Don Juan the impassioned philsopher who knows the illusions of romance and the bitter possessiveness of love. Moreover, the two most striking elements in Act III have no parallels at all in the rest of the play. The whole theme of withdrawal to a world of eternal contemplation can have no equivalent in the "trumpery comedy," for it is the pointlessness of that very comedy that Don Juan seeks to escape. Ostensibly Don Juan's withdrawal is an optimistic action, a union with the Life Force, but in fact it is a retreat from the life of the ordinary world made under the impetus of the second element unique to Act III, a painful vision of human nature. The Devil's long speech on man's taste for destruction and death embodies a concept so distasteful for Shaw that he rarely allows himself to entertain it. But there is no doubt that Shaw is speaking here; at one point, in fact, the Devil's voice becomes that of the Shavian socialist. "What is his [man's] morality?" he asks. "Gentility! an excuse for consuming without producing." But the Devil is less a critic of society than of man's essential nature, which he maintains is given over to the worship of death:

> . . . the power that governs the earth is not the power of Life
> but of Death; and the inner need that has nerved Life to the
> effort of organizing itself into the human being is not the need
> for higher life but for a more efficient engine of destruction.
> The plague, the famine, the earthquake, the tempest were too
> spasmodic in their action; the tiger and crocodile were too
> easily satiated and not cruel enough: something more con-
> stantly, more ruthlessly, more ingeniously destructive was
> needed; and that something was Man. . . .

Although Shaw allows Don Juan to contradict this speech, it remains the longest and most striking utterance in the entire act.
However, Tanner's final decision embodies a kind of contradiction
to the Devil's view. For Tanner finds man only misguided, and
therefore, though with some hesitation, he stays in the world to
reform it, to marry Ann, and perhaps to help breed the superman.
But, though Shaw says that Ann is a vital genius, he does not
portray her as such. If he did, Don Juan might not need to reject
that world of comic futility—or worse, of genuine evil—and ascend
to his heaven of contemplation.

It would seem that the question of man as evil—as ultimately
devoted to death rather than life—is encountered directly in *Major
Barbara,* which Shaw produced two years after the completion of
Man and Superman. But Undershaft, though he is the developer of "a
more efficient engine of destruction," is not an embodiment of
human evil, and the question of man's ultimate nature and worth
is glimpsed here, as it usually is in Shaw, only obliquely. Indeed,
the whole matter of the morality of the cannon works, in which
man's propensity for destructiveness would seem to appear, is essentially an irrelevance, or at least a false theme, postulated at the
beginning of the play but never developed. Shaw cannot afford to
pursue this question very rigorously, for he is—consciously at
least—committed to the Rousseauistic view that man is essentially
good and that actions suggesting the contrary are the results of
social circumstances. "It is quite useless," he says in the Preface to
Major Barbara, "to declare that all men are born free if you deny
that they are born good. Guarantee a man's goodness [presumably
by an adequate income and a just social order] and his liberty will
take care of itself." Any doubts or reservations that lie at the back

of Shaw's mind cannot appear in the intellectually controlled Preface but must work their way out symbolically in the play itself.

As a result, the earlier part of the play, which largely reflects Shaw's conscious, optimistic view, is controlled, incisive, brilliant; the later part, in which the attitude is more divided, is elusive, symbolic, not less interesting but less coherent. In Acts I and II Shaw is dramatizing, as he so often does, a process of education in which a character, in this case Barbara, is taught something about the nature of the world by another, Undershaft. That the pupil is a virtuous daughter, the teacher a "wicked" parent, and that the social lesson is learned in a confrontation at the climax of the second act all remind us of *Mrs. Warren's Profession,* and not surprisingly since the later play was to have been entitled *Andrew Undershaft's Profession.* Once again the morality of the conventionally "good" child collapses before the onslaught of the morality espoused by the parent-teacher, who turns out to have the firmer grip on reality. Undershaft's demonstration of economic truth is as forceful and incisive as Mrs. Warren's of social truth (the precise point made by Undershaft, the supposed exploiter but secret socialist, that in the world of capitalism all money is tainted, is in the simpler, earlier play made by Crofts, the true "capitalist bully"). But even more significantly, after its powerful second act climax, each play becomes curiously murky and less controlled. Vivie's rejection of Praed, Frank, and Mrs. Warren is hardly less strange than Cusins's and Barbara's acceptance of the cannon factory. In each case, Shaw is working with symbols of the impulse to withdraw the self from the world, symbols that are difficult to manipulate, for the impulse is only partially recognized even by Shaw himself.

Moreover, in each case the earlier part of the play must do double duty. Primarily, it presents an aspect of the real human world, subjects it to critical analysis, and makes suggestions for practical reform; but, even as it does so, in portraying emotional complexities and failures it lays the groundwork for the ultimate withdrawal from that world. Thus, reduced to its simplest elements, *Mrs. Warren's Profession* in its opening acts comments on the economic conditions of working-class women and at the same time prepares the way for Vivie's ultimate refusal of all emotional entanglements. In a similar though more complex way *Major Barbara,* while suggesting the futility of charity in a capitalist economy, hints not only at higher social concerns but at visionary ones as well.

When Undershaft gives Mrs. Baines the check for five thousand pounds and teaches Barbara that conventional charity is futile because it depends for money on the very forces it wishes to overthrow, to Barbara he seems to be destroying the faith on which she has built her life. But even at this point in the play we recognize that Undershaft is a good father and teacher who gives his daughter necessary knowledge and who is motivated by "a father's love for a grown-up daughter." This affection, however, is less a matter of personal impulse than of Undershaft's recognition that there is a "power that wields Barbara," similar to the "will of which" as he later says "I am a part." (Both he and Barbara presumably are in the grip of the Life Force.) "I shall hand on my torch to my daughter," he proclaims. "She shall make my converts and preach my gospel—." Barbara, then, is not so much Undershaft's child as his spiritual heir. There is, moreover, a hint that Barbara's relationship with Cusins also transcends the conventional. When she reminds him that "there are larger loves and diviner dreams than the fireside ones. You know that, don't you?" he answers, "Yes: that is our understanding." This statement is never elaborated on, but it suggests that Cusins has agreed that personal intimacy is not to have the first place in their lives.

In striking contrast to these transcendental kinships stands the conventional child-parent relationship of Stephen and Lady Britomart. Although she is lively and often perceptive, Lady Britomart is emotionally possessive and domineering with her son; in response, when Stephen, who lacks any of his mother's generosity of spirit, asserts his independence, he does so cruelly. Thus, although Lady Britomart and Stephen are rich comic creations as well as representatives of certain upper-class social and economic views, they are in the play primarily to suggest the comparative failure of the intimate, possessive, emotional relationship as opposed to the more remote and spiritualized one of Barbara and Undershaft. The human limitations demonstrated in the mother-son relationship justify the nonworldly connections made possible for Barbara by Undershaft and Cusins.

But although the private failures or limitations in the lives of these characters are part of the motive for the removal of the self from this human world, they are relatively minor elements. It is after the mutual challenges of Barbara and Undershaft, the brilliant comic panorama of the West Ham shelter, the climactic demonstration that Undershaft can "buy the Salvation Army," and his ruthless denunciation of Stephen's pretensions to political independence that problems of credibility regarding both place and persons arise. Up to now, Undershaft, although his wit and charm make him an attractive figure throughout, has primarily demonstrated his power as a capitalist exploiter. As such, he is dramatically effective. The hints that he is also something more have been general and symbolic, depending for their effect largely on the thrust of Shaw's rhetoric. "Yes, money and gunpowder; freedom and power; command of life and command of death." Unfortunately, it is hardly possible to make the scope of these suggestions visible in the literal depiction of Perivale St. Andrews. When Cusins first sees the town, he says, "Everything perfect! wonderful! real! It only needs a cathedral to be a heavenly city instead of a hellish one." But it is doubtful that the addition of such an edifice would alter the social structure of Perivale, which as Undershaft describes it is a chain of interlocking snobberies:

> You see, the one thing Jones won't stand is any rebellion from the man under him, or any assertion of social equality between the wife of the man with 4 shilling a week less than himself, and Mrs. Jones! Of course they all rebel against me, theoretically. Practically, every man of them keeps the man just below him in his place.

Perivale is not only snobbish; it is also conventional. If the ruffianly Bill Walker comes to Perivale, Undershaft says, "in three weeks he will have a fancy waistcoat; in three months a tall hat and a chapel sitting; before the end of the year he will shake hands with a duchess at a Primrose League meeting, and join the Conservative Party." When Barbara asks if he will be any better for that, Undershaft justly replies that he will be better fed, housed, clothed, and behaved, and that his children will be healthier. Yet the moral limitation of this claim is evident when Undershaft suggests that his men could indeed benefit from Barbara's efforts as a salvationist. "Try your hand on my men:" he says to her, "their souls are hungry because their bodies are full."

But nothing that we know of Perivale suggests that the souls of its inhabitants desire transcendence. The whole matter of "Barbara's return to the colors," as Shaw calls it in the Preface, of her preaching salvation in Perivale, is extremely unclear. In the first place, the men are already religious; Undershaft has told us that they do not even tolerate agnostics in the high-explosive sheds. Admittedly, Barbara's preaching seems to have little to do with any theology (her appeals to Bill Walker are simple moral exhortations, and she says that she has "got rid of the bribe of heaven"); nevertheless, it is hard to see what she can do in Perivale other than go from house to house, like the unhappy hero of *The Wild Duck*, presenting the inhabitants with a "claim of the ideal." But the author of *The Quintessence of Ibsenism* must have known that the fate of Gregers Werle was to be the eternal exile yearning for the release of death, forever "thirteenth at table."

If Barabara's role at Perivale is rather difficult to comprehend, Cusins's is equally so. He accepts Undershaft's offer to succeed to the management of the cannon business because (in a phrase oddly anticipatory of later political demands) "the people must have power," and "the power that is made here can be wielded by all men." Cusins here seems to be taking very literally Undershaft's earlier injunctions: "Poverty and slavery have stood up for centuries to your sermons and leading articles: they will not stand up to my machine guns. Don't preach at them: don't reason with them. Kill them. . . . Come and make explosives with me. Whatever can blow men up can blow society up." But the vision of Undershaft and Cusins at the gates of Perivale passing out rifles to hordes of aroused workers on their way to storm the Houses of Parliament is too grotesque to be credible. However adroit Shaw's rhetoric, the cannon factory is a phenomenon too real and too horrifying to function adequately as a symbol of the power of socialist idealism.

Major Barbara, then, is brilliant as a human comedy and as a demonstration of the limitations of conventional charity. But when it attempts to deal with the complexities of social and spiritual reform, it becomes elusive and unsatisfying. In part it is so because of the difficulties of translating a discursive and technical subject into dramatic terms. But it disturbs us because the impulse to withdraw from the compromises, limitations, and failures inherent in life is operative even as the Shavian hero commits himself to struggle for reform. At the moment that Barbara accepts Cusins's decision to enter the cannon business, she reveals her ultimate impulses:

> BARBARA. Take care, Dolly, take care. Oh, if only I could get away from you and from father and from it all! if I could have the wings of a dove and fly away to heaven!
> CUSINS. And leave me!
> BARBARA. Yes, you, and all the other naughty mischievous children of men. But I cant.

When Cusins later says that Barbara "has gone right up into the skies," he means that she has joyfully accepted their new life, but even here in the very phraseology there is an echo of that other impulse to "fly away," to remove the self from the world (where men are too perverse—too "mischieveous"—to live humanely), to ascend to heaven.[22]

The education of a girl to a higher state of spiritual being by an ambiguously attractive father figure was obviously an alluring subject for Shaw, but it presented serious problems of dramatic resolution. If Shaw appears not quite to have known what to do with Barbara the transformed salvationist, he had even more trouble with Eliza Doolittle, the flower girl become a lady. As ever, the problem in *Pygamalion* lay in the reconciling of hope and despair, of faith in the vital and distrust of the human. From one point of view, the central story reflects romantic optimism, a faith in material and social progress and even human perfectibility. Not only does it suggest the immediate benefits of money and comfort in overcoming the effects of poverty, but it asserts the belief that by skill and diligence a new and more elevated spiritual being can be developed: in the terminology of Creative Evolution, Eliza is being willed to a higher state of being. Higgins seems to have some consciousness of what he is about when he tells his mother, "But you have no idea how frightfully interesting it is to take a human being and change her into a quite different human being by creating a new speech for her. It's filling up the deepest gulf that separates class from class and soul from soul." Later, when Eliza protests that he does not care for her, Higgins replies, "I care for life, for humanity; and you are a part of it that has come my way." The emphasis on Eliza's spiritual growth is pointed up by contrast with the career of her father. Doolittle, one of Shaw's most inspired comic creations, is comparatively free and vital when we first meet him; as the play progresses, however, he acquires not a new soul like his daughter but money and so falls prey to "middle-class morality."

Yet the last two acts of *Pygmalion* are less the celebration of a newborn spirit than an abrasive conflict between that new being and its progenitor. When Shaw had previously handled similar material in *Caesar and Cleopatra*, he had been able to make his heroine into a willful adolescent and his hero into a remote and aging sage and thus obviate the question of any sexual attraction. Here, however, such limitations do not apply; indeed, one might expect that Higgins, impetuous and enthusiastic, would easily be attracted to the gracious and sensitive young woman whom Eliza has become. The text offers at least two explanations for the failure of the romance to come to fruition, both of which are of interest.

The first is Higgins's involvement with his mother. When Mrs. Higgins mentions that he never falls in love with anyone under forty-five, he replies, "My idea of a lovable woman is something as like you as possible." Shaw elaborates on this matter in the Postcript, suggesting that for an imaginative boy an attractive and cultivated mother effects "a disengagement of his affections, his sense of beauty, and his idealism from his specifically sexual impulses." Many readers would now find rather innocent the assumption that the relations of mother and son are in no way sexual, but there is no doubt that, presumably without Freudian guidance, Shaw had grasped a significant aspect of the oedipal relationship.

It is tempting to suppose on the basis of these comments that Shaw has accidentally let slip the secret of a psyehological problem in himself that, transposed into his art, accounts for Higgins's rejection of Eliza and for much of the denigration of sexuality that appears in the plays. (Mrs. Higgins is by no means a portrait of Shaw's mother, but his family background of a strong-minded artistic mother and a weak father gives some support to this notion.) Although Shaw's plays reflect the personal quirks of their creator, they are not the final determinants of his vision of things. The range of Shaw's mind is too great, his perceptions too penetrating for such a factor to be more than one element in shaping that vision. Ultimately, it is the Shavian sense of life that offers us the final explanation for the failure of the romance between Eliza and Higgins. In Higgins's climactic reply to Eliza's appeal for affection, we hear not merely the rationalization of a sexual neurosis but that profound sense of, and shrinking from, the limitations of human existence that has haunted the plays from the first:

> If you cant stand the coldness of my sort of life, and the strain of it, go back to the gutter. Work til you are more a brute than a human being; and then cuddle and squabble and drink til you fall asleep. Oh, it's a fine life, the life of the gutter. It's real: it's warm: it's violent: you can feel it through the thickest skin: you can taste it and smell it without any training or any work. Not like Science and Literature and Classical Music and Philosophy and Art.

The gutter Higgins refers to here is not merely the working-class world from which Eliza has come but the coarseness of ordinary life in general. The great debate between Eliza and Higgins that constitutes the core of Acts 4 and 5 of *Pygmalion* is in effect (as at the conclusion of *Candida*) a contest between the claims of a world where the freedom of the self is circumscribed by human affection and personal needs and the lures of another where the self may aspire to transcend these demands. When Higgins tells Eliza that one should behave as if one "were in Heaven," he is talking specifically about equality of manners, but there is a significant echo of a metaphor that Shaw has already used to suggest withdrawal and transcendence. It is part of the special quality of *Pygmalion* that Higgins, with his childishness and irascibility, is a fully human characterization and not, like Caesar or Undershaft, a symbolic idealization. He is not a superman, but he does have some connections with that realm to which Don Juan ascends, leaving Dona Ana behind. At the end of the Postscript Shaw points out that "Galatea never does quite like Pygmalion: his relation to her is too godlike to be altogether agreeable."

If *Pygmalion* is one of Shaw's most personal and "domestic" works, *Heartbreak House* seems to be one of his broadest and most "public" ones. The specific identification of *Heartbreak House* in the Preface as "cultured, leisured Europe before the war," Captain Shotover's portentous advice to Hector that his business as an Englishman is to learn "Navigation," followed at once by the appearance of the mysterious bombers that threaten ultimate extinction all combine to suggest a play centered on great political questions raised by World War I, only recently concluded when it was produced. But just as *Pygmalion* has its political element in its implications about class mobility, so *Heartbreak House* has its personal element in the amorous relations of its characters, relations that occupy much of the action and are arguably its most significant elements. Yet *Heartbreak House* has a special place in the Shavian canon, primarily because of the nature of its political and social themes.

In Shaw such themes tend to be specific (e.g., the failure of private charity in *Major Barbara*) and ultimately optimistic; in *Heartbreak House* they are vague and pessimistic. However, one must beware of assuming that because *Heartbreak House* is apocalyptic, it is necessarily profound—or at any rate that it goes deeper than plays whose tone is consistently brighter. Certainly this play reflects the trauma of World War I, the chauvinism and stupidity of which Shaw so clearly recognized, but his work, as we have seen, always had a sense of despair, a darker coloration, which in *Heartbreak House* has not so much changed in quality as spread throughout the play and thus become more visible.

For example, whereas Andrew Undershaft of *Major Barbara* is drawn as a figure of confidence and power who is apparently the owner as well as the manager of his enterprise, Boss Mangan, the equivalent entrepreneur of *Heartbreak House,* is not only a pathetic creature in his emotional life but also in his business life, turning out to be no more than a managerial supervisor living on "travelling expenses" and "a trifle of commission." The factories all belong to "syndicates and shareholders and all sorts of lazy good-for-nothing capitalists." Thus, *Major Barbara* offers us a specific figure who can be turned into a symbol of social hope, but *Heartbreak House* shows us a remote and inaccessible system impervious to change. Mazzini Dunn, the charming and earnest "soldier of freedom," explains what happened when he tried to "do something":

I joined societies and made speeches and wrote pamphlets. That was all I could do. . . . Every year I expected a revolution, or some frightful smash-up: it seemed impossible that we could blunder and muddle on any longer. But nothing happened, except of course, the usual poverty and crime and drink that we are used to. Nothing ever does happen.

A few lines later a momentary sign of hope seems to appear. Captain Shotover says of England ("this ship we are all in," as Hector calls it), "The captain is in his bunk, drinking bottled ditch-water; and the crew is gambling in the forecastle. She will strike and sink and split." When Hector asks what he must do to live, the Captain recommends "Navigation" (the institution of a moral, socialist order?), "Learn it and live; or leave it and be damned." But no sooner has this Shavian demand for positive social action been voiced than we again hear Mazzini Dunn saying quietly, "I thought all that once, Captain; but I assure you nothing will happen." This voice, too, is a Shavian one; like Shaw, Mazzini has joined societies and written pamphlets. Ultimately, Shaw's anger at man's social irresponsibility and his demand for action, voiced through Shotover, remain in balance with his sense of the futility of such endeavors, voiced through Mazzini, even at the end of the play. The bombers, which suddenly appear as the play draws to a close, perform a positive act of social venegeance by destroying Mangan and Billy Dunn, "the two practical men of business," but the most sensitive and sympathetic characters, Hector, Hesione, and Ellie, long for the warplanes to return and either vitalize their futile lives or obliterate them in a kind of Shavian *Götterdämmerung*. Even here, however, there is a small touch of optimism, ironic perhaps, in Randall Utterword's performing "Keep the Home Fires Burning" on his flute.

But though Randall has been a diplomat, he belongs not to the political but to the personal aspects of the play. He and Ariadne are indeed examples of the governing class, but essentially they are representatives of the sexless submission and maternal assertiveness that mark so dangerously certain relationships between Shavian men and women. Randall, pursuing Ariadne eternally but without sexual reward, receives instead maternal discipline. Ariadne's long experience with her children proves useful when Randall "gets nerves and is naughty"; she can "just rag him till he cries." And yet Shaw remains complex and ambiguous about human interactions, for Ariadne is not a Strindbergian monster but a lively comic presence; and Hesione, the other of the "two demon daughters," is one of his most seductively charming creations. It is her charm that allows her to manipulate Mangan and reduce him to tears as easily as, if less brutally than, Ariadne does Randall.[23] Ellie, the heartbroken heroine, is also an attractive feminine figure but like Ariadne and Hesione is also a woman of power. "I only wanted to feel my strength," she says to Mangan as she discards him, "to know that you could not escape me if I chose to take you." Moreover, all three women keep their men at a distance sexually. In a curious line Ellie even implies that this distance is "natural" in a love relationship. She says to Mangan that she does not mind touching him now that he is involved with Hesione. "Not since you fell in love naturally with a grown-up nice woman, who will never expect you to make love to her."

Heartbreak House, in fact, is essentially a world of sterile flirtations, of sexual games that the women almost always win. Its nearest analogue in Shaw's work is the hell of love and beauty, that world of bodiless flirtations, which we hear of in Act III of *Man and Superman.* And not surprisingly *Heartbreak House* is inhabited by a familiar figure. Hector Hushabye, with whose mustache women are always falling in love, is the Don Juan of this world; but he is one who, unable to ascend to his heaven of contemplation, remains trapped "at home all day," as Captain Shotover says, "like a damned soul in hell." Indeed, his surname, with its suggestions of infantile sleep, evokes the condition of his life here "tied to Hesione's apron-string," whereas "Hector" evokes the Shavian philosopher-hero that he would be.[24] Like his father-in-law, Captain Shotover, with whom he has considerable affinity, Hector is a frustrated idealist who knows that his "spark, small as it is, is divine." When the Captain asks, in his anger at human stupidity, "Is there no thunder in heaven?" Hector responds, "Is there no beauty, no bravery on earth?"

A moment later, at the end of Act I, Captain Shotover reveals that he is much more than an old seaman who has taken to rum or than a purveyor of political maxims. When Hesione responds to Hector's question by asking why men are not satisfied with the domestic comforts that women make for them, Captain Shotover suggests the nature of their ultimate aspirations in two lines of verse, which he recites "weirdly chanting":

> I builded a house for my daughters, and opened the doors
> thereof,
> That men might come for their choosing, and their betters
> spring from their love.

Although the lines are no more than doggerel, they reveal Captain Shotover as a conscious ally of the Life Force, like Undershaft a would-be agent of Creative Evolution who had hoped to breed mankind to a higher level. Disappointed in this aim, he must turn to rum—"I drink to keep sober"—to keep himself from escaping the world by drifting off into a realm of dreams:

> I feel nothing but the accursed happiness I have dreaded all
> my life long: the happiness that comes as life goes, the happi-
> ness of yielding and dreaming instead of resisting and doing,
> the sweetness of the fruit that is going rotten.

But "resisting and doing" is no more than a fantasy of destroy-ing people by exploding dynamite with a mind ray. In reality, Shotover's "accursed happiness" is not only an old man's lassitude and self-interest but a climactic expression of that Shavian impulse toward retreat and withdrawal that has always been expressed in his work. Only a few lines before he speaks to Ellie of "resisting and doing," he says to her, "I cannot bear men and women. I have to run away." The seventh degree of concentration, if ever attained by him, guarantees that heaven of contemplation to which Vivie Warren, Eugene Marchbanks, Don Juan, and other Shavian fig-ures have ascended above the terrors, failures, and boredoms of this world.

The other candidate for transcendence is surely Shotover's spir-itual "white wife," Ellie Dunn, the ostensible heroine of the play, though not one of its most successful figures. Although she lacks Vivie Warren's vigor and individuality, she shares her somewhat humorless severity and, more to the point, like her undergoes a significant education during the play. When Ellie discovers that

Hector is a married man and a fraud, she says to Hesione, "I have a horrible fear that my heart is broken, but that heartbreak is not like what I thought it must be." Hesione answers, "It's only life educating you, pettikins." It is this education, which Hesione has already achieved (". . . when I am neither coaxing and kissing nor laughing, I am just wondering how much longer I can stand living in this cruel, damnable world"), that Ellie must now absorb. Just as Frank Gardner and Sir George Crofts taught Vivie the futility of love and the immorality of money, so Hector and Mangan teach similar, if not identical lessons to Ellie. But where Vivie retreats into solitude, Ellie joins Captain Shotover, her "spiritual husband and second father," in his withdrawal. When Hesione says that she hopes the bombers will return, Ellie, "radiant at the prospect," replies in the last line of the play, "Oh, I hope so." She may only wish to relive the excitement of the "glorious experience," as Hesione calls it, but more likely she desires, like Shotover and the other Shavian saints, to withdraw through death from the futile world of mortal men.

Although the story of Ellie Dunn's education in, and withdrawal from, life is the structural basis of *Heartbreak House,* it does not give the play the kind of coherence the story of Vivie Warren gives to *Mrs. Warren's Profession* because the character of Ellie is sketchily drawn and, since other material is so richly developed, not focused on steadily. But it is essentially this story that Shaw tells again, and this time with clear concentration, in the last play in which his powers as an artist were to operate at something near their fullest. Saint Joan is, after all, like Vivie and Ellie, a young girl vital and innocent at the beginning of her play who learns, like her predecessors, that the world has no use for her romantic idealism. Like them she withdraws from it to a place where the self can find safety, to that special heaven where the Shavian rather than the Catholic saints sit in eternal contemplation of the Life Force that ultimately, and tragically, they are powerless to serve.

But whereas Ellie is often hardly to be distinguished against the complex tapestry of *Heartbreak House,* Joan stands out sharply against the comparatively simple background of her play. For *Saint Joan,* full of comic brilliance and narrative vigor, is essentially a direct Chronicle History, focusing for much of its length largely on events. Nevertheless, as one would expect of a play by Shaw, it has an intellectual and social content, the theory that Joan was an early embodiment of Nationalism and Protestantism. This notion seems at first only an intriguing historical speculation, but it is in fact characteristically Shavian and characteristically ambiguous. From the point of view of the optimistic socialist historian, Joan was the precursor of those forces that triumphed over feudalism and medieval Catholicism (or as the Life-Forcer might put it, of the vitality that produced a higher form of social organization). But such a view could be supported only by the isolated scene between Cauchon and Warwick. From another point of view, and a far more pervasive one, Joan is the victim of the great forces of church and state, the embodiments of human weakness and short-sightedness, which destroy those who would alter them.

This view, after all, this Shavian pessimism, informs the whole second part of *Saint Joan.* This darker vision, always present in Shaw's work, is usually disguised, but here as in *Heartbreak House* it appears openly, and it dominates each of the last three scenes of the play. These scenes are in fact all the same scene, rewritten three times over to enforce the message that the Shavian saint, rejected by the world, can only reject it in turn and ascend to his heaven. In Scene 5, Rheims Cathedral after the coronation, Joan is rejected by the King, the Archbishop, and her friends in the army. Comparing her solitude with that of God, she says, "Well, my loneliness shall be my strength too; it is better to be alone with God; His friendship will not fail me, nor His counsel, nor His love." But in the great trial scene that follows, Joan is left alone to confront those who must function in the world according to human institutions and human limitations. Although both the Bishop and the Inquisitor behave with fatherly kindness, Joan rejects them as fiercely as, long before, Vivie Warren had rejected her mother. Indeed, as Joan accepts her death, she turns away from the men about her and speaks again of God: "for I am His child, and you are not fit that I should live among you. That is my last word to you." And finally, having shown Joan rejecting and being rejected by her friends and her enemies, Shaw brings her back once more in the Epilogue to confront them, along with a representative of the modern world, as a glorified saint. But though the tone is comic, the results are the same as they all flee her threatened resurrection. Her last words in the play are only a less angry echo of her last words in the trial scene: "O God that madest this beautiful earth, when will it be ready to receive Thy saints? How long, O Lord, how long?"

This question reverberates through much of Shaw's drama, and certainly through the major plays examined here. *(Back to Methuselah,* in which the highest development of mankind is to withdraw from the world and become a vortex of pure thought, is a highly relevant theoretical document but only intermittently interesting as a play.) Shaw has asked this question, in one dramatic guise or another, throughout his career, but it has remained always unanswered. Inevitably, as for Chekhov, the satisfying social, not to say spiritual revolution lies in the indiscernible future. Yet so persistent in Shaw is the romantic impulse to find a realm in which the self can achieve realization that Shaw is compelled to send his characters over and over again on that half-understood quest. Because the world of perfect fulfillment can never be congruent with the human world, the quest of the Shavian saint, superman, philosopher-artist, always turns into an otherworldly spiritual progress, an ascent to heaven. It is no accident that John Bunyan's name is as much in Shaw's mouth as that of any other author. The pilgrim's progress to the heavenly city is the archetypal pattern of Shaw's plays.

Yet the commitment to spiritual progress never precludes a commitment to material progress. Shaw is both Marxist and mystic. But though the vision of spiritual ascent and that of continuing social (and indeed socialistic) development are both variants on the romantic vision of eternal progress, they are nevertheless profoundly opposed to each other. One derives from the impulse to withdraw from human entanglements and find some point of isolation and repose; the other—equally demanding—to commit oneself to the world of social action and do significant work in it. Whatever their bases, these opposing impulses generate in Shaw's plays a continuing thematic tension and give them much of their complexity and ambiguity.

Such a description of the Shavian world, just as it is, may suggest an altogether grimmer writer than one actually encounters in the plays. The inexhaustible flow of comic gaiety that surges through these works is just as real as the pessimism that lurks within them. Indeed, Shaw's comic genius is a necessary tool of his social activism; through it he can reduce to insignificant buffoons those who would oppose his recipes for progress. But the comedy is an integral part of the darker vision also: the Shavian world, after all, is ultimately a world of fools. Some of them are lovable fools whom one would not alter if one could, but they are not really satisfying company for the superman or the philosopher-artist. They are not ready to receive Saint Joan.

Because they are fools, they reject her and burn her, and so she must ascend to the Shavian heaven to join Saint Vivie Warren and her successors, all of whom have reached it after the same painful progress, having committed themselves to the work of the world, yet, ultimately transcended that sphere for a higher one. The plays are Shaw's instruments for imaginatively achieving these contradictory goals while simultaneously allowing us as readers and spectators to achieve them with him. (The proof, if any is needed, that Shaw is primarily an artist and not a propagandist lies in the fact that only in the realm of art can the unity of such opposites be attained.) Although Shaw's plays are unique in tone and style, the dilemma they project is a great, even traditional romantic one. Tennyson died in 1892 just as Shaw's career in the theatre was beginning, but "Ulysses," written half a century earlier, is a remarkably precise analogue to the Shavian theme. Ulysses leaves an aspect of himself, his son Telemachus, to perform the work of progress in the world of Ithaca, "by slow prudence to make mild | A rugged people, and through soft degrees | Subdue them to the useful and the good." But he himself, a philosopher-king, sets out on a journey beyond the world; as he says at first, "to follow knowledge," then to do "some work of noble note . . . | Not unbecoming men that strove with gods," and finally "to seek a newer world." The confusion of purposes here only masks the fact that the journey is ultimately a suicidal one out of life. Like Tristan and Eugene Marchbanks, Ulysses is entering into the "holy night." For a moment in the poem there appears that note of heroic contemplation that suggests, not despair, but the aspirations of the Shavian saint who, like Ulysses and his mariners, may hope to find a home suitable for a heavenly company, to

> touch the Happy Isles,
> And see the great Achilles, whom we knew.

Jean Giraudoux: Human and Suprahuman

The contrast between the world of common life and action and that other world of "heavenly" contemplation to which so many Shavian characters ascend finds a remarkable equivalent in the great opposition of human and suprahuman that dominates the plays of Jean Giraudoux. Having long haunted the romantic imagination, it has characteristically produced the sense of doubt, the intense ambiguity of feeling, that defines the tone of Giraudoux's work. When Keats's knight-at-arms set the fairy's child on his pacing steed "and nothing else saw all day long," he was turning away from a life of action to contemplate that vision of supreme beauty transcending mortal possibilities that so many artists, Giraudoux among them, have projected through their characters. But that alluring image is also a dangerous and dehumanizing one. Although the knight later escapes from her power, after the pale warriors of his dream vision tell him that the fairy's child is *la belle dame sans merci*, he is left, like Giraudoux—or at any rate like certain of his characters—doubtfully suspended between a mortal world, empty and desolate, and a visionary one, fatal and forever unattainable.

Giraudoux's own stance is hardly that of the hollow-eyed romantic wanderer always searching for the fearful yet enticing vision, but he has seen something analogous to what was beheld by the knight-at-arms, and in play after play he comes back to look at it again. (Not surprisingly, one of his most appealing plays deals, quite literally, with a knight who encounters a fairy's child.) What he sees takes different symbolic forms in different plays—Germany in one, Helen of Troy in another, the world of the water spirits in a third—but it is always essentially the same thing: a realm of beauty, power, and mystery lying beyond the range of human experience yet promising self-fulfillment.[25] More significant still, the glance that is cast upon it is compounded of fascination and repulsion; Giraudoux's attitude toward his vision is at all times profoundly ambiguous.

Yet that ambiguity is not limited to Giraudoux's conception of the suprahuman: his vision of the real world is also a divided one.

Despite the lure of the ideal, the temptation to recognize the world as it is and to accept the limits it inevitably places on the self is never absent in Giraudoux. From one point of view, the world of man is charming, graceful, infinitely desirable. In it nature is fresh and beautiful, and human relations—despite their transitoriness— are full of tenderness and warmth. The very monotony of ordinary existence is magically transformed into variety. Most commonly this aspect of reality appears as an idealized version of a small French town (though in the plays it may be elaborately altered), the Bellac of Giraudoux's childhood, as commentators are fond of noting. When reality is seen in this light, as humane and delightful, it can function as an adequate counterbalance to the vision of ideal beauty. However, when it wears its other appearance, desolation and the threat of destruction replace vernal freshness. Where vices were hardly to be distinguished from whimsical virtues, they are now powerful and dangerous forces. Even trivial antipathies can bring about tragedies both private and public. When the world of reality appears in this guise, the Giraudoux hero, unable or unwilling to accept it, steps aside and continues his quest for a visionary world that, though its pursuit may involve his own destruction, is more tempting, more satisfying than the pain and coarseness of ordinary existence.[26]

Unfortunately, as we have suggested, the world of the ideal can also exert forces that repel and destroy. Although the woman is beautiful, she is also fatal; although the gods are powerful, they are inhuman; although the world of the water spirits is exquisitely mysterious, it is also cruel. The quest for a transcendent world is dangerous to the searcher, for he is necessarily drawn away from the satisfactions of common life. Yet even more dangerous than failure is success. When, through some legerdemain of the theater, Giraudoux allows his searcher to achieve his goal, the results are regularly destructive. The fairy's child becomes *la belle dame sans merci*—consider Judith, Helen, Electra, and Ondine—and the lesser, human creatures near her are destroyed.

This pattern of destruction through a quest for the ideal, which most clearly reveals Giraudoux's attitudes and concerns, dominates four of the series of remarkable plays of the 1930s upon which Giraudoux's reputation as an artist ultimately rests. Not only do these plays—*Judith, The Trojan War Will Not Take Place (La Guerre de*

Troie n'aura pas lieu, performed in English as *Tiger at the Gates),
Electra,* and *Ondine*—form a natural group by reason of their tragic
denouements and certain similarities in the nature of their heroines, but also, because the conclusions toward which they drive are
at once desired and feared, these plays reveal more clearly than
any others the essential ambiguity that Giraudoux's central subject
evokes.[27]

This divided attitude is always present but is less clearly delineated in the lighter plays. In *Siegfried* we greet with pleasure the
return of the hero, an amnesiac soldier, from Germany—the mysti-
cal and romantic—to his true home, France—the rational and
human. However, though Giraudoux succeeds in establishing the
contrast between the "poetic and demoniac" Germany and the
orderly world that the hero desires and ultimately seeks in France,
he is so much occupied in this his first play with shaping the
sprawling discursiveness of his novel *Siegfried et le limousin,* upon
which the play is based, that he loses thematic focus in the mere
business of arranging the action. In *Intermezzo* the happy fulfillment
of the love of the Controller and the charming Isabelle leads us to
accept without reservation her ultimate rejection of the world of
the dead, the immortal charms of which have been only lightly
suggested, and her commitment to the commonplace life of the
town. And finally, in *Amphytrion 38* the genial comedy and the
reunion of husband and wife place the emphasis firmly on the
satisfactions of human life. Yet even here, Jupiter anticipates Ondine in the subtle pathos of his exile from what he calls in Alcmena
"the human infinite," and Alcmena, the quintessentially human
woman, admits the appeal of the divine, which is apparent even in
the childhood she had passed imagining the gods and, as she says
in a phrase later to be used about the idealistic Electra, "making
signs to them."

But it is difficult for Giraudoux to express fully the self's ambiguous longing for the supramundane in his lighter plays. Whatever
their modulations into minor keys, these are comedies, ending with
the bright sonority of the major. His central vision of tormented
aspiration is a tragic one and is most directly expressed in the
darker works. It appears fully developed in *Judith,* the first of
Giraudoux's tragedies, in which the tension between opposing
forces leads finally to mutual destruction. Although Judith alter-

nates between these polarities—first accepting her role as God's saint, then rejecting it under the influence of Holophernes, and finally accepting it again—within each stage of this progression, which is balanced by the ultimate return to the starting point, there is the sense of an opposition of nearly equal forces, even when the characters are not engaged, as they often are, in a Giraudoux debate. Throughout, for example, the essential seriousness, even grimness, of the subject is counteracted by the play of Giraudoux's comic imagination. When, near the beginning of the first act, the young soldier John drags in one of the prophets who have been crying for Judith to save the city by giving herself to Holophernes, her uncle Joseph looks at him and says, "He is dirty and he smells bad. . . . He is obviously a prophet." Not only do we encounter here the classic Giraudoux pattern in which the sublime is deflated to the level of the human, but the very presence of the joke balances the harshness of the initial scene, Moreover, the deliberate intrusion of the modern upon the archaic dignity of the biblical atmosphere suggests the presence of two forces carefully played off against each other.

But these conflicts of playfulness and seriousness, of modern and archaic, are only symptoms of that central Giraudoux conflict between the human and a vision of that which lies beyond it. The major representative of the human in this play is Holophernes, but because he does not appear until the second act, lesser characters perform his function until then. Joseph, for instance, rebukes the Grand Rabbi for calling his house "this place already sacred":

> JOSEPH. Sacred! Why sacred? I hope this place will never be sacred. This is the sitting room where my father had his first attack, where Judith marshaled her dolls and lost her first tooth, where her mother had the first sickness of her pregnancy. . . . Here one eats, one weeps, one spits. Look, I spit! Its sanctity is to be a place that is human, and not sacred. . . .[28]

Emphasizing the same point, John tells the Rabbi that Judith's beauty is not "holy or eternal," that "later Judity will get thin or fat. . . . Her beauty is but a moment!"

Early in the first act John recognizes the nature of the alternatives suggested by Judith's transitory human beauty and her saintly mission. Her name, which, he says, has always suggested "the flower, the secret nearly revealed, so much velvet, such tenderness," now that it is hammered and barked out by the crowd is becoming "for eternity a call of hardness, of sterility." But John's attempt to preserve Judith from these attributes is doomed to failure. From the first Judith shows just that quality of hardness he fears. When he admits that the army is defeated and asks if that makes him less handsome in her eyes, Judith replies, "Hideous, you are hideous." This icy pride and impatience with human weakness show that she is concerned less to rescue her fallen city than to commit herself to her vision of the sublime and the heroic. "Holophernes does not exist," she says, "there exist ways of suffering, of redemption that bear this name. If I go this evening toward him, I will go toward them." In fact, so committed is she to this mode of redeeming the self from the mundane that when Susanna asks to go in her place, claiming that she has patterned herself so closely on Judith as to be able to deceive Holophernes, Judith replies, "One who has a human being for a model cannot resemble me."

But Judith's claims to suprahuman status are abruptly challenged in the second act, which consists essentially of two confrontations, each serving its own purpose, as Judith first meets a false Holophernes, then the true one. When Judith is deceived and humiliated by the impostor Egon, her faith in herself and in the sublimity of her mission is broken down. She is ready then to understand Holophernes when he identifies himself as "a man ultimately of this world, of the world" and to accept when he offers her the pleasure of human self-fulfillment in a place free of gods. Such places as his tent, he tells Judith, are not easily found:

> HOLOPHERNES. This is one of those rare human corners that are truly free. The gods infest our poor universe, Judith. From Greece to the Indies, from North to South, there is not a country where they do not swarm, each with his vices, with his odors, . . . The air of the world, for one who likes to breathe, is that of a roomful of gods. . . . But there are still some places forbidden to them; I alone know how to see them. They subsist on the plain or mountain, like spots of

terrestrial paradise. The insects that inhabit them do not have the original sin of insects; I plant my tent upon these places. . . . By chance, directly in front of the city of the Jewish God, I recognized this one, by a bending of the palms, by a call of the waters.

But the elegant whimsy of "the original sin of insects" and the careful mingling of pagan, Jewish, and Christian religious elements suggest that Giraudoux is not making a theological statement but developing through rhetoric and imagery an opposition to the idealism, the pride, the cruelty that have been presented through the characterization of Judith. If Judith's nature and her divine mission lead us to recognize that her allegiance is to the suprahuman, Holophernes' graceful blasphemy tells us that his is to its opposite. Claiming that he is "the worst enemy of God," he tells Judith, "Dream about breakfast served without promise of hell, about five o'clock tea without mortal sin, with beautiful lemon slices and the sugar tongs innocent and sparkling." As always in Giraudoux these images of bourgeois comfort become emblems of the truly human life.

The third act seems, at first glance, to present a simple reversal of the second. Initially, Judith rejects the applause of Susanna and John, claiming that she has killed Holophernes not for God but for love. When, however, the Angel reveals to her that divine power has shaped her actions, she gives up this claim and accepts her role as God's saint. But both Judith's claim and the Angel's revelation have something contradictory within themselves. Judith tells Susanna that waking "for the first time at dawn near another human being" was a "terrifying thing!" in the sense of loss she endured. "Everything was already the past, everything was yesterday." Resolved on suicide, she contemplated the sleeping Holophernes: "In me, enveloped already in my eternal death, he inspired a pity without limit, so little protected by his ephemeral death against the threats of the coming day! . . . can the sight of a sleeping body call forth anything other than murder as the supreme tenderness!" In this fierce impatience with the imperfections and the transitoriness of life, we see Judith's inherent inclination toward the divine even as she protests that she is moved by the human. But if Judith's love is severe and implacable, that of the Angel who, in speaking directly to Judith, sacrifices his heavenly rank out of devotion to God seems curiously touching and human. It is appropriately to him that Judith will be "a name of tenderness," for, at once angelic and humane himself, he has seen in Judith both human love and that inexorable "supreme tenderness" that answers the threat—that is, the life—of the coming day with death. As so often in Giraudoux, the triumph of the sublime is balanced by the compensating presence of the human.

This balance is maintained in *The Trojan War Will Not Take Place,* though at first glance this play seems to have brought about a remarkable shift in subject matter. For a moment Giraudoux appears to have abandoned his ambiguous contemplation of the conflict between the romantic ideal and the human reality for a denunciation—a most adroit and brilliant one—of man's immutable tendency to destroy himself by war. To a certain extent the play is indeed what it seems to be,[29] but a glance beneath the tendentious surface reveals the familiar Giraudoux materials.

The reality of peace and happiness in the human world is represented by Hecuba, Andromache, Ulysses, and especially Hector. When, during his debate with Ulysses, Hector speaks of his weight in the scale of destiny, he says, "I weigh joy in life, confidence in life, the impulse toward what is just and natural." A universe of loving felicity is envisioned by Andromache as she thinks of the first day of peace as perhaps the "first day of accord between men and beasts."

As the play develops, the force that will defeat such felicity becomes more and more clearly identified with Helen. In the simplest terms, she becomes a symbol of the war itself. When Demokos, the belligerent poet, is composing his war song, he is inspired to compare the face of war to that of Helen, and when the child Polyxena is puzzled and asks, "What does war look like, Mother?" Hecuba drives the point home. "Like your aunt Helen," she replies. Hecuba, however, unlike Demokos, is not thinking of the attractions of war. In the next scene, she makes another comparison. War, she says, resembles "the backside of a monkey. When the she monkey has climbed into the tree and shows us a red bottom, all scaly and glazed, ringed by a filthy wig, war is exactly what one sees, that is its face." But Helen, equated by Demokos and Hecuba, respectively, with the allurement and the ugliness of war, becomes an even more evocative symbol. If, as the ape image suggests, she is the irrational and bestial in man that leads to war, she is also the visible embodiment of beauty. In the elaborate speech of the Geometrician it is suggested that her presence has made meaningful a previously imperfect landscape. Even the dignified Priam tells Hector that the beauty Helen embodies is the "secret vindication" for the failed lives of the old men who now contemplate her. These views are derided by such characters as Hecuba and Hector, but the Helen who finally appears offers some justification for them. Shallow, even foolish, she is nonetheless both mysterious and sinister. (She is indeed *la belle dame sans merci* insofar as the good knight of the play, Hector, falls victim to the power of the irrational impulses she provokes.) Her glimpses into the future suggest that she is attuned to forces beyond the merely mortal. She comes to the human world of Troy from a country where gods abound; Paris has told Hector "that there the heavens teem with them, that the legs of goddesses dangle from the sky." Moreover, she too is distant, like that which is beyond mortal life. "Even in my arms," Paris says "Helen is far from me." But the most suggestive clue to her nature comes during her confrontation with Hector, when she tells him that his ability to control her, in her weakness, will not affect the future. When Hector replies that Greek subtleties and trivialities escape him, she answers, "It is not a matter of subtleties and trivialties. It concerns at the very least monsters and pyramids." If the pyramids suggest the cold, mathematical impersonality of what is above the human level and the monsters the brutal irrationality of what is below it (ultimately found even in Hector when in a burst of rage he kills Demokos and brings about the Trojan War), then Helen encompasses both these extremes and becomes one of Giraudoux's most remarkable embodiments of the forces opposed to such happiness as is offered by the human world.[30]

Finally, however, Helen, though an extraordinary theatrical achievement, is a symbolic outline rather than a fully developed entity. In *The Trojan War* the emphasis falls on the struggle to preserve the human element. Helen retains the allure of beauty and mystery, but there is no doubt that Giraudoux's sympathy lies with Hector and the world of human happiness. In *Electra,* however, the balance is restored and the familiar note of ambiguity sounded more strongly. Although Electra, the representative of the suprahuman ideal, is as destructive as Helen herself, those who stand for the human world are not only noble and endearing but shabby, comic, even gross. The play's almost baroque richness of development and decoration suggests the ultimate complexity of the forces that are played off against each other, but the essential nature of each is recognizable from the first.

When near the beginning of the opening act the President of the Court arrives to dissuade his relative, the Gardener, from marrying Electra, he explains that she is dangerous to human life because she is the "very type of the woman who makes trouble." He asks how it is that given two random groups with "the same amount of crime, of mendacity, of vice or of adultery . . . in one existence flows smoothly, properly, the dead are forgotten, the living adjust themselves, while, in the other, it's hell?" The answer follows: "It's simply that in the second there is a woman who makes trouble." When Orestes protests that the second group has a conscience, the President is unconvinced: "A conscience! Is that what you think! If the guilty do not forget their faults, if the conquered do not forget their defeats, the victors their victories, if there are curses, quarrels, hatreds, the fault does not lie with the conscience of humanity, which has every propensity toward compromise and forgetfulness, but with ten or fifteen women who make trouble!" These women, Orestes replies, "have saved the world from egoism." "They have saved it from happiness," the President tells him:

> I know Electra! Let us admit that she is what you say, the embodiment of justice, generosity, duty. But it is with justice, generosity, duty, and not selfishness and indulgence, that one ruins the state, the individual, and the best families . . . because these three virtues embody the only element truly fatal to humanity, tenacity. Happiness has never been the lot of those who are tenacious. A happy family is a local surrender. A happy epoch is a unanimous capitulation.

As the President speaks, he characterizes not only those aspects of Electra—her exalted nobility, her terrible fierceness, her unalterable commitment to absolute values—that make her the embodiment of romantic ideality in both its most admirable and most destructive forms but also, through Giraudoux's bitter wit, those aspects of common mortal life—its changeability, its cowardice, its impulse to compromise—that make it forever alien to her. To flee from her "toward your radishes and your squash," as the President advises the Gardener, is to return to the secure limitations of ordinary life that Electra inevitably transcends.

This sense of Electra as at once admirable and destructive, that is to say of the ambiguous ideality she represents, is one of the dominant motifs of the play. No other work of Giraudoux's, in fact, expresses this characteristic divided feeling so intensely or so richly. Indeed, it is the effort to project his internal opposition in external dramatic form that leads Giraudoux to introduce into the play so many *doublings,* characters, or other elements that reflect opposed aspects of similar phenomena: Beggar and Gardener, Agatha and Clytemnestra, Clytemnestra and Narses' wife, Egisthus the murderer and Egisthus the hero, hedgehog and wolf.

These two animal images are of special interest, for as metaphorical reflections of Electra herself they express the two contrasting aspects of her nature. Shortly after the President's speeches, the Beggar presents his story of the hedgehogs. Among those commonly found crushed on the roads, he says, there is sometimes one that is young, less dirty, more dignified. Of that one, he says, "one has the impression that he did not die as a hedgehog, but that someone has struck him down in place of another, in your place. His cold little eye is your eye. His bristles are your beard. His blood is your blood." This sacrificial hedgehog, killed by the gods in place of a man, is the redemptive Electra who sacrifices all, including herself, to maintain purity in the world. The opposing Electra is suggested a moment later when the Beggar, recognizing that Egisthus wishes to kill Electra, suddenly interjects another, apparently irrelevant story, that of the wolf cub given to Narses and his wife and treated as a pet that one day, declaring itself a grown wolf, attacked them and killed Narses. The relevance of the story becomes clear as we realize that the wolf is the destructive Electra of whom Egisthus must rid himself. "What day, at what hour," the Beggar asks, "will she declare herself? What day will she become a wolf? What day will she become Electra?" [31]

Closely related to the opposition of hedgehog and wolf is that of Beggar and Gardener, which is revealed after the events of the first act have been played out. Again two elaborate speeches express the contrasting elements. Here, however, they are not so much different aspects of Electra as different aspects of the play as a whole. When the Beggar tells the story of Orestes' fall from his mother's arms and ironically supports Electra's claim that her version of the events is correct, he presents that vision of absolute truth justifying any amount of destructiveness that *Electra* as a tragedy projects:

> Electra, then, did not push Orestes! That means that every-thing she says is legitimate, everything she undertakes un-challengeable. She is the truth that leaves no residue, the lamp that needs no oil, the light without a wick. So if she kills, as she theatens to, all peace and all happiness about her, it is because she is right!

But Electra's perfect truth ignores the mitigating human element, for, as the Beggar tells the story, Clytemnestra dropped Orestes only because she was holding on to Electra. It is exactly this human element that is suggested in the Entr'acte, the elaborate "Lamento" of the Gardener. Although the Beggar, speaking with Giraudoux's bitter whimsy of the ducks who offer men love and brotherhood, says, "As for me, I undertake to teach them to weep," the Gardener, despite his sorrow at the loss of Electra, announces that he has come to speak of joy: "Joy and Love, yes. I come to tell you that they are preferable to Bitterness and Hatred." Even trag-edy, he says, "with its incests, its patricides" is ultimately "purity, that is to say finally innocence." In suicide he finds hope, in mur-der tenderness. (In the tragic world where hatreds and angers are pursued relentlessly and absolutely there is, Giraudoux is suggest-ing, a certain purity in the refusal to accept compromise, a certain innocence in the belief that the absolute can be achieved.) To prove his claim that the gods agree with him, he asks not for a heavenly voice—expanded by celestial amplifiers—or for a storm but for a moment of silence. Although the pathetic charm of the Gardener's request underlines the fact that the paradoxical unity of what he claims to see is only dubiously justified, his very pres-ence, awkward and endearing, provides a kind of counterbalance to the fierceness of Electra and the Beggar.

But the major counterbalance and one of the most significant doublings in the play is its comic subplot, the story of Agatha's betrayal of her husband the President, which parallels in humorous terms Clytemnestra's unfaithfulness to Agamemnon. This double view of the material of the play is suggested at the beginning of the opening scene when, after Orestes notes the "curious facade" of the palace, the Gardener explains that one wing sweats at certain times while the other, made of different stone, upon occasion suddenly glows. The palace thus is said both to weep and to laugh, suggesting the simultaneous presence of comic and tragic elements in the play. That these elements are variations on the same theme is made clear during the second act when, as Electra presses Clytemnestra for the name of her lover, exclaiming, "Who do you love? Who is it?" the President rushes in pursuing Agatha and shouting "Who is it? Who do you love?" In both cases the lover is Egisthus, and in both cases the wives take an extraordinary delight in revealing their hatred for their husbands. Moreover, and more significantly, the President's comic insistence on confronting Egisthus to maintain the honor of the judges of Greece parallels Electra's tragic insistence on having her vengeance though it entails the destruction of Argos. As so often in Giraudoux, the same impulse that, confined within human limits, produces comedy, expanded beyond them produces tragedy.

Perhaps the most striking illustration of the contrast between the human and suprahuman realms, and another of the most important doublings in the play, is found in the parallel set speeches of Electra and Egisthus during their second act confrontation. Explaining his transformation from a shabby seducer to a man of nobility and courage, Egisthus tells Electra how in a moment he had received, as he sensed, the city of Argos as a gift:

> And it was forever! . . . This morning I received my city forever, as a mother her child. And I asked myself with anguish if the gift was not a larger one, if I had not been given much more than Argos. In the morning God does not measure his gifts: he could as well have given me the world. That would have been dreadful. That would have meant for me the despair of one who expects a diamond for his birthday and who is given the sun.

But although Egisthus is now the embodiment of human virtue and seeks only to fulfill his kingly responsibilities, Electra, as the embodiment of suprahuman ideality, still demands that he be punished as a murderer and adulterer even if the punishment entails the destruction of the city. For she, too, received a gift at the same time. But whereas Egisthus' gift was the circumscribed realm of Argos, Electra's gift was a boundless universe of the mind; "Argos was only a point in that universe," she says:

> And it was this morning at dawn, when you were given Argos and its narrow frontiers, that I saw it [the "universe" she has been given] thus immense and that I heard its name, a name that is not pronounced, but that is at the same time tenderness and justice.

If Argos is the country of the specific, the human, the limited, the pragmatic, Electra's country is that of the generalized, the universal, the abstract to which individual human demands must bow.

And yet Electra is more than a walking abstraction, ideality in its exalted and destructive aspects. She is an independent dramatic entity, a character who exists in terms of her relationships to others, most particularly to Clytemnestra. Their double quarrel, over Orestes and Agamemnon, is the most persistent emotive element in the play. The Beggar, who has access to supramortal knowledge, presents a version of Orestes' fall that at least suggests that Electra did not push her brother, but this version is merely a hypothesis dependent upon such dubious elements as the presence of a white cat and Clytemnestra's wearing a diamond brooch. Ultimately, the text does not tell us whether Electra is a loving sister or a violently jealous sibling, nor why she pursues her filial mission of vengeance with such abiding ferocity. The play's most elaborate explanation is that as the embodiment of ideal justice Electra cannot tolerate the existence of so gross a crime and must see it extirpated at whatever human cost. There are, however, alternative explanations, the most obvious deriving from Electra's passionate fixation on her father and consequent hatred of her mother. Giraudoux's Electra seems, in fact, to be a victim of the psychological "complex" that bears her name. If so, her actions stem not so much from an exalted vision of truth as from a perversion of the sexual impulse. So violent a burst of aggression is directed against Clytemnestra less, it would seem, because she is an immoral person than because she is a rival. But beyond the sinister hint that idealism is an illusion, a mere symptom of some psychological malformation, the play offers an even more frightening suggestion. Goaded by Electra, Clytemnestra finally confesses her hatred of Agamemnon, an arbitrary and irrational physical repulsion symbolized by her distaste for his curly beard and perpetually upraised little finger. In contrast to Clytemnestra is Narses' wife, who calls Electra her daughter, and for whom Agamemnon's beard was "a sun. A curled undulating sun" and his hand "the most beautiful hand I've ever seen in the world." That Electra's destructiveness should stem from the thrust of secret psychological forces is a sufficiently disquieting idea, but at least such forces derive from impulses that are human and comprehensible. That it should stem from something absolutely arbitrary and meaningless, a trivial antipathy, is a notion almost too painful to contemplate. And yet these suggestions are inherent in Giraudoux's presentation of his material. As the play draws to its conclusion and the Eumenides appear in Electra's form, we cannot ultimately know whether that form symbolizes a suprahuman idealism, a psychological malformation, or a capricious irrationality that makes humanity its victim.

Nevertheless, we do know that neither the world of shabby compromises represented by Agatha, the President, and the others nor Electra's world of harsh ideals, whatever their psychic roots, can offer a satisfying refuge. But in *Ondine* the central figure seems to draw us toward just such a place. Ondine is not only literally a creature from a world beyond the mortal one but the embodiment of charm, intelligence, and beauty. The innocence with which she speaks of Hans's attractions and the ingenuousness with which she offers herself and her affection endear her to us at once. Moreover, her ideal of an eternal, all-encompassing love is genuinely noble. But despite Ondine's graces and her commitment to an ideal affection, there are disquieting touches in her words and attitudes. Although she is sweetly playful as she practices her future wifely duty of awakening her husband from sleep, when Hans—too hungry to join in the game—continues relishing Eugenie's ham, she realizes she has been in error:

> I am very wrong to wake you! Why waken him whom one loves? In his sleep everything pushes him towards you! As

soon as his eyes are open, he escapes you! Sleep, sleep, my lord Hans. . . .

Ondine's words might suggest no more than a gentle possessiveness if they did not strangely recall those of Judith awakening beside Holophernes to find that the moment of perfection had passed and that her lover was about to escape back into life. She, too, had Ondine's sense that the beloved was possessed only in sleep. And in her reference quoted earlier, to murder as the "supreme tenderness" is delineated that impatience with human limitations, at once cruel and loving, that is the source not only of the murder of Holophernes but ultimately of the destruction of Hans as well.

The first act of *Ondine,* however, gives no more than a hint of this danger. The amiable, limited, human Hans (the noble voices of the animals in the enchanted forest entirely fail to compensate him for the lack of human company) is not really threatened by Ondine's ideality, which expresses itself aggressively only in a burst of girlish temper. But in the whimsical beginning of the second act, even as the Superintendent of the Royal Theatre and the Chamberlain quarrel over a suitable interlude to be played at Ondine's introduction to the Court, Giraudoux's central theme is already suggested. The Superintendent, after all, wishes to present *Salammbô* (whose heroine is herself a fatal woman), whereas the Chamberlain is concerned with the human exigencies of Court politics. But the human and the ideal collide more forcibly as soon as Ondine enters. Speaking to the Chamberlain of his damp palm, she is without fear and falsity but also without compassion. (When Bertram tells her that she causes pain in reminding people of their ugliness, Ondine replies that they need only not be ugly; after all, she herself is not.) However, the full significance of that lack of compassion does not become apparent until Ondine's interview with Queen Yseult. When we learn that Ondine has made a pact that Hans is to die if he betrays her, the spectacle of Hans stumbling into an entanglement with Bertha—shown in terms of the characteristic Giraudoux humor by the Illusionist—abruptly becomes an example of eternal human fallibility, taking on some of the inevitability of the coming of the Trojan War. Nor does Ondine herself escape. She is obtuse, willful, even cruel, but there is a sense of pathetic loss in her reply to Yseult's suggestion that the pact will perhaps be forgotten:

> Oh! do not believe that. It is very small—that realm in the universe where one forgets, one changes one's mind, or one pardons, humanity as you call it. . . . With us, it is as with the wild beast, as with the leaves of the ash tree, as with the caterpillars, there is neither renunciation nor pardon.

Again we see Giraudoux's eternal dilemma: if there is no permanence, no integrity in the human world, there is no charity in the realm of the ideal.

The impossibility of combining the virtues of both these worlds is suggested at the opening of the third act. While awaiting the moment of his marriage to Bertha, Hans is disturbed by the servant's addressing him in an elevated diction. Among the Wittensteins, he explains to Bertha, when the servants speak in exalted language, catastrophe is approaching; when they speak in verse, death is near. Hans's foreboding is borne out during the act, and we see that—as so often with Giraudoux—what appeared at first to be a piece of elegant fantasy is in fact an expression, in dramatic terms, of theme: an elevation beyond the ordinary level heralds the destruction of human life.

But though Hans has turned back to that human world, he cannot obliterate from his mind the image of something beyond it. Ultimately that Ondine from whose memory Hans is unable to escape comes to symbolize a vision of an existence more beautiful—perhaps more terrible—than our mortal one, a vision that once encountered is never again to be entirely eluded. The burden of such a vision and the discontent it induces are suggested in Hans's reply when he is asked what punishment he demands for Ondine:

> HANS. What I demand? I demand what these servants, men and girls, demand! I demand for men the right to be a little alone upon this earth. Surely what God has accorded them is not very grand, this surface two meters in height, between heaven and hell! Surely human life is not so attractive with these hands one must wash, these colds one must nurse,

these hairs that leave one! . . . What I demand is to live
without having to feel, swarming about us as they insist on
doing, these extra-human lives, these herrings with women's
bodies, these bladders with the heads of children, these liz-
ards with spectacles and the thighs of nymphs. . . . On the
morning of my marriage, I demand to be—in a world empty
of their visits, of their humors and their couplings—alone
with my fiancée, alone at last.

At this moment Hans sees Bosch-like images of horror encircling
the human world because his anger at Ondine's supposed unfaithfulness has converted her beauty to monstrousness; but
Giraudoux, whose voice is also audible in Hans's words, sees them
for other reasons. To him they are the depths of terror and irrationality that lie beneath the warmth and conjugal safety of the
human world just as Ondine's delicacy and beauty are what lie
above it. That one who has glimpsed these things should ask to be
free of them is, as the first Judge says in reply to Hans, "the supreme demand."

But if Hans is haunted by his visions, Ondine too has had hers.
For that world of domestic happiness, transitory and imperfect but
nonetheless rich and satisfying, is, from Ondine's point of view, no
less visionary than her world is to Hans. In her devotion to her
spoon, her stepladder, her "pâte brisée," she too is striving to
achieve the unattainable. If she, as her uncle the King of the On-
dines tells us, is human by taste, it is a taste that she cannot ultimately indulge. As the ideal is unapproachable by Hans, so the
human is finally closed to Ondine. Nor is this pattern accidental,
for Ondine's frustration, like that of Hans, is also Giraudoux's.
With Hans, Giraudoux stands within the human world, but—
haunted by the ideal—he cannot accept that world's limitations.
With Ondine he stands, imaginatively, beyond it, but finds himself
longing to return to its warmth and safety. Sustaining this tension
in perfect equilibrium, Giraudoux modulates to the play's conclusion in which Hans's human mortality is counterbalanced by Ondine's divine forgetfulness.

With the death of Hans, however, there dies also Giraudoux's
major creative impulse.[32] Both in *Sodom and Gomorrah* and *For Lucretia (Pour Lucrèce,* performed in English as *Duel of Angels),* his last

two tragedies, there is a sense of a thinning out of the material and a drying up of the flow of linguistic invention, yet even here the pattern subsists.

In *Sodom and Gomorrah,* a long series of squabbles, primarily between the central characters Lia and Jean upon whose ability or inability to achieve happiness the salvation of Sodom and Gomorrah depends, seems to suggest that the destruction or at least the central failures of humanity derive from an ultimate incompatibility of the sexes. Whatever the personal source of this curious thesis may be, the political circumstances surrounding the play help account for its general blackness of tone (and indeed for the subject matter of a nation on the brink of ruin).[33] Beneath these elements, however, we may perceive a basic Giraudoux pattern, for Lia is one of those uncompromising idealists—like Electra—whose commitment to their vision remains absolute even though it may entail the destruction of their world. Indeed, the recurrence of similar elements suggests that *Sodom and Gomorrah* is, in part at least, a darker pendant to *Electra:* in each play the figure of the Gardener appears, and in each the heroine greets the dawn as catastrophe engulfs her city. *For Lucretia,* though it lacks the wit and fantasy of the earlier plays, has something of their essential character. In the opposition between the severe, inhuman purity embodied in Lucile and the perverse corruption of Paola we recognize a part of the permanent Giraudoux pattern. The false rape arranged by Paola is in effect an attempt to reduce Lucile to the ordinary human level, and Lucile's suicide justifies her idealism by momentarily illuminating the world "in beauty and light."

Nevertheless, *For Lucretia,* though it has a certain grim power, lacks not only Giraudoux's stylistic fantasy but the breadth of vision characteristic of his best work as well.[34] In this play both the human and ideal worlds are essentially sinister; but when Giraudoux's vision is at its fullest, both worlds are at once dark and light, sinister and attractive. Then the full ambiguity, that is to say the full richness and complexity, of Giraudoux's sense of life is apparent. Although each of the four major tragedies considered in this study has its special character—the acerbity of *Judith,* the pathetic optism of *The Trojan War,* the exuberant fierceness of *Electra,* the graceful fantasy of *Ondine*—they all embrace within their particular worlds the full range of doubts and contradictions characteristic of Giraudoux's vision. In *Judith* we see not only the power of Judith's aspiration toward the divine but its tendency to dehumanize as well. If Holophernes shows us the charm of human life, Egon reveals its corruption, the Grand Rabbi its hypocrisy. Although Helen is mysterious and beautiful, she is the source of utter destruction; although Hector is wise and good, he becomes the prey of the irrational. Absolute justice is embodied in Electra, but like Helen, she destroys a city. If humanity is noble as in the transformed Egisthus, loving and innocent as in the Gardener, it is shallow in Agatha, weak and even criminal in Clytemnestra. Ondine is ingenuous yet pitiless, Hans well meaning yet obtuse.

In all of these plays Giraudoux has balanced the claims of the human and the suprahuman worlds so precisely that the scale of our judgment hardly tilts. This equilibrium is one of the central qualities of his art. By maintaining it he is able to reveal to us the complexity of the human situation with its possibilities of happiness in the mortal world weighed against the inevitability of corruptions and limitations. We see the dangers of a pursuit of the ideal with its proneness to lead men away from life itself but also the eternal attractions of a dream of transcendent self-realization.

Part II:

Inner Voyages

3.

Williams and Miller

Tennessee Williams: A Desperate Morality

The true setting for the plays of Wilde and Synge is the world of art, a refuge from the forces most gravely threatening to them: Victorian philistinism in one case, ultimate mortality in the other. But a different response is devised for troubling demands by Tennessee Williams and Arthur Miller, even though their affinities with these unlikely predecessors are significant. Usually thought of together only because they are contemporaries who dominated the American theatre in the years following World War II, Williams and Miller, despite notable differences in style and substance, were finally making the same attempt: to create in their works a metaphorical "world" that would be shelter for the self against the assaults of a hostile reality. But for Williams and Miller this sanctuary is not a world of art but a world of innocence. Like the other visionary worlds we have been considering, this one, too, is occasionally seen as a literal place, but it is always and essentially a psychic condition, in this case freedom from an encroaching sense of guilt. That questions of innocence and guilt are central to the work of Arthur Miller, whose plays are filled with ethical crises, has been evident from the first; it is, however, a good deal less obvious in the case of Tennessee Williams.

To call him a moralist might seem to bestow a strange appellation on a playwright whose works deal so sensationally with rape, castration, cannibalism, and other bizarre activities. But in examining the plays of Tennessee Williams it is exactly this point—that he wishes to judge the self, not analyze it—that must be borne in mind. The world of Williams' plays, though it is founded on his observations of the American South, is essentially an inner world dominated by certain overpowering obsessions: fear, loneliness, death, sexuality, and above all innocence and guilt. In this special world the self struggles to affirm its innocence, but over and over again it is adjudged guilty.

Admittedly, Williams's morality is a curious one, but it is a consistent ethic, giving him a point of view from which he can make his judgments. Yet to say that Williams rewards those who, by his standards, are virtuous and punishes those who are wicked is to oversimplify, for in Williams's plays good often has an unexpected affinity with evil. Beneath the skin of the Christlike martyr destroyed by the cruel forces of death and sterility lies the disease, the transgression that had made the author destroy him, while the character most fiercely condemned may at the same time be the one for whom pardon is most passionately demanded. From the self-lacerating desire simultaneously to praise and to punish stems the violence that agitates so many of Williams's plays.

To understand this violence in Williams's work we must first look at his gentlest plays, those in which the virtuous self is rewarded, for here is most directly revealed the morality by which the guilty one is later so terribly condemned. Surprisingly, one of Williams's most significant plays is an indifferent and undramatic one-acter about the death of D. H. Lawrence, only slightly redeemed by the audacious title, *I Rise in Flame, Cried the Phoenix.* The play is so important because it gives us the central fact we must have to understand Williams's work, the nature of his literary parentage.

Whether or not Williams assesses Lawrence correctly is, for an understanding of Williams's own work, irrelevant. What does matter here is that at a very early point in his career *(I Rise in Flame* dates from 1941) Williams saw Lawrence as the great writer who "celebrates the body" and himself apparently as that writer's disciple. But a disciple is not invariably the best advocate of his master's doctrine; Williams began his career as a neo-Lawrentian writer by basing a very bad play on one of Lawrence's short stories. Called *You Touched Me* (also the title of Lawrence's story), this early work (copyrighted in 1942), of slight interest in itself, is revelatory in the distortions it introduces while transforming the original material and additionally important for establishing a structural pattern that Williams was later to use far more effectively.

Williams's play (written in collaboration with Donald Windham) becomes a stunning vulgarization of Lawrence's tale as the younger sister of the story, Emmie, is changed into a frigid maiden aunt representing "aggressive sterility," and the heroine, Matilda, a thin, large-nosed woman of thirty-two in Lawrence's version, is turned into a pale girl of twenty, the cliché of the frail, sheltered maiden. Hadrian, in the story a neat, scheming little soldier with a common-looking mustache, is transformed into "a clean-cut, muscular young man in the dress uniform of a lieutenant in the Royal Canadian Air Force," much given to speeches about faith, the glories of the future, and the conquering of new countries of the mind. And finally, the elderly pottery manufacturer is turned into a spry, if alcoholic old sea captain. Given this set of popular-magazine characters, the play has no trouble reaching its predictable conclusion as the captain helps the handsome airman defeat the aunt and win the shy Matilda.

What is significant is not that at this early stage in his career, Williams should write a poor play, but that, while retaining the essential Lawrentian theme, he should so alter Lawrence's material as to produce an unmistakable Tennessee Williams play. The light but subtle characterizations around which Lawrence built his story are in the play coarsened to the point where the characters are obviously marked out simply as good and bad. Williams here is very little of a psychologist; rather, he is a moralist, a special kind of sexual moralist, whose creations are judged virtuous only if they owe their allegiance to the sexual impulse. Although Williams distorted and sentimentalized Lawrence's story, its central action—the awakening to life, and particularly to sexual life, of one who had previously been dead to it—was one that Williams, with an unquestioning faith in romantic vitalism, saw as profoundly good.

Developed roughly in *You Touched Me,* it was then placed at the center of two of his most pleasing works, *The Glass Menagerie* and *The Rose Tattoo.* In each of these plays a woman who has retired from life is confronted by a man, like Hadrian, the sexual force designed to release her from bondage. But whereas he succeeds in one case, in the other he fails. The reasons for this difference are worth noting.

The figure of Laura in *The Glass Menagerie* has clearly been developed from that of Matilda in *You Touched Me,* who is described by Williams as having "the delicate, almost transparent quality of glass." Both are shy, fragile creatures, remote from the life around them. But whereas Hadrian awakens Matilda to life, Laura's gentleman caller gives her only a momentary glimpse of normal existence before she drifts back into the fantasy world of glass animals. Although in Williams's moral system the rejection of life is a crime demanding punishment, Laura is adjudged innocent; she is not frigid and hostile; she does not reject but rather is rejected, not because of her limp, which does not exist in "Portrait of a Girl in Glass," Williams's own short story upon which he based his play, but because she is the sensitive, misunderstood exile, a recurrent character in Williams's work, one of the fugitive kind, who are too fragile to face a malignant reality and must have a special world in which they can take shelter. The vigorous Serafina Delle Rose of *The Rose Tattoo,* however, deliberately rejects life after the death of her husband, leading an existence as solitary and sterile as that of Laura among the glass animals. Fortunately, when the truck driver Alvaro Mangiacavallo, who has the face of a clown but the body of her husband, appears, she escapes guilt by disclaiming her rejection, returning to the world of life, and accepting sexuality again.

A later and less likable work, *Period of Adjustment* belongs with this group of gentle dramas, for at its conclusion the two couples are permitted to enter the haven of sexual harmony as the phallically named community of High Point sinks farther into the cavern beneath it. But before the playwright allows these consummations, each of the two men who are its central figures is humiliated and forced to admit his guilt. They have been great fighters and war heroes, but one has abased himself to marry for money, and the other has rejected his homosexual nature or at least pretended to a virility he does not possess. Ultimately the play collapses because the author, vaguely hostile to his masculine characters, cannot decide whether they are to be forgiven or punished.

Although Williams's impulse to forgive and grant entrance to the realm of innocence has produced attractive plays, his need to punish has led to his most powerful work. Invariably, the central crime in Williams's moral code has been that from which Matilda and Serafina were preserved, the rejection of life. The theme of punishment for an act of rejection is at the center of a group of plays very different from that already examined, but it is expressed most explicitly in a short story, "Desire and the Black Masseur," from the volume *One Arm and Other Stories.* In this story the central character, Walter Burns, who has yielded to the loveless life around him, is haunted by a nameless desire that is fulfilled only by the manipulations of a gigantic black masseur who first beats Burns and then, as the story veers toward fantasy, kills him and proceeds to eat his body in the atmosphere of a sacred ritual. Bizarre, perhaps a little ridiculous, the story nevertheless makes of its hero a broad symbol of human guilt and desire for atonement. Claiming that the sins of the world "are really only its partialities, its incompletions, and these are what sufferings must atone for," Williams attempts to suggest a wider vision comprehending the world and the place of suffering in it. "And meantime," he concludes, "slowly, with barely a thought of so doing, the earth's whole population twisted and writhed beneath the manipulation of night's black fingers, the white ones of day with skeletons splintered and flesh reduced to pulp, as out of this unlikely problem, the answer, perfection, was slowly evolved through torture."[1]

We need not believe that anything like perfection could be evolved from the process described here (nor linger over the element of erotic gratification in these masochistic images) to see its significance in relation to Williams's major work. The story concerns an elaborate, ritual punishment of one who has rejected life and, more specifically, rejected sexuality. A whole group of plays including some of the most remarkable—*A Streetcar Named Desire, Summer and Smoke, Cat on a Hot Tin Roof,* and *Suddenly Last Summer*—centers not only on Williams's refusal to grant the world of refuge sought by so many of his characters but on his inflicting terrible punishments for sexual rejection, for him an act synonymous with the rejection of life itself.

The stage action of *A Streetcar Named Desire,* still Williams's best play, consists almost entirely of the punishment its heroine endures—even as she desperately seeks a place of safety—as atonement for her central act of rejection, her sin in terms of Williams's morality. Since Williams begins the action of his play at a late point in the story, the act itself is not played out on stage but only referred to. Unaware that she is describing the crime that condemns her, Blanche tells Mitch of her discovery that her adored young husband was a homosexual and of the consequences of her disgust and revulsion:

> BLANCHE. . . . He'd stuck the revolver into his mouth, and fired—so that the back of his head had been—blown away! *(She sways and covers her face.)* It was because—on the dance floor—unable to stop myself—I'd suddenly said—"I saw! I know! You disgust me . . ." And then the searchlight which had been turned on the world was turned off again and never for one moment since has there been any light that's stronger than this—kitchen—candle. . . .

While Blanche delivers this speech and the ones surrounding it, the polka to which she and her husband had danced, the Varsouviana, sounds in the background. At the end of the play, when Blanche sees the Doctor who is to lead her off to the dubious refuge of the asylum, her punishment is complete and the Varsouviana sounds again, linking her crime to its retribution.[2] As Blanche flees from the Doctor, "the Varsouviana is filtered into a weird distortion accompanied by the cries and noises of the jungle." These symbolize both Blanche's chaotic state and the instrument of her destruction, Stanley Kowalski, the complete sensual animal, the equivalent in function to the black masseur.

Although Kowalski's primary mission, to destroy Blanche, is clear, his role evokes certain ambiguities. By becoming Blanche's destroyer, he also becomes the avenger of her homosexual husband. Although he is Williams's exaggeration of the Lawrentian lover, it is appropriate from Williams's point of view that Kowalski should to some degree be identified with the lonely homosexual who had been driven to suicide, for Williams saw Lawrence not only as the propagandist of sexual vitality but as the symbol of the solitary, rejected exile. (In the poem called "Cried the Fox" from Williams's collection, *In the Winter of Cities,* Lawrence is seen as the fox pursued by the cruel hounds.) But however gratifying it may be to identify the embodiment of admired male sexuality with the exile artist and thus by implication with the exile homosexual, the identification, even for Williams, remains tenuous.

Though an avenger, Kowalski is as guilty of destroying Blanche as she is of destroying her husband. For Blanche, who has lost the plantation Belle Reve, the beautiful dream world of safety and gracious gentility, is an exile like the homosexual; her tormentor, the apelike Kowalski, from one point of view the representative of Lawrentian vitality, is from another the brutal, male torturer of a lonely spirit. But however much she wishes to find herself safe and see herself as innocent, Blanche remains, in Williams's moral vision, guilty, unworthy of rescue. She has in effect killed her husband by her cruelty, and her belated acknowledgment of sexuality, turning away from death to its opposite that she had so denied— "the opposite is desire," as Blanche herself says—leads only to her ultimate destruction.

Although a variant on the act of rejection is performed in *Summer and Smoke,* guilt is not absolute and punishment is mitigated. The heroine is similar to those already encountered: the frail, spinsterish southern girl with her sensuality repressed by a puritanical background. Like many of Williams's characters, the hero needs love as an escape from solitude: at one point, while giving Alma an ironic anatomy lecture, he shouts, "This part down here is the sex which is hungry for love because it is sometimes lonesome." At the crucial moment she refuses his advances and rushes off. Alma, having committed the sin of rejection, is condemned, as Blanche was before her, to be tormented by the very urges she had fled from and to turn to promiscuity.[3] Yet because her sin has been somewhat diminished by her realization of it, there is a suggestion at the end of the play that the traveling salesman she has picked up may lead her to salvation rather than destruction.

Like *Summer and Smoke,* a later play, *The Night of the Iguana,* has affinities with both the severity of *Streetcar* and the gentleness of *The Glass Menagerie.* Its heroine, Hannah Jelkes, a New England spinster artist, is like Blanche confronted by an appeal for help from one with abnormal sexual inclinations (a homosexual in Williams's original story but converted for stage purposes to an unfrocked minister with a taste for pubescent girls). But instead of driving him to suicide, she offers him what limited help she can. Because like Laura and Alma she is too delicate and repressed to take on a full emotional relationship, Shannon's rescue is finally left to the sexually vital hotel proprietor, while Hannah must continue in loveless solitude. By her sympathy for Shannon and for the pathetic fetishist she had previously aided, she has earned, however, a fate far gentler than the breakdown meted out to Blanche and to her own predecessor in the source story.

In *Cat on a Hot Tin Roof*, however, Williams produces something much nearer the pattern of *Streetcar*. In fact, from one point of view *Cat* is simply a reworking of the materials of the earlier play, but with a crucial change that made it almost impossible for Williams to bring his new play to a reasonable conclusion. Again, the motivating figure, who does not appear on stage, is the rejected homosexual; the rejector, whose youth like Blanche's is fading, has also like Blanche turned to drink, attempting to find a sheltered world in a state of alcoholic dissociation. But because the one who has rejected, the sinner who must atone, is not a woman but a man, certain problems arise. The audience, although it sympathizes with Blanche, can accept her as guilty. She could not only have given her husband love instead of contempt but at least the possibility of a heterosexual life. But, confronted with Skipper's telephoned confession of a homosexual attachment, Brick has fewer possibilities before him. The audience is likely to feel that sympathetic understanding is the most that Brick can offer—short of admitting to a similar inclination. Yet Williams, although he is ambiguous about several points in this play, is not ambiguous about Brick's guilt. Big Daddy himself, who despises mendacity, condemns his son. "You! dug the grave of your friend," he cries, "and kicked him in it!—before you'd face the truth with him!" But it is beyond Big Daddy's power to tell Brick just what he was to do.

In a play designed for the commercial theatre, Williams could not at that time openly punish Brick for failing to be an honest homosexual. When he showed *Cat* to the representative of that theatre, Elia Kazan, and Kazan suggested certain changes, Williams accepted his advice. As a result, the comparatively optimistic third act performed on Broadway contains the shift in Brick's character that leads to the possibility that his sexual quiescence, a symbolic castration suggested by his broken ankle, will not be permanent. There is no reason to disbelieve Williams's claim that he had agreed to Kazan's suggestions to retain his interest, but it is worth noting that by mitigating Brick's suffering Williams was relieved of the necessity of asking his audience to agree that Brick deserved punishment for an act much of that audience would not have considered reprehensible.

Although the tentativeness of Williams's condemnation of Brick makes it difficult to know whether Brick was so condemned for rejecting his homosexual friend or for rejecting his own homosexual nature, in *Cat,* at least, homosexuality itself carries no stigma. Although Big Daddy is a man of almost ostentatious virility (the latent antifeminism in his sexual revulsion from Big Mama is not stressed) [4] as well as the most powerful and sympathetic figure in the play, he had served and respected the two idyllically conceived homosexuals, Straw and Ochello, and received his land from them as a kind of benediction. Yet in *Suddenly Last Summer,* a later play of what may be called the "punishment" group, Williams has produced a work in which the homosexual—so often for him the symbol of the lonely, rejected exile—becomes the rejector, the sinner who must be punished.

But neither this shift in Williams's usual pattern nor the *bizarrerie* of the play's atmosphere should conceal the fact that *Suddenly Last Summer* follows closely the structure of the other plays in this group. Once more the pivotal figure, the exile homosexual, has met a violent death before the opening of the play. As the sterile Brick is contrasted with Big Daddy, the life-giving father of *Cat,* so the cruel Sebastian is played off against the loving and merciful Catharine who gives herself not, it seems, out of desire but as an act of rescue. "We walked through the wet grass to the great misty oaks," she says, "as if somebody was calling us for help there." Remembering that this act of rescue is exactly what Blanche, Alma, and Brick failed to perform, we realize that Williams means us to accept Catharine as entirely good. Although Sebastian is the loveless rejector who is punished for his sins, there is a surprising similarity between his vision of a world dominated by remorseless cruelty—as expressed in the description of the Encantadas, the Galápagos Islands, where baby sea turtles are killed and devoured by carnivorous birds of prey—and the vision of a world undergoing perpetual punishment expressed in "Desire and the Black Masseur." However, in punishing Sebastian, Williams is not disclaiming this vision. Sebastian's sin lay not in perceiving the world as, in Williams' darkest vision, it is, but in his believing, with a pride bordering on hubris, that he could exalt himself above his kind, could feed upon people like one of the devouring birds of the Encantadas. But as Sebastian had cruelly watched the turtles being eaten and fed the fruit flies to the devouring plant, so he is fed to the band of children whom he has perverted and is devoured by them.

Sebastian's crime, then, is the very one committed by Blanche, Alma, and Brick—turning away from suffering fellow creatures and offering hate instead of love. And yet there is a difficulty for the spectator in accepting the nature of Sebastian's punishment. It is not merely that Sebastian's fate is so grotesque but that, unlike Blanche and Brick, he has not performed a specific act that brings his punishment upon him; he is punished as much for what he is as for what he does. He is not only a rejector but also a homosexual, always in Williams's work an object simultaneously of sympathy and of revulsion.[5] In the intimate connection between the guilty rejector and the martyred homosexual, the punishment visited on the former often echoes the fate of the latter, so that the two characters are not always distinguishable. In *Streetcar* the rejector and the homosexual victim were separate, but both met desperate ends. In the ambiguous Brick these figures began to converge, and in *Suddenly Last Summer* they have completely coalesced.

They remained linked in *Kingdom of Earth*—called the *Seven Descents of Myrtle* in its New York acting version—in which the sickly and effeminate Lot Ravenstock (whose elegantly sinister southern name skirts perilously close to that of Gaylord Ravenal) attempts, in a futile denial of life, to keep his property from falling into the hands of Chicken, his virile half brother (that Chicken is half black and that his domain is a rough kitchen are evident signs of an irresistible earthiness) through his unconsummated marriage to an amiable hysteric named Myrtle. As the procreative flood sweeps over the farm, however, Chicken easily takes over wife and land while Lot expires of tuberculosis after dressing himself in the clothes of his adored mother. Although Chicken is a mere caricature of virility (". . . what's able to happen between a man and a woman, just that thing, nothing more, is perfect"), Lot, the despairing transvestite, reveals a certain complexity, for he is at once shelter-seeking victim and cruel life-denier.

Once again we see the ambiguity in the vision of corruption pervading so much of Williams's work. Not only is retribution visited on the rejector of the homosexual victim, but in certain plays the homosexual himself—sterile and guilty—must be punished as well. Again and again in Williams's plays those to whom he most wishes to offer refuge and to perceive as innocent are ultimately denied their world of safety and adjudged guilty. A group of Williams's plays—*Camino Real, Orpheus Descending,* and *Sweet Bird of Youth*—develops this vision of pervasive corruption through the story of a wanderer, usually only dubiously innocent, who while searching for shelter enters a world of blatant evil and is destroyed by it.

Williams has said flatly that the sinister fantasy world of *Camino Real* "is nothing more nor less than my conception of the time and world that I live in." It is a time in which greed and brutality are the ruling forces and a world in which those pathetic souls who attempt to show some affection for their fellow creatures are remorselessly crushed and then thrown into a barrel and carted away by the street cleaners. Although this is admittedly a nightmare world, it does not differ in any essential way from the American South as it appears in *Orpheus Descending* and *Sweet Bird of Youth* where greed, brutality, and sterility rule and where those who love are castrated or burned alive. As an epigraph to *Camino Real,* Williams has selected the opening lines of Dante's *Inferno;* the setting of the play is the world to which Orpheus descended.

As we would expect, the ruler of hell is Death; more specifically, he is the god of sterility. In *Camino Real,* Gutman, the proprietor of the Siete Mares hotel, is cruel and sinister enough, but he always remains a little remote from what happens on stage. Like Gutman, Jabe Torrance, the proprietor of the mercantile store in *Orpheus Descending,* takes little direct part in the action, but he is a far more heavily drawn figure and a far more violent antagonist. The evil creature who destroys life wherever he can find it is, as Williams describes him in a stage direction, "death's self and malignancy." He is not only "death's self" but the personification of sterility and

impotence. Nurse Porter, who seems to have supernatural perception, can tell at a glance that Lady is pregnant and that Jabe is not
the father. As he had burned the wine garden of Lady's father
where the fig tree blossomed and true lovers met, so he calls upon
the fires of the hell of impotence to burn her and her lover. (It
should be noted that whereas Williams's work has changed in tone
from the gentleness of *You Touched Me,* where the impotent clergyman was a figure of fun, it has not shifted in point of view.) Even
more heavily than Jabe, however, Boss Finley of *Sweet Bird of Youth*
is drawn as the symbol of malignant impotence. Miss Lucy, his
mistress, has scrawled in lipstick across the ladies' room mirror,
"Boss Finley is too old to cut the mustard." By implication, at
least, he had presided over the castration of an innocent black and,
as the play ends, is about to preside over that of its hero, Chance
Wayne.

When Boss Finley's impotence is contrasted with Chance's attitude toward the emasculation of the black, the natures of the opposing forces in the play become clear. "You know what that is,
don't you?" Chance cries. "Sex-envy is what that is, and the revenge for sex-envy which is a widespread disease that I have run
into personally too often for me to doubt its existence or any manifestation." Boss Finley, Chance says, "was just called down from
the hills to preach hate. I was born here to make love." Each of the
three wanderers, Kilroy, Val, and Chance, had been born to make
love, but each has been wounded by a hostile world. Kilroy's heart
condition prevents him from continuing as a prizefighter or from
staying with his "real true woman." Of the three he is the only true
innocent and, significantly, the only one who is alone. Val and
Chance both speak of the corrupt lives they have lived and of the
waning of their youth, but in reality each is bound, not by time or
by his past, but by his relationship with an older woman.

If the suggestion of homosexuality that underlies the relationship between the older woman and the younger man in Williams'
novella, *The Roman Spring of Mrs. Stone,* is extended to *Orpheus* and
Sweet Bird (in each case the ostensible woman is an older person
having a forbidden affair with a beautiful young man), these works
fit very easily into the pattern of ambiguity in the "punishment"
group. From one point of view, the wandering love-giver—Val,
whose phallic guitar is an obvious symbol, and Chance, proclaim-

ing his vocation as lovemaker—enters the nightmare world of Hades in *Orpheus* and of what the Princess in *Sweet Bird* calls "the ogre's country at the top of the beanstalk." In the innocent attempt to rescue a lover he is brutally destroyed by the giant. (Since "Jack and the Beanstalk" is a classic oedipal fantasy, in which a boy destroys a father symbol and thereafter possesses his mother undisturbed, the imagery here has an extra level of appropriateness.) In a special variation on the wanderer material, *The Milk Train Doesn't Stop Here Anymore,* the beautiful young man comes to a ruthless but vital older woman not to rescue her through love but to preside benignly over her death.

From another point of view, however, the wanderer is not innocent but corrupt. Beneath the apparent heterosexual relationship lies one that is homosexual (the "eccentric" were among Chance's lovers; Val has "lived in corruption"), and from it spreads an aura of guilt that pervades the plays. Chance, who calculates his age by the level of rot in him, and Val, who has been "on a party" in the bars of New Orleans since he was fifteen, are trying vainly to flee from their pasts and find the sheltered realm that Williams's corrupted innocents always seek. But as before, the seeming innocent is found to be guilty and must be hideously punished. Once his moral sense has been appeased, however, Williams can allow himself the luxury of a sentimental apotheosis. *Orpheus* and *Sweet Bird* take place at Easter, and in both plays there is a suggestion that the dead wanderers should be viewed as martyred Christ figures whose spirits are resurrected respectively, in Carol Cutrere and the Princess. (Whereas the suggestion that Val Xavier does indeed have something of the savior about him is not entirely incredible, the idea that the pathetic gigolo of *Sweet Bird* could be a Christlike martyr is merely grotesque, as is the notion that Christopher—also significantly named—in *Milktrain* could be an "Angel of Death" who would "mean God" to the dying Mrs. Goforth.) Yet, whatever the wanderer's ultimate state as an object of reverence, he is allowed to reach that exalted condition only after he has been destroyed.

The absence of this conflict between the need to condemn and the desire to pardon is what distinguishes Williams's later plays and what, more than anything else, accounts for their weaknesses. Several of them—*In the Bar of a Tokyo Hotel, Small Craft Warnings,* and *Out Cry*—are indeed rambling discourses with little or no sense of movement toward a climax. Moreover, both in *The Mutilated* and *Gnädiges Fräulein* Williams attempts to use elements of the absurdist style, for which he has no essential affinity. But these miscalculations in technique and style are merely symptoms of an underlying problem. For whatever reason, in these plays Williams has ceased to project the opposing elements of his consciousness outward into self-sustaining dramatic entities, characters who stand in conflict with each other and upon whom Williams exercises his ambiguous judgment of innocence or guilt. Now all are innocent. All significant characters are pathetic victims—of time, of their own passions, of immutable circumstances—and all receive the playwright's sympathy in unbounded measure. But since these characters are so recognizably close to Williams and his concerns, the pity extended to them is ultimately self-pity, an emotion of very limited dramatic appeal.

The most obviously personal, and even self-indulgent, of these late plays is *Out Cry,* in which a brother and sister (suggestive of the figures in *The Glass Menagerie),* the leaders of a traveling acting company, find themselves immured alone in a mysterious foreign theatre. There—on a stage dominated by a terrifying black statue, the symbol of their psychic torments—they act out a play about a brother and sister immured alone in a house dominated by ghosts of a past domestic tragedy. Unfortunately, the Pirandellesque element of the play within the play is handled without sufficient theatrical flair, and the obsessive concern with finding a private world sheltered from the assaults of external reality finally becomes stultifying. Even less appealing is the distracted artist of *In the Bar of a Tokyo Hotel,* whose madness makes him the easy victim of his cruelly vital wife, herself a victim of passing time. This contrast between inert pathos and comparative vitality, regularly presented though pairs of women in the later works (Celeste and Trinket in *The Mutilated,* the Molly-Polly figures and the Fräulein in *Gnädiges Fräulein,* Leona and Violet in *Small Craft Warnings),* runs through Williams's other plays of the late 1960s and early 1970s. But whereas this motif was handled with evocative complexity in Williams's earlier work (Amanda and Laura, Stanley and Blanche, Maggie and Brick are the most obvious examples), here everything is awash in a flood of sentimentality that invites, though it cannot induce, total sympathy for the suffering victims.

Williams's best work derives its force from the strength of his moral temper, which leads him to censure even what he most wishes to exalt. He remains committed to his romantic, neo-Lawrentian view, that the natural equals the good, that the natural instincts welling up out of the subconscious depths—and particularly the sexual instinct, whatever form it may take—are to be trusted absolutely. But in his earlier work Williams was far too strong a moralist, far too permeated with a sense of sin, to accept such an idea with equanimity. However pathetic he made the martyred homosexual, however seemingly innocent the wandering love-giver, the moral strength that made him punish the guilty Blanche also impelled him to condemn Brick and Chance. Because he was judging the self as guilty when he most wished to believe it was innocent, because he was condemning where he most wished to offer a sheltering absolution, in order to condemn at all he sometimes had to do so with ferocious violence.

This violence, however grotesque, was never in itself the real problem in Williams's work. Nor were the disguises, transpositions, even evasions in his handling of the theme of homosexuality. They were, in fact, arguably a source of his strength, for they protected him from oversimplifications and encouraged the genuine complexity of his moral attitude to assume symbolic form in his plays. Williams's problem, then, is not that he dealt obliquely with homosexuality (the oblique view, after all, often reveals what is invisible when the object is contemplated directly) but that, especially of late but to some degree from the first, he sentimentalized. One of the central dangers confronting a romantic writer is that his commitment to the idea of the natural innocence of the self will lead him not only to see this quality as inherent in the child or man in a state of nature (Kowalski is a curious late variant on the Noble Savage) but to affirm its existence in characters who have lived all too fully in the fallen world of mortal corruption. When this easy sympathy is extended without qualification, Williams's work slips over the edge of control into the maudlin just as it slips over the opposite edge into hysteria when the opposing impulse to punish the self is dominant. When these conflicting impulses are held in some degree of balance, Williams renders perceptive judgments on his characters; then he is a moralist of some force, a playwright of some distinction.

Arthur Miller: Eden and After

What binds Arthur Miller and Tennessee Williams together far more than being the two most eminent American playwrights of their generation is their commitment to the same central theme: the quest of the self for a state of innocence. As we have seen, the sheltered place that so many of Williams's characters seek as they flee from their conviction of guilt is often a metaphor for this condition. That Williams in his more recent plays has allowed his characters ever easier access to this realm of innocence crucially distinguishes his work from that of Miller, who has moved in the opposite direction, making it steadily more difficult for his characters to achieve the state of assured virtue they desire. Indeed, in his most recent play to date, the biblical fantasy *The Creation of the World and Other Business,* Miller turned to what is for the Western imagination the primal image of the loss of innocence and of a sheltered world where the self is content, the expulsion from Eden. In most of Miller's plays, however, the certainty of virtue that for him constitutes self-fulfillment is less clearly linked to a particular metaphorical place. Nevertheless, the two areas in which Miller's characters function—the public arena of politics and economics and the private, familial circle (in Miller typically composed of father, mother, and two brothers)—have the characteristic intense identity that makes one think of them as the playwright's "worlds."

But in these worlds the quest for innocence has not proceeded at an unvaried pace; rather, after an eight-year hiatus at the midpoint of Miller's career, it became arguably more intense, certainly less successful. Between the premiere of *A View from the Bridge* and that of *After the Fall,* the vast confessional meditation that began the second phase of his career, Miller produced only one work, a screenplay of dubious merit called *The Misfits.* Despite its shallow characterizations and passages of blatantly bad prose, it demands attention because it reveals with painful clarity the difficulties and confusions characteristic of even the best of the preceding plays. And in so doing it helps us to understand Miller's attempt, after returning to the theatre, to move beyond the fervent simplicities of his earlier works toward a certain balance and sophistication, to mute his first romantic optimism and yet retain some measure of moral confidence.

In the story upon which the screenplay is based, three men are hunting mustangs with plane and truck in the Nevada mountains. The hunting is unprofitable and even distasteful, for the horses, remnants of the great herds that had once roamed the area, are to be slaughtered and their flesh used in canned dog and cat food. Nevertheless, the men continue with the job because, in their recurring phrase, "it's better than wages," that is, better than becoming part of the commercial civilization around them that they sense as alien and corrupt. In a world dominated by this civilization the men are misfits with no objectives or ambitions. "I don't want nothin' and I don't want to want nothin'," says the younger cowboy. "That's the way, boy," the older encourages him.[6] Miller finds this individualism that keeps them from accepting wages both admirable and tragic: admirable because it lets them retain a degree of integrity and tragic because the only task left for such men is painful and brutalizing. Only the mountain horses are at one with their environment, and they are to be hunted down and killed.

The story has been expanded and transferred to the screen with only one major alteration, the character of Roslyn, the older cowboy's mistress. In the original she is not more than a rich easterner who will taunt them for failing to make money, but in the screenplay she has flowered out into a symbol of the acceptance of life. She has "that big connection," as one of the characters says with a gaucherie remarkable even in so comparatively awkward a stylist as Miller; she is "really hooked in," so that the emotions of others are as real to her as her own. After a few days in her company, two of the mustang hunters come to understand the futility of their task, and one, through his union with her, finds the strength to reject his aimless life.

The *ewig Weibliche* that leads man on to a higher state of being is, of course, an ancient and respectable romantic notion, but the character in whom it is here embodied offers only a vague sentimentality, more likely to induce exasperated annoyance than spiritual exaltation. Yet in this awkwardly conceived character Miller was not merely creating a desirable role for Marilyn Monroe, then his wife.[7] Rather, he was attempting to create a solution, however fumbling and inadequate, for the problems that afflict not only *The Misfits* but all of Miller's works. These problems stem from two closely linked concerns, one with man's relation to the world of society and the other with his relation to the private world of the self, upon which the whole structure of Miller's writings has been reared. It is no accident that the cowboys of *The Misfits* are exiles wandering in the desert. Each of the heroes of Miller's early plays in some way suggested a criticism of an oppressive environment, but it is a criticism too limited and too confused to deal with the complexities of reality. And just as Miller's oversimplified view of society led him to the aridity of the Nevada desert, so his oversimplified view of character led him to the foolish sentimentality of Roslyn. Ultimately he comes to the desperation of Adam and Eve wandering in the archetypal desert of *The Creation of the World and Other Business,* separated from that realm of natural innocence, the reality of which Miller seems no longer fully to credit. Earlier, however, from *All My Sons* through *A View from the Bridge,* his allegiance to that realm had led him to grant his characters access to it too easily, to make them virtuous too cheaply, and finally to invent the semi-mystical Roslyn to account for such unmotivated regeneration. But *After the Fall* and the three plays that follow it show a genuine alteration of temper and attitude. Whether because of personal trauma or the natural development of mind and sensibility, Miller turned from the celebration of innocence to a search for the roots of guilt.

The basis of this shift in dramatic concerns will be clarified by an examination of the social and psychological difficulties of Miller's earlier plays. His problems in dealing with man in society appear most clearly in *Death of a Salesman,* still his richest play and yet the one in which his failure to develop an adequate view of the external, social world is especially apparent. The parallel dilemmas Miller encountered because of his view of the inner self are revealed in other plays from the same period as well as in his treatment of Willy Loman.

Although the difficulties of the aging salesman of Brooklyn seem remote from those of the mustang-hunting cowboys of Nevada, they are in fact intimately connected. Whereas the cowboys have rejected the wages of the commercial world and are struggling to find another way of life in which each can keep his dignity and his individual identity, Willy Loman has given himself entirely to shallow dreams of commercial success that distort the characters of himself and his sons and that finally destroy him. *The Misfits,* then, by far Miller's worst work, is one side of a coin and *Death of a Salesman,* still his best, the other. But whereas the central weakness of *The Misfits* lies in the vagueness and inadequacy of the solution to the cowboys' dilemma as embodied in Roslyn, the central weakness of *Death of a Salesman* lies in the difficulty of perceiving just what Willy's dilemma is. Why his actions have led him to his pathetic destiny and what attitude we should take not only toward him but toward his society remain elusive questions.

We commonly expect the conflicting forces that have set a play in motion to clash decisively in its climactic scene and there to reveal its central motive. In *Death of a Salesman,* however, this scene is strangely inconclusive. The nearest thing to it is that in which Biff's faith in his father and his father's ideals, and thus in himself, is shattered. The scene has been held back out of chronological sequence till just before the end of the play and is obviously meant to reveal the hollowness of Willy's philosophy as the source of Biff's degeneration. But it does nothing of the sort. When Biff finds Willy with a woman in his hotel room, he at once concludes that his father's total view of life is erroneous, that his character is worthless, and that he, Biff, is irretrievably lost. But why should he? In extenuation Willy says truthfully that he was lonely and that the woman meant nothing to him. Biff himself, we are told, has cut a considerable swath among the high school girls. Sons less devoted have forgiven their fathers more. At this point in the play, Miller clearly wishes to show through Biff the nature of Willy's error. Yet, strangely unable to do so, he is forced to invent irrelevant, psychologically untenable emotional entanglements that hardly conceal his failure.

If we set aside the play's structure and attempt to examine Willy's philosophy directly, similar problems arise. Willy is a man so foolish as to believe that success in the business world can be achieved not by work and ability but by being "well liked," by a kind of hearty popularity that will open all doors and provide favors and preferential treatment. So convinced is Willy of the rightness of his doctrine that he raises his sons by it and, without intending to, subtly undermines their moral character, turning one into a lecher and the other into a thief. If the death of Willy Loman is to be any more significant than the death of many another pathetic incompetent, and Miller clearly wishes it to be so, then Willy's doctrine, the ultimate cause of his downfall, must be both dangerous and widespread. When pushed to Willy's extreme, it is no doubt dangerous, but that it is widespread is doubtful. That many Americans are obsessed by the idea of commercial success is surely a truth, though hardly an original one; that large numbers of such persons intend to achieve their goals primarily by cultivating the art of camaraderie is most unlikely. We are, in other words, being elaborately warned against a danger that is not dangerous. Indeed, Willy's touching desire to be liked often strikes us as one of his most endearing characteristics. For all his bluster and his terrible incomprehension, we do like him. His death moves us, perhaps because he so obviously wanted us to be moved. The desire to be liked functions in the play emotionally, but intellectually it is meaningless. It is not at the root of the socioeconomic ills of modern American society, and a critique of that society based upon it would be entirely without validity. Yet a critique of some pretensions seems to be present in the play: if it is not based on Willy's doctrine, we may reasonably ask what it is based on.

Unfortunately, the question is more easily asked than answered, for the play, when closely examined, yields not one critique but at least three, each distinct and each negating the other. From one point of view, Miller's dissatisfaction with the society that Willy Loman exemplifies stems from an implicit comparison between it and a previous one that was stronger, simpler, and more noble. So considered, Willy's society is no more than the corruption of the pioneer vision of a pastoral edenic world peopled by a dignified race finding fulfillment in its labors. Willy, then, represents the degeneration of an older, stronger stock, described by his brother Ben:

Father was a very great and a very wild-hearted man. We would start in Boston, and he'd toss the whole family into the wagon, and then he'd drive the team right across the country; through Ohio, and Indiana, Michigan, Illinois, and all the Western states. And we'd stop in the towns and sell the flutes that he'd made on the way. Great inventor, Father. With one gadget he made more in a week than a man like you could make in a lifetime.

Willy's father, too, was a salesman, but he was also a pioneer and sold the artistic products of his own hands. The end of this speech is colored by Ben's character, but even that character is ambiguous, for Ben's business in Alaska and his offer to Willy suggest the pioneer developer as much as the capitalist exploiter. It is this character of the hardy, simple man, happy in a rural environment (as the cowboys of *The Misfits* might have been happy) that Willy's dreams seem to have corrupted. Biff says that he and his brother should work outdoors; Willy is never happier than when doing manual work about the house. But this life is not possible. Brooklyn is no longer a place where one can hunt rabbits (again, a hint of the lost Eden) but a place where the few anachronistic houses like Willy's are ringed by the characterless apartment buildings of an industrial-commercial civilization. Dave Singleman, the eighty-four-year-old salesman upon whom Willy had modeled himself, derived respect and friendship from his work, but Willy is alone in a world that ignores him.

If the central motive of this play is a critique of American society as the corrupted remnant of a great pioneer vision, then Willy has much to answer for. If the thousands of Willies whom Miller evidently finds in our society have through their stupidity and vulgarity destroyed the rustic happiness that Miller appears to see in the American past, then they are guilty of a great crime and deserve their fates. But Miller does not seem to condemn Willy, at least not very forcefully, for there is a strong suggestion that his fate has been thrust upon him by forces beyond his control or indeed his comprehension. The pathetic picture of the tired old salesman, helpless in an overwhelming environment, does not suggest the righteous destruction of the wicked. There are other men in the play far worse than Willy. The speech about Willy's pioneer-flutist father is delivered by Ben (no one else is available to give it), but he is a very different sort of person. Ben presents his philosophy when he says, "Why, boys, when I was seventeen I walked into the jungle, and when I was twenty-one I walked out . . . and by God I was rich." When sparring with Biff, Ben trips him, threatens him with the point of an umbrella, and then advises, "Never fight fair with a stranger, boy. You'll never get out of the jungle that way." The jungle is clearly the brutal, competitive modern world in which the strong and ruthless like Ben will triumph and the weak like Willy will go under.

Here, then, is no image of Willy as destroyer but rather of Willy as victim, coldly fired by the firm he has served for thirty-four years. "Business is business," says the young employer whom Willy has known as a child.[8] Willy agrees that business is business, but he does not really believe it. When he tries to explain why he chose to remain a salesman, he says, " 'Cause what could be more satisfying than to be able to go, at the age of eighty-four, into twenty or thirty different cities, and pick up a phone, and be remembered and loved and helped by so many different people?" Willy's error, as we see him here, is a failure to understand the harshness of the world he has attempted so ineptly to conquer. He has tried to find a world of private affections where there was only a jungle.

The critique suggested here is not so much of Willy as of Willy's world. Since it implies that Willy is essentially innocent and has been destroyed by the competitive system, we may call it the socialist critique (though the author's personal politics are not made explicit). Such an attitude would seem to underlie the requiem spoken by Willy's friend, Charley: "You don't understand: Willy was a salesman. . . . He's a man way out there in the blue, riding on a smile and a shoeshine. And when they start not smiling back— that's an earthquake. And then you get yourself a couple of spots on your hat, and you're finished. Nobody dast blame this man. A salesman is got to dream, boy. It comes with the territory." If this speech means anything very specific, it means that Willy was, in essence, not at fault. His foolish and dangerous dreams came with the territory; that is, they were the inevitable product of an evil system for which he was not responsible.

Yet there is still another critical point of view in the play, and Charley is its spokesman as well. In fact, he and his son, Bernard, offer a continuing contrast with Willy and his sons. Because Miller so clearly extends to Charley and Bernard a degree of approval which he withholds from the Lomans, he has, intentionally or not, made Willy's neighbors a symbolic commentary on Willy himself. They have self-understanding where Willy does not; they are at ease in a world where Willy is tormented. When, in desperation, Willy comes to his friend after he has been fired, Charley tries to show him his error: "The only thing you got in this world is what you can sell. And the funny thing is that you're a salesman and you don't know that." "I've always tried to think otherwise, I guess," Willy answers. "I always felt that if a man was impressive and well liked, that nothing—"; "Why must everybody like you?" Charley cries. "Who liked J. P. Morgan? Was he impressive? In a Turkish bath he'd look like a butcher. But with his pockets on he was very well liked." Charley does not say that the commercial world of salesmanship is inherently wrong but that Willy has confused it with something else. Because the world of J. P. Morgan is hard, one cannot get ahead in it by means of a false impressiveness but by work and ability. The exemplar of this doctrine is his son, Bernard. While Biff was playing football and being taught by his father that he could get what he wanted simply by being liked, Bernard was working at his studies. When we see them later, Bernard is a successful young lawyer on his way to argue a case before the Supreme Court, and Biff is a failure and a near kleptomaniac. Bernard and his father, then, represent reliance on the bourgeois virtues of honesty and hard work rather than a socialist rejection of competitive society.

That in some way Miller intends to criticize our society through Willy Loman is unquestionable; that he clearly understands the nature of his own criticism, however, is doubtful. After all, he has suggested, with a kind of naive romanticism, that the Loman ethic has corrupted a simple and noble pioneer dream; he has seemed to portray Willy as the pathetic victim of a ruthless competitive system; he has also managed to imply that Willy's error has been his attempt to substitute an empty creed for the solid qualities of honesty and work. That Miller has held these incompatible views and embodied them in his finest play suggests that he has written out of a deep dissatisfaction with the social world and an almost equally severe confusion about one's role in it.

Moreover, just as he has been unable to present a coherent attitude toward the external world, so Miller has offered a view of the self too simplified to convince us that his work is an adequate representation of reality. Miller's central characters, each the living emobodiment of his point of view, have been engaged in an action their creator clearly considers the most significant one a man can undertake, the personal search for dignity and identity in a hostile world. In this search Willy Loman resembles the cowboys of *The Misfits* as well as Miller's other significant characters, for each of them, though he lives most explicitly amid the problems of the modern social world (Miller's one historical play is a thinly disguised presentation of the McCarthy era, and his biblical fable derives from personal material), is on a private quest for a self in which above all he will find an ultimate core of virtue. When he has achieved this aim—and a Miller hero of the early plays almost inevitably does so—he has, in the mind of his author, reached the point of rest at the end of his journey. This faith in the efficacy of self-recognition as a mode of achieving virtue is far more central to his view of life than any of his ideas, however serious, concerning the immediate problems of society. But as with many a faith the difficulties of acquiring and retaining it are great.

These problems exist in *Death of a Salesman,* to which we will return later, but they are more readily visible in Miller's simpler works. The play most closely related to *Death of a Salesman, All My Sons,* reveals many similar events, including the same vague condemnation of competitive economics. During the war Joe Keller has shipped cracked engine heads out of his factory, causing the deaths of twenty-one pilots. When his son Chris accuses him, Keller defends himself by pointing to the pressures that were put upon him:

> You're a boy, what could I do! I'm in business, a man is in business; a hundred and twenty cracked, you're out of business . . . they close you up, they tear up your contracts, what the hell's it to them? You lay forty years into a business and they knock you out in five minutes, what could I do, let them take forty years, let them take my life away?

When Keller fears that Chris will send him to jail, he protests that others were as bad: "Did they ship a gun or a truck outa Detroit before they got their price? Is that clean? It's dollars and cents, nickels and dimes; war and peace, it's nickels and dimes, what's clean? Half the Goddam country is gotta go if I go!" Even the idealistic Chris finds these arguments convincing. Without ever refuting them, Miller convinces Keller of his guilt by producing, with an aplomb worthy of Sardou, a crucial letter from Keller's older son revealing that he had committed suicide because of his distress at his father's actions. (He seems to have heard his father's arguments, for he does not accuse Keller of murder, only of "doing business.") After reading the letter, Chris triumphantly challenges his father: "Now blame the world," he says. But Keller could quite reasonably answer that the world has forced him to kill his son and that he himself is not guilty. In fact, his defense is never answered. The result of letting it stand is not to exonerate Keller, who is patently guilty, but to condemn all other businessmen. For Keller has identified himself with them, and if the identification holds, they are as guilty as he. As it happens, the identification is false. Chris has said to his father, "I know you're no worse than most men," but Joe Keller is a great deal worse than most men and Chris does not really need a letter from the grave to prove it. Keller has not merely made profit from manufacturing war materials, which may or may not be reprehensible; he has knowingly sent out materials that killed the soldiers of his own country, which is certainly reprehensible and rather different from "doing business." As in *Death of a Salesman,* Miller seems to censure commercial society without adequately suggesting the basis for his condemnation.

But there is more here to trouble us than some dubious economics. When Keller reads his son's letter, something very curious happens. For no logical reason, he is instantaneously convinced not only of his own guilt but of the universal brotherhood of man as well. That is to say, he becomes both sensitive and virtuous. The psychological implications of what has occurred here are quite remarkable. In Joe Keller, Miller has postulated an ordinary man, well intentioned and devoted to his family. Such a man, he asks us to believe, could be responsible for the deaths of twenty-one men yet feel nothing but a natural apprehension at being caught.[9] When convinced of his guilt, however, Keller finds the burden intolerable, and, rushing into the house, he shoots himself. But surely a man coarse enough to carry that first guilt, or devious enough to rationalize it, could attend to the second one. The playwright, however, will not have it so. For him, virtue, or at least the striving after it, is automatically attendant upon knowledge of the self. It is for this reason that, in defiance of psychological probability, Keller suddenly realizes that all the dead flyers were his sons and that his crime must be expiated.

The pattern of moral regeneration through self-discovery, though apparent in *All My Sons,* is somewhat obscured by the suggestion that the central character is merely a victim of social forces and, therefore, not entirely responsible for his actions. In Miller's early novel, *Focus,* and in his play *The Crucible,* however, the pattern stands out sharply, though these works are even more clearly set in the social world than *All My Sons.* But the enemy that Miller chooses to fight in each of these two works is so clearly an evil, as it is not in *All My Sons* and *Death of a Salesman,* that when the hero finally summons up strength to combat it, his virtue need not be questioned. *Focus* tells the story of Lawrence Newman, a gentle man in his mid-forties who finds that he must wear glasses even though they so alter his appearance that he is regularly taken for a Jew. He suffers all the indignities of anti-Semitism and finally is forced to defend himself physically against a gang of toughs sent by a virulenty anti-Jewish group. Under these pressures Newman changes from a mild soul accepting and even helping to perpetuate the common bigotries of life into a determined fighter for human dignity. When a policeman to whom he has taken his story assumes that he is Jewish, Newman accepts the assumption and the new identity it gives him. At the moment he comes to know himself as a Jew, Newman achieves courage and moral vision.

In *The Crucible* almost exactly the same pattern of the regenerative force of self-discovery is found in the upstanding farmer John Proctor. Though much given to self-reproach for having betrayed his wife in a moment of passion, he has no self-doubt about publicly opposing the Salem witch hunts. After he himself has been seized and finds that he can preserve his own life only by confessing to witchcraft, he signs his name to the confession but will not let the document out of his possession. When the Deputy Governor asks him why, he cries, "Because it is my name! Because I cannot have another in my life! . . . How may I live without my name? I have given you my soul; leave me my name!" When the Deputy Governor continues to demand the document, Proctor tears it in half and accepts his fate. "You have made your magic now," he says, "for now I do think I see some shred of goodness in John Proctor." In fighting to maintain his self, Proctor finds that, despite his personal transgressions, that self is essentially innocent and that he is capable of battling the social enemy. Exactly who that enemy is Miller has not made clear, for despite his later protestations that the Salem judges are consciously evil, the text does not tell us whether they are sincere but narrow believers in the supernatural, authoritarians who find witchcraft a convenient instrument for oppression, or merely sadists. But however ambiguous Miller may once again be in discriminating the evils of the social world, he is precise in showing the roots of virtue, which for him always lie in the inner world of the self.

In the simple realms of *Focus* and *The Crucible,* where the good are very good and the bad are monsters, the link between public virtue and inner strength seems clear. But in what purports to be the heroic domain of classical tragedy, virtue does not attend so immediately on self-knowledge. That Miller should choose to enter here after dealing directly or symbolically with social themes in all his previous plays is significant, for it suggests the beginnings of a discontent with these themes or with his ability to handle them.

Miller wants his audience to recognize the effects he is aiming for; at the beginning of *A View from the Bridge* he has his chorus, a lawyer named Alfieri, tell us that the story of Sicilian dock workers about to be unfolded has parallels in antiquity: ". . . every few years there is still a case . . . and the thought comes that in some Caesar's year, in Calabria perhaps or on the cliffs at Syracuse, another lawyer, quite differently dressed, heard the same complaint and sat there as powerless as I, and watched it run its bloody course." In the story itself the simple longshoreman Eddie Carbone is unknowingly consumed with sexual passion for his wife Beatrice's orphaned niece whom he has raised as a daughter. When she falls in love with the younger of two illegal immigrants, cousins of his wife whom the family has been sheltering, Eddie in a helpless, jealous rage betrays them to the immigration authorities. Marco, the elder of the two, publicly accuses Eddie of the betrayal, an unforgivable sin in this society, and later kills him in a fight. Throughout the play, Alfieri comments on the action, even explaining that he has consulted an oracle, a wise woman of the neighborhood, who is as helpless as he. The sense of inevitability, which Miller here creates, is less impressive than it might be, however, for it lies not in the circumstances or even in the genuine strength of Eddie's passion but in his lack of sophistication about sexuality. Alfieri and even Eddie's wife know perfectly the nature of his feelings but cannot bring him to understand them. Miller has not tried to make Eddie admirable by giving him heroic virtues but rather by having him, especially in the revised published version of the play, insist on a kind of stubborn self-affirmation. In defiance of circumstances, Eddie maintains that he has the right to an honorable name (he has, in fact, betrayed his guests) with all the sincerity of John Proctor defying the Salem court. "Because it is my name," Proctor had said in refusing to give up his confession. "I want my name!" Eddie cries. ". . . Marco's got my name!" Fortunately, Eddie's—and Miller's—faith in his character turns out to be justified. As he lies dying (having provoked his own death), his passion for his niece suddenly evaporates, and his love for his wife returns. "My B!" he gasps as he dies in her arms. It is Alfieri who suggests that Eddie is not merely an unfortunate victim of his desires but somehow innately noble. "I confess," he says in a brief requiem, "that something perversely pure calls to me from his memory—not purely good, but himself purely, for he allowed himself to be wholly known and for that I think I will love him more than all my sensible clients." In other words, for Eddie to have been wholly himself, whatever that may have been, was to have been enough. To exist, maintaining one's own identity, then, is sufficient to be virtuous, to be innocent, and to be enshrined in a tragedy.[10]

But it is not enough. To reveal one's self is not necessarily to reveal anything admirable. Yet Miller, profoundly committed in these early plays to the Rousseauistic assumption that an essential virtue lies within any man not hopelessly corrupted by society, seems to believe that it is. In *Focus* and *The Crucible,* comparatively simple, polemical works, the heroes are so obviously superior to the monsters about them that we may accept Miller's faith in their virtue with little difficulty, but these works are limited by their very simplicity. In those plays that more nearly approach the complexity of life, we can less readily grant the writer's presuppositions. We need not believe that Joe Keller will shoot himself or that Eddie Carbone will die with his wife's name on his lips as soon as they understand what they have done.

Even *Death of a Salesman,* Miller's richest, most complex work, is limited by his special view of man. Miller has always needed a character—Joe Keller, John Proctor, Eddie Carbone—who would discover within himself that ultimate virtue his creator so admires and so strongly wishes him to find there. But because that discovery often stems less from the character's nature than from the author's conviction, what should be the emotional culmination of a work at times seems unreal or arbitrary, and much good playwriting goes for nothing or at least for less than it should. One of the virtues of *Death of a Salesman,* however, is that Willy Loman is not subjected to this arbitrary regeneration. The easy strength that supposedly attends on a recognition of the self is foreshadowed in a moment of crisis by his son Biff. "What am I doing in an office," Biff asks, "making a contemptuous *(sic)* begging fool of myself, when all I want is out there, waiting for me the minute I say I know who I am!" In the short requiem at the end of the play, Biff says of his father, "He had the wrong dreams. All, all wrong. . . . He never knew who he was." The assumption here is that if Willy had known who he was, had realized the limitations of his nature, he would automatically have had the right dreams. Biff may believe so because the dreams he finally comes to are very limited: work, food, and time to sit and smoke. But need we share the belief that had Willy recognized his own incompetence he would have ceased to long for success? Happily we are not asked to do so. Because Miller was able to present in Biff the ennobling self-knowledge that he so wished to see, he was not forced to distort the character of Willy Loman who, still uncomprehending and lost in his empty dreams, stumbles on to his death with a terrible directness and with a credibility no other creation of Miller's possesses. Had Biff not been conveniently present to carry, fortunately not conspicuously, the burden of Miller's beliefs, we might have been faced with the spectacle of a regenerate Willy. It is the salvation of *Death of a Salesman* as a work of art that Willy never achieves either easy self-knowledge or the automatic innocence that Miller associated with it.

Miller's return to the theater after his eight-year period of silence emphasized his abiding concern with the necessity for self-knowledge. But, significantly, he was no longer so profoundly committed to the notion that an essential innocence could be discovered by plumbing the depths of the self. Although the generalized tone of moral earnestness remains, the shift away from public concerns, already visible in *A View from the Bridge* (which despite its classical trappings is set in Miller's private family world), continues in these later plays even though some of them seem, at first glance, directly involved with politics. *Incident at Vichy,* after all, deals with Nazi anti-Semitism in occupied France; *After the Fall* returns at least in part to the material of the McCarthy era previously dealt with by implication in *The Crucible.*

Whatever attractions it may or may not possess as personal revelation, *After the Fall* has as a play, despite its rambling structure, sections of considerable intensity and power. Moreover, it not only marks beginning of the second phase of Miller's career, but it is the seminal work from which all of the plays he has written since have in one way or another derived. Whatever its ultimate merits, it is worth considering in some detail, for its sprawling assemblage of plots and characters reveals not only the themes and materials that have occupied Miller in his recent plays but their relations to his past work as well.

When Miller treats once again the inquisitions of the McCarthy period, he is still concerned, as he had been in *The Crucible,* with the question of self-identity. But in his first handling of this material, he had created a moral melodrama in which entire goodness and entire evil were opposed. The self-doubts of the hero were unconvincing and, in any case, irrelevant to the central issues of the play. Now, however, things are less simple. In *After the Fall* a crisis of conscience comes to the central figure, the attorney Quentin, through two of his friends, Lou, a law professor, and Mickey, a colleague, both of whom have been called before a congressional committee and questioned about communist affiliations in their past. Although Lou is essentially a sympathetic victim, he has lied by writing a book falsely defending Soviet law. Mickey, in spite of being Lou's betrayer, is also presented sympathetically and even humorously.

Moreover, Mickey, who is about to be called back before a congressional committee, cogently defends his plan to give names, insisting that his honesty and his identity are at stake. Speaking of his first hearing, at which he had not revealed anything, Mickey says, "Lou, when I left the hearing room, I didn't feel I had spoken. Something else had spoken, something automatic and inhuman. . . . I ought to be true to myself now." In his own fear and distress at being betrayed, Lou forgets that he had used Mickey's very words a few moments earlier. Speaking to Quentin of his desire to redeem his false book by publishing an honest one, he had said, "And that's why, now . . . with this book of mine, I want to be true to myself." The unresolved opposition here reveals how Miller, though he has freed himself from the hero-villain pattern of *The Crucible,* remains, however doubtfully, committed to the romantic postulate that in knowledge of and truth to the self lie virtue. Although after Lou's suicide Quentin reflects, "Maybe it's not enough—to know yourself," throughout the play he is on just that quest for self-knowledge the validity of which he has come to doubt. Even if he can no longer find the comforting assurance of his own virtue, he now seems to hope that the very knowledge of his guilt will somehow release him from its burden.

For through his relations with Mickey and Lou, Quentin has come to see not only their guilt but his own. Although he has undertaken Lou's legal defense, Quentin feels himself secretly relieved and even pleased when Lou's suicide frees him from a crisis that threatens his career. But despite his own sense of guilt and all the aggressions he has seen released, Quentin still finds himself maintaining that "underneath we're all profoundly friends." At this point, his instinctive confidence in man's innate goodness has only been shaken, not destroyed. But as he reviews other aspects of his life, his convictions are subjected to even greater stress.

In no part of the play are Quentin's discoveries about himself and others more harshly opposed to these convictions than in those showing his relations with his family, and especially with his mother. Once again the central theme of this material is betrayal, but in even more intimate circumstances. Quentin's mother had put aside a romance with a penniless medical student ("Who knew he'd end up so big in gallstones?" Miller makes her ask, with the sense for Jewish humor that he has shown of late) and agreed to marry a prosperous businessman, only to make the traumatic discovery soon after the wedding that her husband could not even read. Frustrated in her visions of wider horizons, she begins undermining Quentin's faith in his father by pointing out her husband's crudities and shortcomings. When the family business collapses during the depression, all her aggressions break through, and, totally estranged from her husband, she screams at him, "You're an idiot!"

To Quentin, the observing adult, this estrangement parallels the total alienation of the Nazi executioner from his victim. Moreover, it anticipates the rage of Elsie, Lou's wife, at her husband's weakness and of Louise, Quentin's first wife, who in the course of one of their quarrels repeats the mother's abuse in almost precisely the same words. Through his family and friends Quentin comes to know how even those who should be intimates can learn to betray and become strangers. Nor is he himself guiltless; as a child he had felt so wounded at being left with a maid while the family slipped away on vacation that upon their return he had attempted suicide, knowing instinctively that he could thus destroy the mother at once so hated and beloved. His angers reappear toward the end of the play when, trying, in a momentary rage to strangle his wife Maggie, he finds himself choking his mother as well. Miller is here suggesting that Quentin's attempted suicide, dramatically insignificant compared with Maggie's, is as much an act of hostility, indeed an attempt at murder, as hers.

It is through Quentin's relationship with Maggie, in fact, that the questions of guilt and innocence are most significantly developed. Whatever the interest of the relationship of Quentin and Maggie as a glimpse into the private life of Miller and Marilyn Monroe, it has the greatest psychological subtlety and dramatic force of any in the play. As Quentin relives in memory his marriage to Maggie, he becomes aware that there had been from the first an element of hypocrisy in his feeling for her. He, too, had laughed at her and had refrained from a quick conquest out of fear rather than respect. Yet he lets her believe otherwise and accepts her adoration. "Why did I lie to her, play this cheap benefactor?" he asks. But Quentin has in fact been haunted by the answer to this question from the start. On the wall of his room are two light fixtures a certain distance apart. As he remembers Maggie's offering herself, he recalls his temptation to stand between them, extend his arms, and assume the attitude of the crucifixion. Maggie, too, has grasped Quentin's longing for absolute innocence inherent in his desire to play the role of a Christlike savior and rebukes him for failing in it. In the depths of their final confrontation, Maggie abruptly asks Quentin, "What's Lazarus?" He replies, "Jesus raised him from the dead. In the Bible." A few moments later as Quentin admits that he has lied and that his patience has been exhausted, she suddenly exclaims, "But Jesus must have loved her. Right?" When Quentin asks "Who?" she replies, "Lazarus?"

If Quentin has sinned by pretending to a limitless, Christlike love that could raise this Magdalen from the state of psychic death into which she had fallen, he was not alone in sin, for Maggie too has pretended to a more-than-human love. When she first offered herself to him, Quentin, astonished at the ease and charm with which she did so, had exclaimed, "You're all love, aren't you?" "That's all I am," she had replied. Her promiscuity, she says, had been a kind of charity. "Like I give to those in need?" (Maggie's equation of sexuality and virtue here is strikingly reminiscent of Williams.) Throughout, even in her final drug-induced stupor, Maggie's words recur till the phrase "that's all I am" becomes the symbol for Maggie's illusion that she is "the sweet lover of all life" whose perfect innocence has been betrayed by the world's cruelty. Despite her impulsiveness and generosity, Maggie has, in actuality, been cruel and vengeful just as Quentin has been vain and hypocritical. They are, as Quentin comes to see, alike in their guilt, each having used the other to foster a deceptive illusion of the innocence and virtue of their own selves.

But beyond the personal guilt that Quentin finds in his life and in the lives of those about him, there exists, Miller wishes us to understand, a larger universal guilt of which these are only examples. Throughout the action the symbol of that guilt looms over the stage in the form of the shattered watchtower of a Nazi concentration camp. When at the end of the play Quentin attempts to sum up the meaning of his relations with Maggie, the tower lights up, as it has previously, to signify a crisis of guilt. At this point, however, as Miller tries to establish an equivalence between Quentin's guilt and that of the mass murderers of Nazi Germany, his argument becomes unconvincing, his meaning uncertain. Quentin recalls that at the beginning of his last meeting with Maggie he had noticed the first signs of barbiturate poisoning but had stayed to argue, rather than call medical help, in an attempt to regain his innocence. "To get that back," he explains, "you kill most easily." Miller hardly means to imply that the exterminators of Dachau were endeavoring to reacquire their lost innocence, but his phraseology almost suggests as much. A few moments later Quentin asks, again with reference to the concentration camp, if it is possible that he is not alone in his feelings and that "no man lives who would not rather be the sole survivor of this place than all its finest victims." To which one can only reply that it is more than possible and that the sense of guilt at surviving a painful and destructive marriage is not justly analogous to the survival guilt of those who endured the Holocaust.

In fact, neither Quentin's search for innocence nor his pangs of survival have any convincing relationship with either the murderers or the survivors of the concentration camps. That connection lies entirely in Quentin's discovery that, his own survival threatened, he too has felt "the wish to kill." Miller here postulates in Quentin, and in all of us, depths of aggression in some degree analogous to those that led to the horrors of Nazism. That such depths exist is surely a tenable contention; that Miller has demonstrated them in Quentin is doubtful. Neither Quentin's impatience with his first wife, nor his understandable sense of relief at Lou's death, nor the childish tantrum in which—he contends—he tried to destroy his mother through his own attempted suicide reveals anything profoundly sinful in his nature. Of all Quentin's guilts only those that stem from his relationship with Maggie are dramatically credible. Through his blindness and vanity Quentin has done her genuine injury, but even here the effects of his actions are mitigated by the portrayal of Maggie. Not only does Miller show that the roots of her psychoses extend far deeper than her marriage, but he so powerfully portrays the strength of her self-destructive alienation that the tendency is finally to exonerate Quentin. He is, after all, helpless in the face of Maggie's suicidal impulses. Paradoxically, then, although Miller has chosen the most profound symbol of human guilt offered by our times, the mass murders of Nazism, he has presented us with a hero who is ultimately innocent, or at any rate with one whose guilts are inadequate as that symbol's correlative.

The simplest and most obvious explanation for Miller's exculpation of Quention is that, since *After the Fall* is at least partially autobiographical, Miller has yielded to the temptations to absolve himself. However, Miller's immediate return to the subject of the Nazi mass murders of Jews in *Incident at Vichy* suggests not only the significance it has for him but a possible dissatisfaction with his first treatment of it. Intriguingly, when he returns to this material, the result is again an equivocal affirmation of innocence in a world of guilt. Although the play touches on the motivations for the sadism of the Nazis as well as the acquiescence of the Jews, it centers on what was also a major concern of *After the Fall,* the limits of human responsibility. When Leduc, a Jewish psychiatrist who, along with various other people, has been rounded up for deportation to the death camps, asks a sympathetic German major to risk his own life and help him escape, the major refuses, pointing out that Leduc, by his own admission, would not sacrifice himself for the others. Ultimately, however, the sacrificial act is performed. Although Leduc insists to Von Berg, an Austrian nobleman who has been rounded up by mistake, that men are "full of murder," that he has "never analyzed a gentile who did not have, somewhere hidden in his mind, a dislike if not a hatred for the Jews," the prince denies it and denies Leduc's further insistence that men are alienated from each other, that "each man has his Jew; it is the other. And the Jews have their Jews." Finally Von Berg vindicates his denial when he chooses to "make a gift" of himself in giving his exit pass to Leduc and, like Newman in *Focus,* realizes himself in accepting another identity. Although Miller has come very far from the easy confidence in instinctive virtue that marked his early plays, he has made *Incident at Vichy* a morality play both in the rather doctrinaire arrangement of its characters (the artist is called Lebeau, the businessman Marchand, the most morally elevated person Von Berg, etc.) and in its ultimate demonstration of an abiding moral consciousness.

But the extremity of the circumstances in *Incident at Vichy* and the absoluteness of Von Berg's sacrifice produce a sort of *exemplum,* removing this troubled affirmation of an ultimate virtue in the self from the ambiguities and complexities of life. Turning in his next play to precisely the same subject, the gift of a life, but shaping the action more flexibly and drawing the characters more richly and humanly, Miller produced in *The Price* the best play thus far of his second period. For his basic material he went back again to the seminal play, *After the Fall,* where, almost lost in the movement of other events, the family world of *The Price* had first appeared. For a brief moment at the beginning of the second act we saw the father ruined by the depression, the rejecting mother, the son who sacrifices himself by staying to help the father, and the brother who leaves to develop his own life.

In *After the Fall* Miller focuses on this brother, but having left his family is only one of Quentin's guilts, indeed the least of them; in *The Price,* however, Miller is primarily interested in Victor, the brother who remains at home, sacrificing his promising career in medicine to support his father. As the two brothers reveal the roots of their quarrel, each rebukes the other. Victor implies that his brother had allowed the sacrifice and refused to help him out of envy; Walter, the brother who had left and become a successful physician, maintains that Victor "with this saintly self-sacrifice" had set out to prove his brother treacherous. Although Miller balances out the claims of the brother committed to self-sacrifice and the brother who has reached for self-fulfillment, letting each argue his case fully and even allowing Walter the last word, he has given Victor (a suggestive name once again) the final action, which vindicates his life. For Victor, in disposing of the family furnishings, refuses the financially advantageous arrangement suggested by his brother, and instead sells them to Gregory Solomon, the ninety-year-old furniture dealer, who had retired to his shop to wait for death and for whom the new project is a return to life. In reenacting with this surrogate father his original sacrifice, he affirms his commitment to it, and the theatrical strength of the characterization of Solomon affirms its value. For Gregory Solomon is so charming a dramatic creation, so wise and sympathetic in his utterances (though his wisdom is as much Sophoclean as biblical—witness his final words: "Good luck, you can never know till the last minute, my boy") that we give our approval to Victor for preserving him.[11]

Nevertheless, both brothers have been involved in a complex relationship in which neither is entirely free of guilt. (Nor, indeed, is the father, who—though he had some resources—knowingly accepted Victor's sacrifice; drawn back to the psychic essence of his material, Miller touches briefly on something like the crimes of Willy Loman and Joe Keller, who had also blighted the lives of their sons.) Although Von Berg's act attests to the existence of a radical innocence in the self, it is performed in a world of disturbing evil. If *After the Fall* is, in its simplest terms, a play about a man who fails to sacrifice himself for another person and *Incident at Vichy* and *The Price* are plays about men who do, all three works evoke an ambiguity of feeling far different from the apparent certainties of the earlier plays. Nor are any certainties achieved in Miller's latest play, *The Creation of the World and Other Business*. A more attractive work than its brief run and unfortunate notices would suggest, it shows Miller turning to the materials that, in our culture, embody most strikingly the themes now dominating his work, the loss of innocence and the responsibility for, in the ultimate sense, one's brother. The expulsion from Eden, latent in the title and theme of *After the Fall,* now appears on stage literally, but even this loss of the archetypal realm of innocence is mitigated by being presented in terms of amiable Jewish humor: after God has rebuked Eve for her part in the Fall, he turns in exasperation to Adam: "As for you, schmuck. . . ." Moreover, God's refusal near the end of the first act to grant Lucifer equal status with himself testifies to Miller's refusal to relinquish some degree of faith in an independent and uncorrupted goodness. Even in his treatment of Cain a similar mixed feeling survives. It was probably inevitable that the rival brothers who have appeared in so many of Miller's plays should eventually reveal themselves as Cain and Abel, destroyer and victim. Yet, though the Abel who appears here is the conventional "good" victim, Cain is not a monster of evil but a young man victimized at birth, aspiring to devoutness, anxious for praise, tormented by jealousy. If in Miller's treatment Cain is not the solution to the riddle of evil, he is a viable embodiment of impulses as destructive to the self as to the other.

In *The Creation of the World* Miller attempted to summarize the concerns of his more recent work. If he has not made a fully successful play, it is at least in part because in the whimsical treatment of mythic materials (a mode more congenial to French writers—and audiences—than American), his efforts at playfulness mingle uneasily with a sometimes ponderous moral earnestness. Nevertheless, the play, which has moments both of charm and dramatic force, is significant for its confirmation of the steady development of Miller's work. Although the theme of moral responsibility for the life of another appears as early as Joe Keller's recognition that all the pilots for whose deaths he was responsible were his "sons" (the pervasiveness of the family world in the work of this "social" writer is suggested by the latest form this theme has taken, the murder of a brother), it becomes crucial in Miller's plays with *After the Fall* when Quentin attempted, so unsatisfactorily, to equate the failure of his responsibility to Maggie with the crimes of the Holocaust. But in Prince Von Berg and the tormented Victor, Miller reasserted, through those who give their lives as the ultimate token of responsibility, his faith in an abiding core of innocence in man.

It was this essential innocence that Miller, like his improbable companion playwright Tennessee Williams, had from the first wished to confirm. Although sexuality is hardly the obsessive concern in his plays that it is in Williams's, Miller, too, wishes above all to see his characters safe in a world where they may know their selves as innocent. To achieve that aim, whether his characters were in the public world of politics and economics or the private one of family conflicts, Miller offered them the gift of self-knowledge, for in Miller's eyes to know the self was to know its virtue and to discover its strength. Thus, John Proctor could find the courage to defy the Salem court, Biff could have the right dreams, Joe Keller could acquire honesty and dignity, Eddie Carbone could demand his name. Only Willy Loman remains unregenerate and—in defying his creator's convictions—most richly human. If Miller's faith in the ultimate innocence of the self is severely tested in the crucible of his later work, his continuing, though troubled commitment to it attests to the steadiness, if not the fullness of his vision. To find that fullness of vision in which the self and the world that it longs for are seen in all their complexity, we must turn to the playwright justly recognized as Miller's dramatic master, Henrik Ibsen.

4.

Ibsen, Pirandello, Pinter

Henrik Ibsen: Impulse and Ideal

The quest for innocence in the work of Williams and Miller shares some intriguing elements with the quest for art in Wilde and Synge. Both Wilde and Williams were seeking a way to avoid certain moral strictures; both Synge and Miller were attempting a mode of political involvement: affirming "Irish" values, questioning American ones. And just as the world of art functions for Wilde and Synge as a refuge from and an evasion of threatening experience (Shaw, Chekhov, and Giraudoux—more powerful writers—do not distort reality, their visionary worlds always lying beyond it), so the commitment to ultimate innocence, difficult and even tormented as it is, allows Williams and Miller to evade a full confrontation with the complexities of the self. Nevertheless, examining their concern, however limited, with the inner direction of the self is an appropriate prelude to the central considerations of this chapter. Whereas the playwrights dealt with in the first part of this book have always looked outward and upward to visionary realms for self-fulfillment, those in the second part of this study have turned or retreated to darker realms within. The visionary surge persists in Ibsen, but in Pirandello and Pinter the world constricts to the boundaries of the self—self and world, in effect, coalesce—and the dream of fulfillment becomes an effort to maintain and control that self against assaults both from external reality and from the depths within.

Although Ibsen explores these darker areas of the self as profoundly as any playwright of modern times, his work still embodies the full force of romantic transcendence. Indeed, this impulse is visible in Ibsen himself from the first. On one of the brief visits the young Ibsen made to his family after moving to a nearby town to become an apothecary's apprentice, the usually reserved and even secretive boy spoke openly to his sister of his aim to attain "the utmost perfection of greatness and clarity." "And when you have reached that," she asked, "what do you want?" "Then," he replied, "I want to die." [1] Whatever their element of adolescent bravado, these words were prophetic, if not of Ibsen himself, at least of his creations, for many of his plays from *Brand* through *When We Dead Awaken* concern heroes who die on the heights having achieved, or striven for, whatever "greatness and clarity" they could apprehend. The typical Ibsen hero is obsessed with some exalted ideal of the self and some vision of a transcendent realm in which by force of will that self can achieve realization. Yet for all the fierceness of their striving, their highest achievement often coincides with destruction for these melancholy figures. This pattern is more than the projection of a boyish fantasy. Not only do the limits of the commonplace world make ordinary existence intolerable to the romantic idealist, but the very nature of his aspiration, intense and elusive, prevents its steady continuance. Thus, Rosmer and Rebecca, confronting the reality of their desires and rejecting their environment of politics and middle-class living rooms, seek their end in a *Liebestod* not unlike that of Tristan and Isolde.

Moreover, a further element often impels the Ibsen idealist toward a disastrous consummation. His aspirations to self-transcendence conflict with an impulse to fulfillment through self-gratification, sometimes embodied in another character, sometimes found within himself. Just as that soaring idealism may ambiguously induce both nobility and repressive inhumanity, so its alternative impulse may bring about both a vital joy and a weak self-indulgence. The special quality of Ibsen's work develops not so much from his observation of provincial Norway as from his apprehension of the interplay between these complex and dubious forces. In the plays they often take the form of symbolic environments, "worlds" as we have been calling them, whose differing characteristics suggest the opposing elements they represent; the glittering icepeaks and the corrupted house of *Ghosts,* for example, or the true and false forests of *The Wild Duck.*

The thematic richness and psychological complexity of Ibsen's later plays have sometimes concealed not only their mutual relationships but their line of development from the earlier writings. Ibsen did not, as has sometimes been claimed, put aside in mid-career an early poetic manner and begin a rigorous investigation into the ills of contemporary society only to end with a series of symbolical-autobiographical plays expressing the ills of his own psyche. On the contrary, moving from play to play, he considers from different points of view and under different guises the central themes that obsessed him throughout his life.

To understand Ibsen fully, then, we must do as he himself suggested, follow him from the beginnings, in this case a heroic verse tragedy called *Catiline,* composed shortly after the revolutionary stirrings of 1848. Ibsen began his career as a playwright in the grand romantic manner with a nocturnal meditation:

> CATILINE [after a pause]. I must! I must! Deep
> down within my soul
> a voice commands, and I will do its bidding; . . .
> I feel I have the courage and the strength
> to lead a better, nobler life than this. . . .[2]

Though few would recognize the author of *The Wild Duck* and *The Master Builder* in this piece of adolescent rhetoric, he is there, for Ibsen's heroes remain to the end of his career on a quest for "a better, nobler life than this." And like John Gabriel Borkman destroyed by the exposure of his financial maneuverings, so Catiline—trapped in his vulgar conspiracy—remains an exile from the fulfillment he longs for. Moreover, Catiline is destroyed less by the pitfalls of Roman politics than by an almost forgotten crime emerging from his past. The result of his own passionate impulses now rises to confute his idealism as similar crimes confront Ibsen characters from Rebecca West to Arnold Rubek. Although in the later plays the past is made to impinge on the present with skill and subtlety, it here bursts in with gaudy theatricality in the person of a Vestal Virgin named, with suitable latinity, Furia. Learning that Catiline had seduced her sister and caused her suicide, she pursues him vengefully and, despite their attraction to each other, is instrumental in his downfall. The vehemence with which the young playwright presents this character verges on the comic, but Furia is an intriguing element, the first of Ibsen's fatal women—fierce, destructive natures who eventuate into such richer figures as Hedda Gabler and Hilde Wangel. Ibsen's concern with the contrasting figure of the gentle, devoted woman who comforts the hero in his distress and attempts to save him, begins here as well. Although tempted to accompany the implacable Furia to some nameless perdition, Catiline is preserved by the love of his gentle wife Aurelia, which triumphs over "all the powers of darkness." Ibsen's handling of the eternal feminine, like his treatment of the fatal woman, grows vastly in sophistication; but the sympathetic, faithful woman, sometimes victim, sometimes savior (Solveig, Ella Rentheim et al.). is a romantic archetype that reappears in his plays to the last.

If Catiline tells us little about the psychologist, realist, and craftsman that Ibsen was to become, it suggests in the opposition of desires—toward transcendence and passionate self-gratification—how profoundly Ibsen's mind and temperament were, from the first, shaped by the romantic ethos. Indeed, the whole group of plays produced before he found himself as a writer in *Brand* reveals in differing ways the same conflict between these extremes of the romantic temper. In several of them, for example, *The Warrior's Barrow,* the one-act play that followed *Catiline,* that conflict takes the form of an opposition between Christian spirituality and pagan vigor, but in *Lady Inger* [*of Ostraat*], it is embodied in Lady Inger's hesitation between the impersonal ideal of freedom for Norway and the intimate claims of the self, her secret love for her son.

None of these earliest works, however, has the inherent dramatic interest of the three plays that immediately preceded *Brand.* The first of these, *The Vikings at Helgeland,* offers, instead of the unlikely intrigue of Ibsen's earlier and somewhat similar *The Feast at Solhoug,* a grimly fatal clash of character and attitude as well as the remarkable portrait of Hjordis, who anticipates something of the frustration and neurotic aggressiveness of Hedda Gabler, the fierce aspiration of Rebecca West, and the icy will of Gunhild Borkman. Moreover, Sigurd's failure to take the woman he loves looks forward to similar failures by Karsten Bernik and John Gabriel Borkman himself. But most significantly, in the destruction of Hjordis's pagan love for Sigurd on the rock of his Christianity we see that conflict between the impulse to self-gratification and the striving toward the ideal that reappears in remarkably similar dramatic terms in *Rosmersholm*. If the love of the poet Falk and his beloved Swanhild in Ibsen's satiric verse play *Love's Comedy* results only in separation rather than in the death, chosen by Rosmer and Rebecca, the frustration of that love derives from a similar recognition that the ideal cannot be realized in the world of common life. And in *The Pretenders*, Ibsen's powerful drama of rivalry among the kings of medieval Norway, Duke Skule can achieve fulfillment neither by exalting the self nor by gratifying its impulses. Trapped between the blind desire for self-aggrandizement suggested by the conscious Machiavellianism of Bishop Nicholas and the unattainable ideal of true kingship represented by Haakon, Skule, like Solness, finds no solution except death. But just as Skule's destruction is qualified by Haakon's benediction, "Skule Baardsson was God's stepchild on earth," so the deaths of Brand, Peer, and the Emperor Julian, the heroes of Ibsen's next three major plays, are presented with similar ambiguity of tone. Because the characters represent aspects of the same unsolved problem that occupied Ibsen in *The Pretenders*, they die like Skule, half condemned and half condoned. Moreover, the plays that focus on them form an extraordinary triptych, Ibsen's last efforts in the heroic mode.[3] Brand and Peer, as students of Ibsen have recognized, are opposites, each possessing something of what the other lacks, each developing one aspect of Ibsen's persistent antithesis. It was these opposites that in the third play, *Emperor and Galilean*, Ibsen, with such vast labor and such little success, would attempt to reconcile.

As always in Ibsen, however, the conflict is far more interesting than the reconciliation (witness the weak endings of *The Lady from the Sea* and *Little Eyolf*). Seemingly the more powerful of these opposites is Brand, the steel-willed preacher whose demand of all or nothing leads him to sacrifice mother, child, wife, and ultimately himself. The source of Brand's unyielding aspiration (it lies deeper than Ibsen's anger with the Norwegian people for failing to come to the aid of Denmark in the war over Schleswig) appears early in the play as the solitary Brand meditates in the romantic mountain landscape. A discontent with the imperfections of the human condition is the essential force behind the ruthless will that drives him toward the ideal:

> When I was a boy, there were two secret thoughts
> That made me shake with inward laughter;
> They got me many a hiding
> When the old schoolmarm was feeling nasty:
> I tried to imagine an owl afraid
> Of the dark, and a fish afraid of water.
> They used to make me laugh out loud.
> I tried to put them from my mind, but still
> They stuck there, like burs. . . . What gave me
> Those sudden fits of laughter? Well, I suppose
> It was the dimly-apprehended gulf
> Between what is, and what ought to be . . .
> Between having to bear the burden, and
> Finding the burden too heavy to bear. . . .
> Nearly every man in this land, whether sick or well,
> Is just such an owl, just such a fish.
> He was created to toil in the deep,
> And meant to have his being in the dark.
> Yet those are the things that make him tremble.
> He flounders in fear towards the shore;
> He dreads his own star-bright chamber,
> And from him the cry goes up
> "O, for air! O, for the fires of noon!"

Yet the very metaphors that Brand chooses suggest the sense of tragic futility that haunts him from the first in finding no realm propitious for existence. Although the owl should be best adapted to the world of night, the fish to that of water, they are alienated from their own elements by fear and desire. It may be admirable to flee from darkness and the depths in order to struggle for light and the heights, but it is also a futile, perhaps merely obdurate undertaking. Knowing that he is born one of those "meant to have his being in the dark," Brand himself aspires toward the world of the sun and endures the frightening guilt that aspiration entails.

How far Brand is condemned or exculpated, however, remains doubtful, possibly as much to Ibsen as to the reader. The symbols that suddenly accumulate around the end of the play are merely suggestive. When Brand drives away the Phantom Agnes, which he calls the spirit of compromise, and it metamorphoses into a screaming hawk, this act appears to be a victory over a base temptation.[4] On the other hand, it is only when he rejects the exaltation to Christ-like status offered by Gerd, his *alter ego,* (symbolically, also the child of his mother) that he can weep and Gerd can shoot the hawk. Even the structure of the play helps to balance our sympathies. The satire on the vulgarity and small-mindedness of the townspeople that occupies the first part of Act IV is placed after the scenes in which Brand's demands of All or Nothing destroy his family so that Brand's will, whatever its consequences, contrasts with the ignobleness of the Mayor, the Schoolmaster, and the Dean. Because Brand's strivings stem from an attempt to escape and surpass an immutable condition, they are at once noble and perverse. The meaning of the voice that calls through the avalanche "God is Love" must remain ambiguous because, for Ibsen at least, Brand's problem ultimately had to remain unsolved.

If *Brand* is unclear, as to whether the *deus caritatis* of the original text condemns the hero for lack of love or shows him mercy for having nobly striven, *Peer Gynt,* Brand's comic antithesis, is at least equally equivocal.[5] Certainly the plays are intended to complement each other. Peer's whimsically affectionate kindness to his dying mother stands, as Archer noted, in direct contrast to Brand's harsh refusal to come to his mother's deathbed. Where Brand seeks to ascend to the realm of a superhuman ideal, Peer is entirely immersed in the world of impulse, fantasy, and self-gratification.

The one point on which Peer and Brand seem paradoxically to agree is the question of selfhood. Ultimately, Brand is not preeminently a Christian (Ibsen himself said he could as well have been a sculptor or a politician) but rather the apostle of a demonic morality that sacrifices everything to the integrity of the self, whatever that self may be: "If you cannot be what you ought to be," Brand asserts, "Then try to be whatever you honestly can / Be utterly a man of clay." Soon after resolving to find his calling within his self, he asks for a realm where that self may be fulfilled.

> O, for room in the world's wide arch, a place
> Where I may be myself entirely! That is the lawful right
> Of every man! This granted, I should demand no more.

Peer, also obsessed with the question of his own identity, again and again insists that he is above all himself. To the sycophants who surround him in his prosperity, he delivers an oration, exulting in the claim that his personality is the sum of his appetites:

> The Gyntian "Self"—it's the regiment
> Of wishes, appetites and desires;—
> The Gyntian "Self" is the sea of ambitions,
> Needs and demands; in fact, whatever
> Causes my breast to heave uniquely,
> And makes me exist as the "I" that I am.

But even this dubious notion is braggadocio. Peer, Ibsen tells us, has never committed himself wholly to a life of indulgence but has always stood freely poised, ready to retreat when it seemed advisable. As the button molder later tells him, he has been a failure even as a sinner. Unconsciously he has carried out his threat to Solveig at the wedding feast: he has turned himself into a troll, "himself-sufficient" only to whatever the occasion demanded, never making direct choices but going, as the great Boyg commanded, roundabout.

Yet for all his weakness, there is more than a half suggestion that Solveig's semimaternal love will save him:

> My mother; my wife; purest of women!
> Hide me there, hide me in your heart!

Despite the fact that Solveig is an idealized figure, almost a pure abstraction, her sudden appearance to rescue Peer from his deserved fate does not grate on our sensibilities as much as it might. If Peer were really as vapid as Ibsen would seem to have us believe, his moment of sentimental penitence would hardly be enough to redeem his life. But though he has lacked a guiding idealism, Peer has not been a characterless nonentity. He has after all carried off the bride, seduced the daughter of the Troll King, fought the Great Boyg, become a millionaire, a prophet, a traveler in distant lands, and above all he has through the power of his imagination cast over his adventures an aura of glamour and daring that is a creation in itself. If Brand is the self constrained by the ideal, Peer is the self liberated, exuberant, free to indulge its vitality and appetite. He is both dangerous and contemptible, but he has more of the virtues that Brand lacks than Ibsen himself could admit.

Although *Emperor and Galilean,* the "world historic" drama on the life of Julian the Apostate through which Ibsen hoped to resolve the clash of opposites, ultimately cost him more labor than any of his other creations, he was less interested in Julian's career in itself than as an occasion for expressing the "positive world-philosophy" that he felt called upon to utter. He comes nearest to presenting it explicitly when the youthful Julian, finding both religion and philosophy unsatisfactory, seeks out Maximus the Mystic, who offers what appears to be a resolution of Julian's conflicts:

> MAXIMUS. There are three empires.
> JULIAN. Three?
> MAXIMUS. First that empire which was founded on the tree of knowledge; then that empire which was founded on the tree of the cross. . . .
> JULIAN. And the third?
> MAXIMUS. The third is the empire of the great mystery, the empire which shall be founded on the tree of knowledge and the tree of the cross together, because it hates and loves them both, and because it has its living springs under Adam's grove and Golgotha.

Although Julian labors under the impression that he has been elected to establish the third empire, presumably identical with Ibsen's "positive world-philosophy," he fails to do so, and not surprisingly it remains, a "great mystery," for the Hegelian synthesis that is to result from the conflict of pagan and Christian lies inevitably outside the limits of the text.

The phenomenon of thesis and antithesis here is, as it was in relation to Brand and Peer, essentially symbolic of the central clash of impulse and ideal. Indeed, the Christ so fearfully envisioned by Julian immediately evokes the fierce God worshiped by Brand. "Oh, he is terrible," cries Julian, "this mysterious . . . this merciless god-man! Wherever I wanted to go, he loomed up, large and forbidding in my path, adamant and pitiless in his demands." Christan idealism is opposed by pagan self-gratification as Julian, like Peer, loses himself in delusions of splendor and pleasure, and also like him receives at his death a benediction from a saintly woman because he is one of those who have striven. But though Julian may be forgiven, nothing can save *Emperor and Galilean* with its pages of flat characterization and weighty dialogue. It is ironic but not entirely surprising that to the end of his life Ibsen seems to have thought it his masterpiece, for it remains the most sustained and ambitious of his attempts to reconcile the great opposites of his universe.

With the completion of *Emperor and Galilean* Ibsen turned to the realistic play of modern life, the form that, steadily enriched and expanded by his efforts, thereafter occupied him exclusively.[6] The first three plays in that mode already constitute a remarkable progression, which suggests the continued refining of Ibsen's art and anticipates its psychological and—ultimately—its symbolic manifestations in the plays that follow. *Pillars of Society,* encompassing a large family, friends, dependents, business associates, and eventually the entire community, is confident and optimistic in tone, broad and tumultuous in scope. In *A Doll's House,* however, the focus narrows to a married couple and their immediate associates, although they are still actively involved in the life of the town. In *Ghosts* the tone is now grim, the atmosphere one of seclusion, the community distant; and only the remnants of a family still struggle with the past. As Ibsen concentrates and subtilizes his material here, it becomes steadily more powerful and more tragic. Yet we are still far from the richness of texture, the suggestiveness, the depth of character analysis in *The Wild Duck, Rosmersholm, The Lady from the Sea,* and *Hedda Gabler* and from the scope of vision in *The Master Builder, Little Eyolf, John Gabriel Borkman,* and *When We Dead Awaken.*

Pillars of Society, however lively and carefully contrived, remains inadequate as a play,[7] yet it is still a representative production of

Ibsen's mind. Beneath the melodrama of commercial conscience lie the central concerns for the self and the ideal. Indeed, Hilmar Tonnesen, Mrs. Bernik's inquisitive cousin, refers to "the flag of the ideal" at every opportunity, and there are many. But he is only an ironic foil to the play's true idealist, Lona Hessel, who arrives at the end of Act I "to let in some fresh air" upon the hypocritical and restrictive society that is frustrating all self-fulfillment for those trapped within it. In *Emperor and Galilean* Ibsen had conceived of a third empire, in which idealism and self-gratification would be reconciled. Here he suggests through Lona Hessel that the pillars of that empire, if it is to be founded on earth, must be "the spirit of truth and the spirit of freedom." The pat optimism of this conclusion and behind it the easy acceptance of the romantic confidence in man's essential goodness (Dina Dorf says that people should not be moral and respectable but "natural") are strikingly uncharacteristic of Ibsen. Never again was he to suggest so explicitly the route to the third empire or to stamp his characters with such unqualified approval.

In *A Doll's House,* where the achievement of the ideal and the full development of the self are still conceived of as, to a considerable extent, the same, the conclusion is even more problematic than that of *Pillars of Society.* Through a rich psychological variation on the Scribean quiproquo, the idealistic Nora reads into Helmer's assurance that he is capable of handling any threat that Krogstad might present a promise that he will take upon himself whatever consequences may result from the exposure of her forgery. Although Nora has taken pleasure in her hidden life of work that was "almost like being a man," she has also accepted her childlike role as coddled household plaything. But now this supposed confirmation of her vision of Helmer as a heroic martyr (secretly treasured for eight years), the "miracle," as she calls it, releases her concealed aspirations. She sees the miracle as an emblem of life lived fully, ideally, of the self expressed without compromise or limitation.

When her husband turns out to be an obtuse, self-centered, conventional-minded bourgeois rather than the heroic martyr she had fantasized, Nora experiences a psychic transformation involving both death and rebirth. The self that had lived through childish gratifications is destroyed utterly (Nora and Dr. Rank are both embodiments of Ibsen's obsessive symbol, the murdered child), but the hidden self of her dreams begins to flower forth. Although she no longer believes in miracles (nor in law nor religion), Nora is no less resolved to find fulfillment. With a tragic determination worthy of Brand himself, she cuts herself off from children, husband, and the social world she has known and goes off to create her new self and to find a realm in which it can be fulfilled.

But beneath the confident assertion marked by the sound of the slamming door at the end of the play, there lies a dilemma. Without reopening the profitless debate on the morality or probability of Nora's desertion of her children, we should observe that Ibsen has finely balanced Nora's abrogation of her role as a mother with her abrogation of her role as a child. Both must be sacrificed if the self is to bloom. For all her newfound strength, Nora cannot make self-gratification and self-transcendence entirely coincident.

Even less so can Mrs. Alving, whose moment of decision, unlike Nora's, has long since passed. Indeed, she has not made the same kind of decision, for the opposition between the two women is not quite what at first it seems. It is true that Nora leaves her husband, presumably for a fruitful life, and that Mrs. Alving returns to hers with hideous consequences. But the solutions to Mrs. Alving's problems did not lie in a life of ecstatic iniquity in the company of Pastor Manders, himself the representative of the hypocritical and repressive code of life that dominates her society, passing from generation to generation warping instincts and destroying joy as the secret and terrible disease that is its symbol destroys the lives of Dr. Rank and Oswald Alving. Ironically, had Mrs. Alving followed her own first inclinations and married Manders, this free union based on affection, which Ibsen could approve, would probably have been little more successful than that of Nora and Helmer. It is, by a further irony, Lieutenant Alving, the man she is coerced into marrying, who has the "joy of life," the unfettered assertion of the self, that might have produced genuine happiness. Whereas Nora may well succeed because she is able to reject her husband, Mrs. Alving may have failed because she could not accept hers.

She takes the blame for this failure upon herself in her climactic confession to her son, maintaining that it was her coldness and insistence on duty that had killed the exuberance and joyousness of the young Alving. "Everything seemed to come down to duty in the end—*my* duty and *his* duty. . . . I'm afraid I must have made the house unbearable for your poor father, Oswald." Some of the tragic dignity that lingers about Mrs. Alving stems from this assumption of guilt, but the reader is inclined to look beyond to the pettiness and ignobleness about her. Essentially, Mrs. Alving is trapped between two worlds, which, since Ibsen is a dramatist and an artist rather than a commentator, appear in the text primarily through symbolic suggestion. One is the conventional and repressive middle-class world, idealism degenerated to duty, joy corrupted to debauchery, suggested by rain, gloom, disease, and the ironic triple symbol of house, orphanage, and brothel. The other is the world of the free self suggested, however awkwardly, by Oswald's description of the artists' life in Paris and by his attempts to evoke joy in his painting and symbolized in its exaltation and unattainable remoteness by the sun and the morning light shining on the glacier and the mountain peaks at the end of the play. Because Mrs. Alving has not understood the nature of either until too late, she is caught between them and destroyed.

If Mrs. Alving's fate results from her failing to demand truth and self-fulfillment soon enough, the destiny of Dr. Stockmann, the enemy of the people, stems from his doing just that. Like Nora, he is a romantic rebel who gives his allegiance to a moral code that, he maintains, is superior to the one generally received. That he is patently in the right does not prevent him from suffering the doom of many such figures, exile. (Ibsen himself, after all, whose anger and sense of rejection at the outraged reception of *Ghosts* Stockmann embodies, was literally an exile from his native country for most of his career and a spiritual exile for the whole of it.) But though a martyr—the twelve disciples the doctor sets out to find at the end of the play suggest an even more exalted role—Stockmann is subject to certain qualifications in our sympathies. For all the affection that his courage and innocence evoke, he is, as his brother Peter correctly points out, reckless, irritable, and self-involved, a sort of bumbling, comic Brand. Indeed, like Brand, he puts his ideals before his family, though with less disastrous results. Even in this, the simplest and most direct of the plays of Ibsen's maturity, there is a sense of ambiguous balance, of tormented contradiction. Stockmann is both exalted idealist and comic butt. As always, aspiration and truth to the self are at once admirable and destructive; here it is even suggested that they may be absurd.

This sense of precarious balance and a deeper probing of his characters are the central features of Ibsen's middle group of "psychological" plays. A new depth of character analysis that gives us, in the range of figures extending from Hjalmar Ekdal to Rebecca West to Hedda Gabler, the most extraordinary portrait gallery in the modern drama stems from a developing view of man that no longer lets Ibsen suggest, even in so qualified a way as he already has, that impulse and ideal can unite to form a free and fulfilled self.

Although there clearly is a shift in attitude related to the deepening of Ibsen's perceptions, it would be a notable oversimplification to take *The Wild Duck* as a negation of the apparent optimism of *Pillars of Society*. It is true that in the latter play Lona Hessel's exposure of the lie on which Bernick's life has been founded reestablishes it on the basis of truth and freedom while in the former Gregers's revelations cause only destruction. But the point is not that there is reversal of meaning but that *The Wild Duck* is vastly richer, subtler, and more elusive.

In the earlier play, for example, the true representative of the ideal is clearly Lona Hessel, but in *The Wild Duck* no single character, not even Hedvig the pathetic victim, plays that role. To some degree it inheres in the image of the wild duck aloft in the skies as it was before being shot. But essentially it lies in the world of freedom and beauty evoked by the forests of Hoidal that appear again and again in the speeches of the characters. When Gregers's blundering has run its course and Hedvig lies dead, Old Ekdal speaks again as he had when Gregers described the felling of the trees at Hoidal, "The forest's revenge." The destruction of the life of the forests, then, becomes symbolically equivalent to the destruction of the life of the child, and no one in the play escapes the taint of corruption that stems from these acts. Even Old Ekdal, who seems, next to Hedvig, most the victim, has been a destroyer. He has, as we are told more than once, shot nine bears. Ibsen is unlikely to have been so specific about the number, which does not appear in the first drafts, without reason. If the nine bears parallel the nine dolls of Mrs. Solness, they may suggest the months of pregnancy, reinforcing the sense of the destruction of life.

The elusive weakness of the Ekdals is no less dangerous than the open ruthlessness of the Werles. Where the Ekdals frustrate life through lassitude and self-indulgence, the Werles do so with impossible demands or with an open blow. But even toward Haakon Werle, who has felled the forests, struck down Old Ekdal, and shot the wild duck, we take an ambiguous attitude. Along with Mrs. Sörby, he has the robust conscience, a strength of will that lets him carry his guilt with dignity. Moreover, his sins were evidently not entirely of his own making. As a young man he had been forced to endure endless sermons on his misdeeds, imaginary as well as real, from a rigidly moralistic wife. The husband-seducer whose secret passions produced an illegitimate daughter we knew before as Captain Alving; reincarnate, he stands before us too strong to be a prey to drink and disease, too stunted to be in spirit anything but what he is becoming physically—blind.

Gregers, who has something of his father's strength of purpose coupled with a certain "blindness" in his inability to see through Hjalmar's facade, has inherited from his mother a "sickly conscience." Unable to bear the sense of guilt implanted in him by his mother, he demands of those about him an inhuman perfection; but he can escape from his guilt only in thoughts of suicide. Hjalmar shares at least one characteristic with Gregers; he too has been brought up under pious feminine domination. His "soul-mothers" are, in Relling's words, "two crazy, hysterical maiden aunts," in Gregers's "women who never shut their eyes to the claim of the ideal." Under their influence Hjalmar's weakness has turned to indulgence and self-deception while Gregers's self-reproach has become fanaticism. But whereas Hjalmar destroys through a weak self-aggrandizement, Gregers does so through a fierce self-abnegation and a destructive aspiration. The two men are in fact mirror images, each reflecting the other in reverse. (The morbidity of Gregers's thoughts of suicide is balanced by the comedy of Hjalmar's; Gregers's determined resolve, as his father asks him what he is going to do in life, "I shall fulfill my mission, that's all," is a grim echo of Hjalmar's fatuous boast, "As truly as I have a mission in life, so shall I fulfill it!") They are the two poles between which the other elements in the play fluctuate, the great opposites of Ibsen's universe, impulse and ideal, but here expressed in their lowest, most distorted forms, the ideal of Faustian aspiration become deadly fanaticism, the impulse to self-gratification become poisonous dream, at home only in the fantasy world of the attic. In opening this new phase of his art, Ibsen returns to the archetypal figures with which he inaugurated his European career. But Hjalmar is Peer Gynt futile and without vitality; Gregers is Brand fumbling and devoid of grandeur.

Ibsen seems at first kinder to Hjalmar than to Gregers, but Dr. Relling, Hjalmar's defender, is less a *raisonneur* than a rationalizer, invented to oppose Gregers's view because Hjalmar, the self-deceiver, can never understand his own position well enough to do so. It is not that Hjalmar-Relling is right and Gregers wrong but that each in his own way is profoundly destructive. Notice, for example, the precision with which Ibsen distributes the responsibility for Hedvig's death. Gregers suggests the pistol and the idea of sacrifice; Hjalmar's self-centered cruelty drives her to the act of suicide.

But if the scale may have been tipped toward impulse in *The Wild Duck*, it is leveled again in *Rosmersholm*. Here the elements are of equal weight; they move at equal velocity; their collision produces both destruction and triumph. Like Gregers, Rosmer has had a vision of an ideal life. As Gregers had presented his claim at the doors of the cottages of Hoidal, so Rosmer had dreamed of something similar. "You wanted to go from house to house," Rebecca says, "like a messenger of deliverance. . . . Creating all about you a nobility . . . in ever wider circles. Noble men." But whereas Gregers had merely presented an inflexible demand for elevated conduct, Rosmer, more sensitive and discriminating, knows that he must alter the natures of those about him if he is to lead mankind to realize the ideal.[8] Nevertheless, for all the sympathy that Rosmer's character and views evoke, there is in him a central lack. Like Oswald and Gregers before him, he is the victim of an inherited disease, "a sort of infection," as Mrs. Helseth terms it, that touches all the children of Rosmersholm, who do not cry and later, as adults, do not laugh, and spreads from that realm of exalted frigidity throughout the district. The "Rosmer philosophy of life" kills what Ibsen earlier called "the joy of life." In the case of Rosmer himself the lack of that central creative vitality is suggested by his sexual coldness, which had prevented him from fulfilling his wife's physical needs. "I told you, didn't I," he exclaims to his brother-in-law, "about her wild fits of sensual passion . . . which she expected me to respond to. Oh! how she appalled me." Ultimately, Rosmer, noble but essentially lifeless, is a prey to the white horses of Rosmersholm, messengers of purity and death.

Rebecca, too, has a taint within her, represented like Rosmer's in sexual terms. She has, the play suggests, been unknowingly involved in an incestuous relationship with Dr. West, her adoptive, and secretly her real, father.[9] But whereas Rosmer's frigidity suggests an inherent inhumanity, Rebecca's passionate excesses symbolize the destructive possibilities of an uncontrolled impulse toward self-aggrandizement. Urged by the force of creative energy and hardly impeded by scruples, she has swept Beata into the millrace only to find that the stain of corruption and the coldness of idealism have together overwhelmed her. By the time Rebecca has been ennobled and Rosmer vitalized, neither can escape the guilt of the past.[10]

As the play draws to its close, the destinies of the central characters are reflected in the career of Ulrik Brendel, a kind of *Doppelgänger* who possesses something of the Dionysiac energy of Rebecca and the exalted idealism of Rosmer, whose mind he has helped to form and whose clothes he wears as he goes forth to place his ideals before the world. As Rosmer's faith is broken by the crass rigidity of the conservatives, so is Brendel's by the shabby opportunism of the liberals. At the end of the play he comes back, embittered and half mad, to tell them that only through the mutilation of Rebecca's beauty can Rosmer's mission succeed. Holding Rebecca by the wrist, he speaks of what is required for Rosmer's triumph:

> That the woman who loves him goes out into the kitchen and gladly chops off her dainty, pink and white little finger . . . here, just here near the middle joint. Furthermore, that the aforesaid woman in love . . . equally gladly . . . cuts off her incomparably formed left ear. [*Lets her go and turns to Rosmer.*] Farewell, my conquering Johannes.

Astonishingly prescient in regard to sexual symbolism (the finger suggesting the male organ, the ear the female), the speech evokes the fierce sacrifice of vital gratification that aspiration demands and that a few moments later helps draw Rosmer and Rebecca into the millrace.

The idea of a mysterious fate rising from the waters carries over from *Rosmersholm* to *The Lady from the Sea.* In fact, Ibsen's symbolic vision of the ocean first emerged in his jottings for *The Wild Duck.* His note is of interest, for the manner in which it is ultimately developed helps explain the failure of *The Lady from the Sea.* "People are sea creatures," Ibsen wrote, "—like the wild duck—not land creatures—Gregers [Hjalmar in the final version] was made for the sea. All people will in time live on it when dry land is inundated. Then family life will stop." [11] As first conceived, the sea is a realm of both ideality and gratification, a third empire that will ultimately supersede ordinary existence. Transferred to Ellida's character, this concept becomes, as her husband puts it, a "craving for the unattainable . . . for the limitless, for the infinite." But when the infinite appears on stage as the Stranger, he is only a rather seedy version of that romantic archetype, the demon lover. In a sudden, awkward reversal, Ellida rejects him for a slogan, freedom and responsibility, that abruptly intrudes on the action of the play. Usually Ibsen's dramatic vision encompasses both a romantic longing for the ideal and a sense of the moral restraints of life. But because here he forces himself to choose between simplistic alternatives, an empty slogan and cliché figure, the play collapses in confusion.

Although *The Lady from the Sea* is ultimately a failure and *Hedda Gabler* is one of Ibsen's most notable successes, the two works are closely related, the later play constituting, from one point of view, a more powerful working out of earlier materials. In each play the heroine is a woman of great attractions married to an amiable but in some way unsatisfying husband. Each woman finds herself alienated from the household of which she would normally be the center, Ellida by her feeling that she is neither needed nor desired, Hedda by a parallel sense of exclusion as well as her intense distaste for what she believes to be a sordid domesticity. Moreover, each woman has concealed in her past a lover of greater vitality and attractiveness than her husband. When the lover reappears, the plot rises to its climax, and the heroine's destiny is determined.[12]

These parallels would be intriguing but hardly crucial if it were not that the heroine's alienation and her vision of the forces embodied in her lover are the central elements in each play and determine its direction and meaning. For Ellida, as we have seen, her lover is the sea and what it symbolizes—the unattainable, the limitless, and the infinite. But in *Hedda Gabler* the lover from the past, Ejlert Lövborg, is not a representative of the ideal but rather an embodiment of its opposite, the passionate, liberated self. The stories of his revels have allowed Hedda a glimpse of a world of masculine freedom that in her own life she can know nothing of. He has roused in her a sexual interest that none of her other admirers has evoked. But primarily Hedda envisions Lövborg "with vine leaves in his hair" as a Dionysiac embodiment of the courage and self-fulfillment she at once fears and longs for.

Despite his intellectuality Lövborg is, within the terms of the play, a representative of the impulse to self-gratification. Like his forerunner Peer Gynt, he is passionate, lacking restraint; like Peer, he is succored by a faithful woman. From their union comes his book, the "child," destroyed by Hedda. Although she is drawn toward the impulses embodied in Lövborg, Hedda is ultimately committed to an antithetical ideal, her sterile dream of a world of aristocratic elegance in which a life can be lived beyond the "paltry circumstances" that make existence "so positively ludicrous!" At its most petty, her dream leads to small-town snobbery, but at its most exalted and its most dangerous it leads to the moment at which she gives Lövborg the pistol so that in killing himself he may transfigure her commonplace world by performing "an act that has something of unconditional beauty." When Lövborg, who shoots himself accidentally in the abdomen rather than deliberately in the temple, fails to achieve her ideal of frigid beauty and she is in the power of Judge Brack (the sensuality she had toyed with, denied in herself, and frustrated in Lövborg now returns, with perfect Ibsen irony, to dominate her), she can only put the pistol to her own temple and attempt to achieve that ideal herself by dying "beautifully." From the first *Hedda Gabler* has been discussed by critics as the portrait of a destructive, near psychotic woman, and such indeed it is. But it is also the portrait of one of the most extraordinary of Ibsen's idealists, without the nobility of Brand or the dedication of Gregers, but with an obsessive exaltation that, no less destructive than their strivings, ultimately grants her some of their tragic stature.

Although the relationships between *Hedda Gabler* and *The Lady from the Sea* on the one hand and *Rosmersholm* and *The Wild Duck* on the other divide these dramas of psychological analysis into contrasting pairs, the interconnections among the more essentially symbolic plays make them an indissoluble group. In each play the central figure is a man of some stature, a philosopher, a financier, an artist. Linked to him are two women, one comparatively gentle, the other passionate and demanding. Concealed in his past lies a secret crime, in three cases specifically the destruction of children—Ibsen's persistent symbol for the dangers in an excess of impulse or ideal—and in the fourth case, *Borkman,* an analogous destruction of human affection. As so often in Ibsen, the central action is a confrontation with the past and, in life or in death, some new adjustment to it.

Ibsen conveys this dramatic action through more overtly symbolic means than previously, but the difference in technique is only relative. As the sun and the shining mountaintops of *Ghosts* remind us, he had long been a symbolic writer. Similarly, though a specific autobiographical element in *The Master Builder* and *When We Dead Awaken* does not appear earlier, the conflict between ideal aspiration and human self-aggrandizement around which these plays revolve has consistently been central to Ibsen's work.

Therefore, it seems best to discard the autobiographical approach to *The Master Builder,* which in the history of Ibsen criticism has been consistently attractive but notably unhelpful in elucidating what is in many ways the richest and most powerful of Ibsen's works.[13] Halvard Solness, whether or to whatever degree he is an incarnation of Henrik Ibsen, stands in the line of those Faustian idealists whose pursuit of a suprahuman perfection ultimately dehumanizes and destroys them. As in the cases of Rosmer and Hedda, Solness' dehumanization is presented in terms of a lack of sexual force. The tower and the wreath, when linked with the adolescent Hilde's orgasmic experience during Solness' ascent and his advances, real or imagined, toward her afterward, become unmistakable erotic images. Solness' tendencies to dizziness symbolize some degree of sexual incapacity, and the barren nurseries of his home suggest not only his wife's sterility but his own.

But *The Master Builder* is not merely a pre-Freudian case history, nor is Solness' sterility only the result of a personal trauma. Part of a wider context, it stems from Solness' overwhelming urge to build, to achieve his aims as an artist. For in *The Master Builder* art itself becomes the ideal. Like Brand, Solness has set himself a more-than-human goal and like Brand, he has sacrificed wife and off-spring to realize it. The helpers and servers who, he believes, have achieved his aim are the creatures of his own will, servants of the troll, the blind, demanding, unreasoning self that hides beneath the rational element in man. It is Hilde Wangel, the embodiment of vital impulse in this play, who tells Solness that there is a troll in him as well as in herself. But whereas the troll impulse in Hilde is natural, almost unthinking, that in the master builder is the slave of an inspiration at once noble and perverse. For in Solness, as in other late Ibsen heroes, that sense of soaring aspiration is allied to a ruthless self-aggrandizement that crushes any natural human life in its way.

Not surprisingly, then, our attitude toward Solness is profoundly ambiguous. His aims as an artist, after all, have been admirable. Moreover, since he lacks the robust conscience that Ibsen both admires and fears, he is, like Gregers, obsessed by an agonizing sense of guilt. "And these helpers and servants," he cries, "go flaying off skin from other people's bodies to patch *my* wound. Yet the wound never heals . . . never!" Nor is Solness alone in his torment and guilt. Like Captain Alving and Old Werle before him, he is chained to a woman whom he has profoundly injured and who has injured him by substituting for human warmth the cold and life-less ideal of duty. The plot of ground that the fire freed for Solness to build upon is regularly referred to as the great garden, and the theme of the lost Eden, of the man and woman searching with pathetic futility for a happy world they have destroyed (a poem on this theme was Ibsen's starting point), pervades the play, especially in the persistent contrast between the homes Solness has built and his own empty house with its aspiring tower.

Because our attitude toward Solness is so equivocal, our feelings toward his destroyer are also mixed. Hilde's youth and grace, her enthusiasm, the freshness of her sympathies all make her an appealing figure. So does the childlike, imaginative quality of her yearning for the kingdom of Orangia, though the tropic lushness of its name hints that it is a realm of passionate self-gratification. Moreover, the near perversity of her erotic fixation and the ruth-lessness of her greed for sensation, for anything that will be "thrill-ing," suggest a temperament that, like Hedda's, is dangerously unstable. Although Hilde is one of Ibsen's most remarkable achievements as an intuitive psychologist, she is, like Solness, more than a case history. Young and ardent, Hilde is the living embodiment of the impulse toward self-gratification that Solness has crushed in others while furthering his own aspirations. The fear of youth dominates *The Master Builder* not only because Ibsen had, at the time of its writing, recently attended a lecture at which the young Knut Hamsun denounced the senior Norwegian writers, but because childhood and youth, the results of ordinary procreative impulses, are what Solness' urge toward suprahuman creativity has destroyed. But Solness, for all his sterility, has roused the very creature that will crush him. Ten years later the child whose sexual feelings he had awakened arrives, identifies herself with his own dead children by sleeping in their nursery, and strikes him down.

But though Solness has so deeply sinned against life that that the embodiment of blind vitality must ultimately come as an avenger, nonetheless he yearns for the joy of existence. Alfred Allmers of *Little Eyolf,* on the other hand, though he writes of human responsibility and talks of devoting himself to his son, in reality desires only "the peace and serenity that comes from the nearness of death." Despite the radical shift in character of the protagonist, however, the two plays are closely connected. The first version of *Little Eyolf,* in fact, included the poem "They Sat There, the Two," the original basis for *The Master Builder.* In it a husband and wife search among ashes of their burnt-out home for the jewel of love that they have lost. Allmers, whose marriage like Solness' is burnt out, also has a hint of sexual corruption about him. Not only does he reject with frigid repulsion the demands of his passionate wife, but his love for his supposed half sister, Asta, has in it a touch of the incestuous and the homosexual. (Asta used to dress in boy's clothes for him.) And just as Solness had ascended his tower to proclaim himself, so Allmers has ascended to that special Ibsen world, literally above the human one, "the mountain peaks and . . . the great desolate open spaces." But there he finds that his ideals lead not toward human responsibility but toward death. So also does the uncontrolled impulse of his wife, Rita, for they share the guilt for the crippling of their child, little Eyolf (exactly as Gregers and Hjalmar share the guilt for the death of Hedvig). Enlightened by his new knowledge, Allmers resolves to put aside his empty moralizing and devote himself to the education of his son. Yet not until the child, the symbol of their guilt, is drowned, does Allmers fully understand his coldness and Rita her lustful possessiveness. But now they can only expiate their guilt by such acts of charity as they can perform and wait for death.

In *John Gabriel Borkman* even expiation has ceased to be possible. For those not directly involved in the central tragedy—Frida, Erhart and Mrs. Wilton, who in her strength and amoral honesty is a kind of reincarnation of Mrs. Sörby—there is escape from this claustrophobic world, the guilt-haunted house, to a more human life in the South. (All three of Ibsen's final plays show this pattern of a younger, more hopeful group juxtaposed with an older, tragic one.) But for Borkman and the two women indissolubly bound to him there is no such possibility. Like Allmers, and indeed like Consul Bernick long before, he has married without love to further his dreams of success. In effect, he has chosen the ideal over the human, and both have eluded him. No speeches in Ibsen so precisely express the lure and the danger inherent in the realm of the ideal as the final exchange between Borkman and Ella Rentheim:

> BORKMAN. Ella, you see those distant mountains there—ranging, soaring, towering. That is my vast, my infinite, my inexhaustible kingdom!
>
> ELLA RENTHEIN. But it's an icy blast that blows from that kingdom, John.
>
> BORKMAN. To me it is the breath of life. To me it comes like a greeting from loyal subject spirits. I sense their presence—those captive millions. I feel the veins of metal reaching out their twisting, sinuous, beckoning arms to me. Standing that night in the vaults of the bank, a lantern in my hand, I saw them as living shadows. You wanted to be freed. And I tried. But could not succeed. And the treasure sank back into the depths. [*With outstretched arms.*] But let me whisper this to you, here in the stillness of the night. I love you: you who lie in a trance of death in the darkness and the deep. I love you! You and your life-seeking treasures and all your bright retinue of power and glory. I love you, love you, love you.

Still bound to his vision of the ideal kingdom that he is never to rule, Borkman feels the "icy hand of iron" upon his heart and dies, hardly understanding the human self-fulfillment he has denied.

For Professor Arnold Rubek of *When We Dead Awaken,* however, understanding comes all too clearly. He knows that in expanding and mutilating the statue of Irene, *The Day of Resurrection,* (the embodiment of Rubek's icy aspirations), he has committed child murder, Ibsen's unpardonable sin. Irene, too, who regularly refers to the statue as her child, knows that she has committed an analogous crime (the very one that so long ago Nora Hellmer had avoided) in giving up herself to Rubek. "But I was a human being—then!" she cries to Rubek. "I, too, had a life to live . . . and a human destiny to fulfill. And all that I put aside . . . threw it all away in order to serve you. It was suicide. A mortal sin against myself." In denying, for the sake of his art, the passion that animated both Irene and himself, Rubek has in effect condemned them both to death. His work has degenerated into sterile caricature, her life into degradation and madness. But even though Rubek's wife, Maja (named for the Greek earth mother), and her lover, Ulfheim, apparently go to a life of freedom and fulfillment, their final movement is a descent from the mountain. There is still something alluring in the ascent of Rubek and Irene to the ice world of the ideal, "the summit of the tower that shines in the sunrise." In the avalanche that destroys them and in the *pax vobiscum* of the Sister of Mercy we hear the echo at the end of Ibsen's career of the conclusion of *Brand,* the play with which its greatness began.

Not only is there again the imagery of the mountain, the avalanche, and the lonely figures carried to their deaths, but the sense of simultaneous attraction and repulsion one feels for Brand is almost precisely reproduced in Ibsen's final play. From first to last the figure of the aspiring, demanding idealist dominates Ibsen's work. Sometimes, as in the cases of Lona Hessel and Dr. Stockmann, he is the admired truth speaker; on other occasions, as with Hedda Gabler and Arnold Rubek, he is the castigated sinner. But, however wide the range of attitudes evoked—Gregers, for example, partakes of both—his demands and aspirations are always central. He is, as Croce said of Ibsen, "all absorbed in anxious longing for the felicity to be attained by attaining to the sublime and the extraordinary, and at the same time most sensible and intransigent in the consciousness of responsibility and guilt." [14]

However intensely the Ibsen idealist strives toward the world of the mountain peaks where in Ibsen the sublime and the extraordinary so often reside, a consciousness of responsibility and guilt stands ready to send the avalanche hurtling down upon him, crushing his aspirations into nothingness. For he is the victim of the disparity between two impulses profoundly contradictory yet both integral to the romantic consciousness that Ibsen inherited. One is the Faustian urge that leads him to reject the limitations of the earthly self and aspire to a suprahuman perfection. The other is the impulse (resting on the Rousseauistic view that man's nature is essentially admirable) to fulfillment, not through transcending the self, but through gratifying and aggrandizing it. From this dialectic no synthesis can result. For the idealist, fixed on his vision of the sublime, there is the danger of icy cruelty and inhumanity; for his opposite the urge to self-aggrandizement often produces a demonic greed, an equally cruel demand that the self be gratified at all costs. However much Ibsen may desire happiness, he senses that the "joy in living" inevitably involves a negation of the beauty of the ideal and that the pursuit of the ideal kills the possibilities for the gladness human intercourse allows.

Anticipating Freud's insights, Ibsen evokes the forces of the demanding superego and the desiring id. From Brand through Arnold Rubek his characters—noble yet tyrannical, yearning for greatness yet murdering joy—whose aspirations lead them toward the exalted frigidity of the ice worlds project the nature of the exacting superego, which both demands and punishes, uplifts and yet tyrannizes. In the same way, from Peer Gynt through Hilde Wangel, those creatures of Ibsen's—vital yet childish, seeking gratification yet achieving corruption—who live by the impulses of the self rather than the dictates of the ideal suggest the id that must be controlled but that cannot without danger be repressed. Yet Ibsen's vision is not to be reduced to a psychoanalytic paradigm, however complex and ambiguous, for the plays are at once realistic and metaphorical, literal and symbolic, an analysis of life and an image of it. A character such as Rosmer, for example, is at once a self-sustaining psychological being, an evocation of the superego, an embodiment of ideal aspiration to higher realms of experience. Ibsen's work does more than present an abiding dialectic. In the variety and complexity with which the plays explore the conflicts between their opposed forces, the alliances they form or attempt to form, and the consequences of their interactions, we see dramatized before us the variety, complexity, and elusiveness of existence itself.

Luigi Pirandello: The Imprisoned Self

When in 1935 Domenico Vittorini, Pirandello's biographer and critic, showed the proofs of his recently completed book to the Maestro, the reaction was not auspicious. Told that the first chapter traced his relation to the school of naturalism, Pirandello exclaimed violently, "My art has no connection whatsoever with naturalism. Giovanni Verga, the great representative of that movement, wrote me that there was a new force and a new light in my art. I have a letter written to me by him after the publication of my novel *L'esclusa* [*The Outcast*]. Indeed, I feel I am at the opposite pole from naturalism." [15] Despite the unfortunate Vittorini's hasty assurances that he considered naturalism no more than the starting point of the Maestro's art, Pirandello, only partly appeased, continued to claim that his views on life and art had remained substantially unchanged since the early days of his career.

Pirandello's insistence on this point is suggestive of more than the difficulties of dealing with a living and irascible writer. If he is correct, then *The Outcast*, though a very early work (dating from 1893 when its author was only twenty-six), ought to anticipate the vision of life expressed later in the plays. If we look for that vision in convoluted discourse on illusion and reality or on the multiplicity of personality—the sort commonly associated with Pirandello—we will be disappointed, for there is none here. However, much of what is central to Pirandello's plays will appear if we recognize in the treatment of his heroine's exclusion from her village society an image of the self barred from genuine commerce with external reality and condemned to the ultimate solitude of an interior world. If we look further in this novel at the desperate efforts of the self to transcend the limits of that world, we can see a crucial link between Pirandello and the other playwrights of this study.

Although a bare summary of *The Outcast* cannot convey the

power in the delineation of the Sicilian milieu and in the projection of the characters' feelings, it does reveal a typically Pirandellesque irony underlying the action. In a Sicilian town, probably modeled on Pirandello's own Girgenti [Agrigento], a young married woman, Marta Pentagora, has allowed herself to receive admiring, even passionate letters from a successful attorney and rising politician, Gregorio Alvignani, though she has done no more than engage him in a literary duel of wit. When her husband, Rocco, finds her reading one of the letters, he instantly assumes that she has been guilty of adultery and drives her out of his house. The entire town believes in her supposed guilt; her father, a man of violent passions, locks himself away in his room out of shame and ultimately dies of a stroke. Reduced to poverty, Marta resolves to support her mother and sister as well as herself by teaching, but though she wins a post it is made intolerable by her students' hostility. Through Alvignani's intervention she finds a new post at Palermo where she finally becomes his mistress. Now, however, her husband has become convinced of her innocence and asks her to come back to him. Even after she tells him of her relationship with Alvignani, he persists, and the end of the novel suggest that, though embittered and loveless, she will return to him.

A heroine who when innocent is universally adjudged guilty and who when in fact guilty is only then accepted as innocent is, of course, the living embodiment of that disconnection between inner reality and external perception so central to Pirandello's work. The bitter comedies that are among the most important of Pirandello's plays are, without exception, based on an ironic interplay between things as they are and as they appear to be. And, indeed, the power of illusion to impose itself on reality and modify the very nature of a self, so significant an element in the plays, appears here with peculiar force, for Marta gives herself to Alvignani, not out of passion or gratitude, but almost without volition, as if to attain reality she has to enter into that image of her self as having yielded to him that has so dominated the minds of those about her.

It is the swirl of illusions those minds create that is the first material in the novel. It begins by showing the agonized reaction of Rocco Pentagora to the discovery, as he believes, of his wife's infidelity, then shifts to Marta's home and the stubborn rage of her father. Only gradually does the reader find himself centering his attention on Marta and coming to know her mind and her emotions. By shifting focus in the early pages of the novel among different points of view, Pirandello suggest the multiplicity of a reality existing primarily in the observer's apprehension. In the plays he will often turn to a *raisonneur,* developing this concept through elaborate philosophical discourse, but its germ is here in the changing viewpoints of the first novel.

However, the treatment of the heroine is the most characteristically Pirandellesque element in the novel. From the moment when Marta Pentagora becomes the center of attention till the book's end when, bitterly and even unwillingly, she gives up her thoughts of suicide to return to her husband, we see her as a creature existing in solitude. Although she is devoted to her mother and sister, she cannot communicate with their simple and commonplace natures. Driven out of her husband's house by ignorance and conventionality, out of her own by poverty, out of her teaching post by malice and envy, and finally out of the very town by vindictiveness, she bears her suffering in a solitude of mind unbroken even during her affair with Alvignani.

The state of near solipsistic anguish in which the only sure reality is that of one's own torment links Marta directly to the heroes of Pirandello's major plays, trapped within the confines of their own selves—more particularly their minds—and doomed to suffer there, relieved only by such self-generated illusions as they can bring themselves to accept.[16] In the anguish with which she recognizes the discontinuity between her inner image of an innocent self and the outer one of an adulteress reflected in the eyes of those about her, Marta anticipates the agony of Henry IV trapped in his identity as madman or of the Father in *Six Characters in Search of an Author,* forever defined by the scene of his shame in Madame Pace's brothel.

These anticipations of the later Pirandello in *The Outcast* suggest that the discursive element in the plays may have been considerably overrated. In fact, Pirandello could express with conciseness and simplicity the ideas he often develops in the plays at such ingenious length. His summary of them in the celebrated Preface to *Six Characters in Search of an Author* is as direct and precise as any:

> Each of them [the six characters] . . . expresses as his own
> living passion and torment the passion and torment which for

so many years have been the pangs of my spirit: the deceit of mutual understanding irremediably founded on the empty abstraction of words, the multiple personality of everyone corresponding to the possibilities of being to be found in each of us, and finally the inherent tragic conflict between life (which is always moving and changing) and form (which fixes it, immutable).

Since Pirandello's "ideas" are so easily separable from the body of his work and since their development, or at least their elaborate philosophic presentation, postdates by many years the appearance of the essential Pirandellesque vision of life in *The Outcast,* we may ask whether the plays are, in fact, about these ideas or whether they are about something far more central that the ideas, as parts of the plays, help to express.

Just as Pirandello, often thought of as an experimental playwright, is essentially a conventional craftsman,[17] so in a somewhat similar way, however widespread his reputation as an intellectual, he remains a dramatist of the emotions. For behind the brilliant facades of intellectualizing and theatrical trickery, his plays are essentially portrayals of man fated to languish in the prison of his own self. Indeed, what is central in the plays is the emotional anguish flowing out from that core in the form of impassioned confrontations, crises of love and jealousy, "operatic feelings and melodramatic climaxes," as Robert Brustein puts it.[18]

But this gaudy emotionalism is not the random expression of a tempestuous nature. The feelings in a Pirandello play, though they flow with great force, are confined to a very narrow channel, the central figures generally undergoing only two significant experiences: one is guilt and the other a very special kind of solitary suffering. Although the repugnance that some Pirandello characters feel at the force of their own sexual passion is not an invariable feature of his work, it is a submerged motif rising to the surface in certain plays. But even the discovery of the naked bestial self behind the external mask is less painful to the Pirandello hero than the mere circumstance of existing behind it. For that mask—the image of the exterior self—is an impassable barrier. If Pirandello is one of the romantic voyagers into the world of the inner self, he is not, like Freud and others, a true explorer of that realm. In that darkest of terrains he has had little more than occasional glimpses of sexual guilt. But he has sensed what it is like to live there. Ultimately, if not truly a dramatist of the intellect, he is a dramatist of the mind, a playwright who has known and projected the loneliness of the inner consciousness. (Significantly, in his later years when he deliberately abandons the inner world and attempts to deal with society, religion, and art in plays he called social "myths"—*The New Colony, Lazarus,* and *The Mountain Giants*—he produces some of his least successful work.) In the world of the Italian bourgeoisie that he usually inhabits the typical Pirandello hero is not often in a position to assume the Byronic stance, alone on the mountaintop (though Henry IV comes close), but he is nonetheless a romantic exile, if not driven by his mind, yet isolated within its confines.

The devices of what was to be called the absurdist theatre were not yet readily available to express this sense of isolation; in any case, Pirandello was not an experimentally inclined playwright. It is accordingly the intellectual concepts that serve to convey the disconnection between external and internal realms on which Pirandello's writing centers. In speaking of "the deceit of mutual understanding irremediably founded on the empty abstractions of words," he is saying less about language than about loneliness. When each of us is isolated by his own vision of reality, words cannot rescue us from the solitary reaches where such visions are formed. The concept of "the mutiple personality of everyone" is, from one standpoint, simply an extension of what Pirandello has already suggested. Since each observer has his own idea of the person he sees, there are in effect as many persons to be seen as there are observers, and no single self can be consistently known. Again, an essential isolation produces a failure of understanding. And from another point of view there is an even greater isolation within the self, since each man knows that at different times he has performed actions or manifested impulses that later he no longer recognizes as his. What greater solitude, Pirandello implies, than to be cut off by the flux of time from aspects of one's own self? Even when he deals with "the inherent tragic conflict between life (which is always moving and changing) and form (which fixes it, immutable)," Pirandello does not deviate from his central theme. With all its fluctuations, existence as it appears in his work is always the sense of lonely interior agony, and form is some exterior codification of it.[19]

But if Pirandello's conception of life—a failure of apprehension linked to some solitary suffering—remains constant, his embodiment of it varies richly from play to play. In certain of them the discontinuity between the world of external happening and internal feeling is, to a greater or lesser degree, bridged over. Some beneficial illusion is achieved or some mode of behavior established that allows life to be carried on with its suffering diminished or held in abeyance. These ironic comedies, which vary in tone from the farcical *Man, Beast and Virtue* to the near tragic *The Rules of the Game,* are the most significant of Pirandello's earlier plays. Around 1920, however, he began to turn away from this genre. *Six Characters in Search of an Author* (1921) used the very circumstances of theatrical presentation as the tools of expression. So convenient were these circumstances for his purposes—and so alluring the brilliant success of *Six Characters*—that he twice returned to them, in *Each in His Own Way* and *Tonight We Improvise,* making up the "trilogy of the theatre in the theatre," as he called it. But despite the renown of *Six Characters,* Pirandello's preference among his plays was for *Henry IV,* the most moving of the third group of works to be considered here, the tragedies of alienation.

The tragic implications of Pirandello's work seem at first far removed from the simplest and most direct of his comedies, *Man, Beast and Virtue* (it is in fact a broad and even rowdy farce), but the play is less atypical than it appears. Whereas the horror of the inner world becomes fully known to the heroes of the tragedies, the central figures of this comedy succeed by a desperate and ludicrous strategy in avoiding precisely that knowledge. The particular device by which the mask of exterior appearances is maintained seems to have had a remarkable fascination for Pirandello, since he had used it at least twice before. The situation in which a husband is induced to accept as his own a child of his wife's actually fathered by someone else appeared as early as the year 1904 in his novel *The Late Mattia Pascal,* in which Mattia fathers a child on the virtuous Oliva to prevent her sterile husband from claiming as his own a child Mattia had already fathered elsewhere. Twelve years later Pirandello reused exactly these materials in his Sicilian folk comedy, *Liolà.* When he returned to them in *Man, Beast and Virtue* (1919), the situation was much simplified, but the characters remained similar: a wife, described at any rate as virtuous; her lover; and a husband who must be induced to accept the child she is pregnant with as his. Unfortunately, Captain Perella, the husband, never has intercourse with his wife on his brief visits ashore, since he has already fathered a large progeny by his mistress in Naples and wishes to avoid any further household expense. After much farcical maneuvering, he is enticed into eating a cake containing a strong aphrodisiac. The next morning Signora Perella, who has agreed to give her lover a signal of success by putting a flowerpot in the window, happily if somewhat wearily carries five pots of flowers to the windowsill in token of the triumphant conclusion of their endeavors.

Yet Pirandello himself said this play was "tragedy stifled by comedy." And when it is looked at closely, certain characteristic touches begin appear. The blustering Captain Perella, so gruff and violent when he is with his wife at home, is, we find, meek and submissive when he is with his mistress in Naples. But the multiplicity of Captain Perella's selves is here only a humorous digression. Essentially, *Man, Beast and Virtue* develops from a typically Pirandellesque paradox, or series of paradoxes regarding appearance and reality in human nature and behavior. Although Signora Perella is described both at her entrance and, in the final words of the play, as the personification of modesty and virtue, she is at its opening two months pregnant by her son's tutor, Signor Paolino. He, in turn, though he lectures on hypocrisy to his "beastly" students, finds that he must basely dissemble and that to preserve the honor of his beloved he must even encourage another man to make love to her. Indeed, to stimulate the laggard interest of the Captain, Paolino personally applies to the face of his mistress—whom he habitually addresses as "my soul," *anima mia*—the makeup of a prostitute. Ironically, the coarse Captain Perella—"the beast," as Paolino calls him—whom these two ostentatiously pure and moral persons are endeavoring so frantically to arouse, desires nothing more than a night of the most chaste slumber.

The ultimate irony, however, comes at the end of the second act when Signora Perella hopefully disposes herself before the door of her husband's bedroom, accidentally assuming the attitude of the Virgin at the moment of the annunciation. Meanwhile Paolino, holding in his hand a pot containing a gigantic lily that is to be the symbol of their triumph the next morning, has himself fallen into the pose of the angel. At this moment Pirandello's comedy is at its harshest. The heavenly messenger heralding the Virgin birth is contrasted with the comic, mortal man frantically encouraging "virtue personified," who is herself pregnant though untouched by her husband. By the conclusion of the play the discrepancy between the external illusion of a virtuous self and the internal reality of a beastly one has been fully developed and the position of man, who longs to find fulfillment in the first but must acknowledge the power of the second, pathetically and comically delineated.

The tragedy behind *Man, Beast and Virtue,* which is "stifled by comedy," lies not merely in the possible discovery of the adulterous relationship between Signora Perella and Paolino but in the full confrontation with the beastliness within their selves they would then be forced to undergo. Because neither discovery nor confrontation occurs, this play can remain in the realm of farce. But in *It Is So! (If You Think So)* the interior reality comes much nearer to breaking through the surface of external life. Although still one of Pirandello's comedies, it has, therefore, a much darker coloration, deriving largely from those characters, Signor Ponza and his mother-in-law, Signora Frola, whose lives are led essentially in the world of interior emotion. Perceived as tragic, or at least as profoundly pathetic creatures, they speak always of their suffering, of what they have endured, of the violence used upon them, and they beg only to be left alone. On the other hand, those characters who live in the world of external fact are conceived in essentially comic terms. In the perpetual frustration of their fumbling attempts to find out the secret of the Ponza household, Councillor Agazzi, his family, and his friends become objects of ridicule, not only for the audience, but for Pirandello's representative on stage, Lamberto Laudisi, whose bursts of sardonic laughter conclude each act.

Laudisi's role, however, is open to misunderstanding, for it is less central than it seems. Although he is a *raisonneur* par excellence and spouts Pirandellesque ideas at every opportunity, he does not finally explain the play. When he tells the devotees of fact that because each sees the world with his own eyes, each inevitably sees a different reality, the dramatic point of the scene is not so much Laudisi's intellectual concept as in the emotional failure of those who cannot sense that an ultimate truth is unfathomable because evanescent. The quite direct explanations that he offers and the

harsh laughter with which he greets the successive failures of their
attempts to solve the riddle of the Ponza family serve mainly to
increase the disconnection between the world of external fact and
that of internal feeling. Indeed, early in the play Laudisi himself
suggests that he is less concerned with his ideas per se than with
the sort of attitude they should induce. "All I'm saying," he tells
Signora Cina, "is that you should show some respect for what other
people see and feel, even though it be the exact opposite of what
you see and feel." [20]

Yet Laudisi's admonitions to be charitable are fruitless. The fact
hunters continue to pry, but inevitably the tragic, interior world of
the Ponzas, delineated visually by the black that all of them wear,
remains impenetrable. Because Signora Ponza, by abnegating her
own self ("for myself, I am nobody. . . . I am she whom you believe
me to be") succeeds in defeating the ruthless and foolish curiosity
of the Agazzi group and in keeping alive those private, interior
visions of reality upon which, however agonizing, the selves of her
husband and his mother-in law depend, the play remains comic
and ends with Laudisi's laughter at the discomfiture of the Agazzi
circle and not with the terrible confrontation of interior feeling and
brute external fact that makes for tragedy in Pirandello's world.

However, Signora Ponza can play her contradictory roles because she appears only for a moment at the end of the play and
therefore need have no psychological reality. More fully developed
characters sometimes find that the roles they must enact (to bring
their interior lives into some bearable relation with the external
world) are themselves the sources of pain. Only when the role itself
is honorable and the circumstances around it congenial can it successfully bridge the gap between interior and exterior. In 1917 and
1918 Pirandello's mind was so occupied with this question that he
produced a group of four successive plays in which role playing is
central, *The Rules of the Game* being the most complex and successful of these.

The two most closely related of these plays, *The Pleasure of Honesty* and *But It's Nothing Serious,* are the two brightest in tone, for in
them the role, adopted as an external expedient, becomes an internal reality that relieves the central figure of the guilt associated
with his previous inner identity. A marriage of convenience turns
into a genuine union, and the protagonists realize themselves by

becoming the best aspects of the roles they have assumed. So Angelo Baldovino triumphs over a tormenting self ("You know I have this horrible beast in me," he tells a friend, "this creature I freed myself from by chaining it here in the conditions imposed by our agreement") to become what he portrays—he constructs himself, to use Pirandello's term—and find a measure of peace in winning the love of his wife. Similarly, in *But It's Nothing Serious* Memmo Speranza, disgusted by his meaningless existence, becomes the genuine husband he had hoped to avoid being by marrying a poor drudge (herself now also transformed by her new life into a charming woman).[21]

In the bitterest and most powerful of all these plays, *The Rules of the Game,* the role played is that of a husband, though here it leads not to salvation from a lost sense of reality but to total alienation.[22] Leone Gala, living apart from his restless, demanding wife, Silia, adopts the role of a complaisant husband, accepting with apparent indifference any demands made upon him. To Silia's uncomprehending lover, Guido Venanzi, Leone reveals that to survive he has been forced to cut himself off from external demands and the needs of the self, that his outward role is a defense against the pain endured in the inner world of feeling. "You must defend yourself," he tells Guido, "from others and above all from yourself, from the pain which life inflicts on everyone. . . . We make each other suffer all the time and nothing can be done about it. That's the way life is." Even though he admits to Silia that he is sometimes tempted to let himself be torn apart by one of the "beasts" of his emotions, he continues to "abstract" himself and play life as a game. Angered at his seeming indifference, Silia maneuvers him into challenging a dangerous swordsman, and Guido, to ingratiate himself further with Silia, becomes his second. At the moment of the duel, however, Leone, as a husband only in name, refuses to fight, forcing Guido, as lover in fact, to take his place and die for Silia's dubious honor. But though Leone has won the game, he has also, because of the scandal of his refusal to fight, locked himself forever within the ignominious roles of complaisant husband and coward. In the effort at controlling the relationship between inner self and outer appearance, the nearest thing to self-realization the Pirandello hero can adumbrate, Leone has "constructed himself" too well and must now, in the solitude of his tortured life, be the character he had impersonated. The exterior form has triumphed over the interior self, but its new realm is as hellish as the old.

It is no accident that in the first of his "trilogy of the theatre," *Six Characters in Search of an Author,* Pirandello should have an acting company briefly rehearse *The Rules of the Game,* for of all his works up to that point it is the most concerned with role playing. Here the Characters, irrevocably committed to the personalities and situations established by their author, will to a certain extent recreate the dilemma of Leone Gala, irrevocably committed to the shameful identity established by himself. Life has been shaped by Leone into a game with predetermined rules and by the author (the offstage character, not entirely congruous with Pirandello) of the Six Characters' story into an artwork, however abortive, with its predetermined forms; in fact, both of these shapings are Pirandellesque metaphors expressing the impulse, alluring but dangerous, to try to control the flux in which the self exists.

Whereas in *The Rules of the Game* the story of Leone Gala provided the entire means by which Pirandello expressed his vision, in *Six Characters* the actual story of the characters is only one of his tools. The earlier play had contained in Leone's decision to "abstract" himself from life that element disconnecting the interior self from the forms of the external world that is the hinge upon which Pirandello's drama regularly turns.[23] But the story of the Six Characters, as Pirandello originally conceived of it, did not place the disconnecting element in sufficient prominence. That element was originally inherent in the material of the plays that preoccupied him before *Six Characters (As Before, Better Than Before,* and *Mrs. Morli, One and Two):* the woman who reestablishes a relationship with her husband after living apart from him for many years. In both the disconnecting element lies in the fact that the lapse of time imposes differing personalities on her, especially in relation to her children, which she must reconcile with her interior self. When Pirandello returned to his material in *Six Characters,* his attention had again shifted—now to the Father and the Step-Daughter relationship—and therefore, though the anguish of the woman (the Mother in *Six Characters*) at finding she has lost her identity as mother to her eldest son is a significant factor in the play, the central element of disconnection is lacking.

Only when he conceived of his persons as characters cast off by their author and trying to re-create their drama for a group of incredulous actors did Pirandello find for his story a device that would reveal the gap between the external view of the action and the internal agony of those caught up in it. Now he had a form suited to his purposes, for not only did each Character have his private world isolated from that of the others but the total group of Characters, by the intensity with which it experienced the suffering of disconnectedness from the external world, constituted a cohesive unit of interior emotion that could be viewed only from the outside by the uncomprehending actors. Since they in turn are observed by the audience, the entire theatrical occasion becomes an arrangement of emotional intensities and isolations that rise in painfulness as the focus of attention descends further into the interior worlds of the Characters. As we move from the audience seated passively and comfortably in its chairs to the actors working at their trade and annoyed at being interrupted, then to the Characters as a group acting out their tangled, even melodramatic story, and finally to the individual Characters each crying out his private, interior agony, we are more and more engaged with a sense of suffering and even of emotional reality.

The development of this progression is one of Pirandello's central purposes in the play, since the interior realm of thought and feeling, represented by the Character, is for him always more significant than the external one of action and appearance. Indeed, the two things the Characters continually tell us about themselves—that they are real and that they suffer—dramatize the two things that for Pirandello are of the essence of man's interior life, that it is painful and that it is more real, more immediately felt, than the exterior. The paradox of the fictitious Characters, whom we apprehend as more solid and vital than the "real" actors, embodies in dramatic terms the Pirandellesque paradox of the unseen, ungraspable, eternally fluctuating interior life that is more substantial and significant than the plain, visible life of the external world.

But still more intense than the inner life of the Characters as a group is the existence that each of them leads within the closed circle of his own mind. Struggling to achieve such tenuous self-definition as he can conceive of, that of being known, each of the Characters attempts to impress upon the actors his own version of their story. In the failure of that effort Pirandello reveals the total isolation that cuts each character off from any external reality. Even the Son, though at first he disclaims any intention of defending his point of view, ultimately exposes the source of his grief and solitude. "What about my case?" he asks. "Haven't I had to reveal what no son ought ever to reveal: how father and mother live and are man and wife for themselves quite apart from that idea of father and mother which we give them? When this idea is revealed, our life is then linked at one point only to that man and that woman: and as such it should shame them, shouldn't it?" Cut off from his parents by the separateness of their identities, he feels with disgust that his existence derives only from the animal moment of conception.[24] The Mother, too, though like the Son comparatively undeveloped as a character, argues about the reasons for which she left her husband and insists that her sufferings are the greatest of all. But the burden of expressing the Characters' torment falls primarily on the Father and the Step-Daughter. Her implacable refusal to let the Father project his view of their story and the single-minded violence with which she cries, "I want to act my part, *my part,*" reveal that she is as isolated as the others. Most tormented, however, is the Father, for he understands the nature of his pain. "Each of us," he tells the Manager, "has within him a whole world of things, each man of us his own special world. . . . We think we understand each other, but we never really do."

Moreover, the Father must express not only his own isolation but the pain that comes to all of them from their situation as characters. "Our reality," the Father cries, "doesn't change: it can't change! It can't be other than what it is, because it is already fixed for ever. It's terrible." Pirandello's ideas about the immortality of art are hardly original intellectual insights (in a stage direction, he himself characterizes the Father's argument that a human personality, since it fluctuates in time, has less genuine identity than a fictional one as specious), but they embody in powerful theatrical terms his emotive sense that in man's interior world his suffering, fixed forever by memory, as art is fixed forever by its creator, never ceases to be fresh.

If neither of the remaining two plays in the theatre trilogy is as moving an expression of the Pirandellesque vision, each has special virtues as well as limitations. *Each in His Own Way,* for example, presents a remarkably complex arrangement of theatrical elements, including the audience in the theatre, an audience represented onstage, the actors as actors, the actors as characters, and the "real" people upon whose lives the play is supposedly based. Unfortunately, the central material of the play does not adequately support so elaborate a superstructure. Although the physical passion of Delia Morello and Michele Rocca, which has resulted in the suicide of her fiancé, binds them together in an agonized union resembling that of the Six Characters, its nature is not clear until near the end of the play when Rocca first appears and, seizing her, cries to the protesting onlookers, "Monstrous? Yes! But she must belong to me! She must suffer with me . . . with me!" Most of the play, however, is taken up with two young men who offer differing and equally erroneous rationales for Delia Morello's actions, reverse their views, and in their exasperation prepare to fight a duel. Their friend Cinci, the play's *raisonneur,* points out how men struggle to create a recognizable personality out of the flux of shifting apprehensions, but his deeper explanation of the "filth and muck and smallness" that lie beneath these constructed personalities has no correlative in the play until we see the animal nature of the relationship between Rocca and Delia Morello, by which time it has lost much of its dramatic force. In addition, the elaborate scenes designed to be staged in the theatre foyer, which culminate in the enactment of the climax by the "real" characters, come to little more than Pirandello's paying himself a dramatized compliment on his own psychological acumen. Essentially, Pirandello spends so much time arranging the masks of external illusion that hide the naked internal reality that the force of his ultimate revelation is largely dissipated.

In *Tonight We Improvise,* however, though the interior torment of the central character, Mommina Verri, is not fully developed until late in the play, it grows more naturally out of what has gone before. At the beginning, the grotesquely comic theater manager, Doctor Hinkfuss, delivers a learned lecture on the immutable nature of art as opposed to the eternal instability of life. This conflict, he claims, can be resolved only when a story (art) is presented onstage as an improvisation (life) under the control of a director as dexterous and imaginative as himself. But from the first, as his name might have led us to expect, things do not go well. Shifting in an out of their roles, the actors quarrel among themselves and with Hinkfuss, who desperately tries to convince the audience that everything onstage is controlled pretense. But, as the fictitious life of their roles comes to dominate the "real" actors, they become less and less amenable to Hinkfuss's direction, ultimately thrust him out of his theater, and play out their drama uninterrupted.

Here again, in outline, is the familiar Pirandellesque paradox in which the world of fiction becomes more real than the external world of actual persons and events. In addition, the drama that is finally enacted contains an even more intensely projected version of this same theme. Although pathologically jealous, Rico Verri has married a girl from a household in which, by Sicilian standards, extraordinary liberties were allowed, and now he is consumed by the fear that within the inaccessible reaches of her mind Mommina is betraying him in memory. Verri speaks of his anguish:

> You stand there looking at me, and what can I do? Can I lay your head open and look inside and see what it is you are thinking? I ask you, and you reply "nothing"; and all the while, you are thinking, dreaming, remembering, under my very eyes, looking at me all the time, and it may be that you have another there within, in your memory; how can I know? How would I be able to see him?

As the fictitious world of the story finally conquers the "real" world of the actors and the manager, so the fictitious visions of Verri's jealousy dominate his wife's faithfulness. At the end of the play, as her longing for self-realization is evoked for a moment in the envisioned performance of *Il Trovatore,* she dies confined within the prison of Verri's house, as man is confined within the prison of his mind.

The contrast between the passion and anguish in the interior story of Verri and his wife as opposed to the comedy in the exterior conflict of Hinkfuss and the actors is typical of Pirandello's use of the relations among characters, actors, directors, and audience to suggest the disconnection between the external and interior worlds as well as the solitude and torment that he finds in the latter. But in the vast majority of Pirandello's plays, which observe the conventions of realistic theater, other devices must project the disjunction of the inner and outer worlds. One of the most common of these is the introduction of a break in the continuity of a character's life so radical that he assumes, at least for others, a new identity. In the failure of this external identity to remain continuous with the character's inner self, that continuity being the nearest approach to self-fulfillment for such a character, lies the essence of Pirandellesque tragedy.

However, in *Henry IV*, the richest and most suggestive of the tragedies, the discontinuity between inner and outer selves had begun to appear even before the great break in Henry's life, the twelve years of genuine madness that confirmed in him the absolute separation of these two identities. When early in the play Donna Matilda and Belcredi attempt to tell the Doctor what Henry was like before his accident, they reveal, without quite understanding what they suggest, that even then he had a special self-consciousness encompassing a sense of the falsity of the external world and a longing to surpass the limitations of the internal one. Of Henry's curious manner Belcredi says, "He was often genuinely exalted. But I could swear, Doctor, that he saw himself at once in his own exaltation. . . . Moreover, I am certain it made him suffer . . . because that immediate lucidity that comes from acting, assuming a part, at once put him out of key with his own feelings." Meanwhile, Donna Matilda has spoken of the intensity of Henry's demand, ultimately a demand that she recognize his inner self, *allow it to enter* her consciousness: "But with him one couldn't joke. . . . When I laughed at him then, it was partly out of fear. One might have almost believed a promise from those eyes of his." As the play progresses, these intimations of his yearnings are developed. Speaking to his visitors in Act I, Henry weaves through his apparent ravings hints and suggestions that the Marchioness and her friends have constructed for themselves external facades that they need in order to get through life. They are, he implies, living a masquerade seriously, whereas he only does so jestingly. "But woe to him," Henry prophetically cries, "who doesn't know how to wear his mask, be he king or Pope."

Only at the end of the second act, however, does Henry fully reveal his perception of the self's tragic isolation and its desire to transcend that state and find realization in knowing and being known, thereby entering another world. But in the present mirror world of artificially constructed selves, each reflecting a different version of reality, no genuine meeting of selves is possible. One must hold on to the commonplace, external "truths," however contradictory, Henry tells his counselors, or suffer the knowledge that one is always alone:

> I would never wish you to think, as I have done, on this horrible thing which really drives one mad: that if you were beside another and looking into his eyes—you might as well be a beggar before a door never to be opened to you; for he who does enter there will never be you, but someone unknown to you with his own different and impenetrable world. . . .

In this speech the image of Henry standing hopelessly alone before his beloved merges with that of the excommunicate emperor standing in the snow at Canossa, desiring yet denied entrance, and becomes Pirandello's symbol of the self's ultimate solitude.

To escape from this world in which, incapable of ever being truly known, one lives successfully only by becoming the mask that others see, Henry turns to another where all is fixed and the mind need no longer feel itself lost, alone in a chaos of illusions. The immutable realm of history can offer a release from the uncertainties and perpetual fluctuations of human life. Even a tragic existence, Henry tells his counselors, can be beautiful when fully known:

> And sad as is my lot, hideous as some of the events are, bitter the struggles and troublous the time—still all history! All history that cannot change, understand? All fixed forever! And you could have admired at your ease how every effect followed obediently its cause with perfect logic, how every event took place precisely and coherently in each minute particular! The pleasure, the pleasure of history, in fact, which is so great, was yours.

As Henry's own description suggests, what is here called the world of history is, in its fixity, in the perfect organization of its form, and in the pure contemplation that it invites, identical with what Pirandello in other places calls the world of art. Here as elsewhere this world is a transcendent alternative, at once feared and longed for, to the ordinary human condition. Once again Pirandello's forte is not intellectual conceptions (the idea of history) but their use in dramatizing an emotion—here, as in Wilde and Synge, the longing to escape to a timeless, safely ordered universe (or one at least conceived as such).

However, the world of art, for Pirandello, again as for Wilde, is not an ultimate solution to the dilemma of life. Even if it were widely attainable, its rigidity would always exclude the fullness of existence, which is forever in flux. Henry himself hints at the end of Act I that, fixed in history as in a work of art, the self he bears weighs heavily upon him. Speaking to the Marchioness, ostensibly to request through her a favor of Gregory VII, he points to his portrait and asks that the Pope "take me away from them; and let me live wholly and freely my miserable life. A man can't always be twenty-six, my Lady." Moreover, when this world is not entered voluntarily or when it forces upon one a painful or degrading identity, it becomes a prison and one's role a masquerade like that Henry sees played around him in ordinary life. Nevertheless, when the representatives of the external world (consciously or otherwise, characteristically cruel) play their trick on Henry to restore, as they think, his sanity, his resentment drives him to contrast his deliberate madness favorably with what he calls the madness of the outer world where everyone plays his role without realizing it. "I am cured, gentlemen," he says, "because I can act the madman to perfection, here; and I do it very quietly, I'm only sorry for you that you have to live your madness so agitatedly, without knowing it or seeing it." But, carried away by his anger and by the power of his own fantasy (for a moment Henry seems to believe he has broken through time and the power of externality to seize fulfillment in the person of the Marchioness' daughter), he kills Belcredi, his rival and tormentor, and finds himself, the beauty of his dream already shattered, trapped forever in the role of a madman.

But where *Henry IV* can conceal the unbearable pain of his interior life beneath the beautiful trappings of history and art, Ersilia Drei, the heroine of *To Clothe the Naked,* can only cover hers with a pathetic lie easily stripped away to reveal the naked ugliness and agony beneath. While Henry's fantasy is a device to make life bearable, Ersilia's is designed only to give a momentary glamour to her death. When her suicide attempt is unsuccessful, however, she returns to life, as Henry had returned to sanity, and finds that, like him, she must confront the disconnection between interior and exterior realities that in Pirandellesque tragedy is fatal if it cannot be bridged. The story, which, supposing herself to be dying, she has told a newspaper reporter, has created for her a new self, that of a pure innocent cruelly betrayed by her fiancé and then, unjustly saddled with the guilt of a child's death, cast out by her employers. As Henry IV had linked the inner and outer selves by assuming in a fantasy realm of history the identity of the emperor, so Ersilia Drei wishes to assume her new self in the fantasy realm of art, the novel that Ludovico Nota, the writer who has taken her in, plans to make out of her story. "Let me be that other one," she cries, ". . . the girl you imagined. If just once I could be something! Just the way you said it was, in your novel, but with myself in it, exactly as I am!"

However, her attempt to attain the self that she has envisioned is a pitiable failure. Shortly after the appearance of Nota and Ersilia, an old man is crushed to death by an automobile in the brutal, turbulent street outside the writer's windows. Just so, Ersilia's fragile effort at fulfillment through identification with her new self is crushed and destroyed by the demands of the external world in which she has previously lived. "For you I might have succeeded," she tells Nota, "because I would have found a new life in your art. But you see, this other life, the life I tried to get rid of, won't leave me alone. It has me in its teeth and it won't let go!" As the layers of illusion are stripped away, the ugliness of her affair with Grotti is finally revealed. (The discovery of the lust of Delia Morello and Michele Rocca in *Each in His Own Way* has a similar effect.) With the emptiness and bestiality of the inner self nakedly exposed, Ersilia can only seek, and this time find, the death that had eluded her before.

Although the plays of Pirandello's last few years rarely achieve the richness of his best writing, one of them, *As You Desire Me,* is intimately connected with earlier ones and shares some of their theatrical vitality. The same inner revulsion that drove Ersilia Drei to invent a new self drives the Strange Lady of *As You Desire Me,* to accept the identification with the innocent Cia, lost in the turmoil of the war, and thus, she hopes, escape the disgust at her life as a café dancer and her liaison with the aging writer, Carl Salter (whose homosexual daughter is an additionally disquieting presence).

Turning away from the bestiality of the interior self and trying to find fulfillment in a new one, the Strange Lady, like Henry IV, creates an image, a work of art that stands outside the flux of time, fixed in a certain form. Pointing to the portrait of the former Cia, she says, "Yes—I am Cia—I am Cia!—I alone! I! I!—not she, the one who was, and—who knows—perhaps was not aware of it herself at that time—today like that, tomorrow what the accidents of life make of her. . . . Being? Being is nothing! Being is becoming! And I have made myself into her!" But the self she has so carefully shaped is, like Ersilia's, vulnerable to the assaults of the uncomprehending outer world. Neither the squabbling relatives nor even Cia's husband understand the validity of the Strange Lady's creation. When the vengeful Salter brings the real Cia, now a gross, mindless creature plucked from a sanitarium, the Strange Lady, not desiring to maintain an image that no one knows how to accept, returns to her former life, leaving to Cia's family the hideous reality that they so blindly desired.

Although *As You Desire Me* is well organized theatrically, certainly as Pirandello's plays go, it fails to project the inner life of the major character. Whereas the agony of Ersilia Drei clearly derives from the depravity she recognizes within herself, the corruption in which the Strange Lady claims to have been immersed appears not in her nature but, rather unconvincingly, in the grotesquerie of the Salter household. Usually, however, Pirandello does not doubt the reality of the inner darkness. We remember that Angelo Baldovino of *The Pleasure of Honesty,* for example, knows that there is a "horrible beast" within him that must be chained up if he is to live in decency.[25] But the function of Pirandello's art is not so much to reveal the depths of this inner world as the vastness of the gulf that separates it from the outer and that makes the expression of the authentic self so difficult.

This emphasis on the dissociation of interior and exterior worlds reminds us that Pirandello's dramatic roots extend back through the romantics to Shakespeare, most particularly to Hamlet, that "prince of the mind," as Erich Heller calls him, for whom nothing "could possibly be in perfect accord with his inner being. . . . Whether he were to kill his uncle or let him off, whether he were to make love to Ophelia or undo her with his cruelty, whether he were to be kind to his mother or thrust words like daggers into her heart—the action chosen would always, whatever he did, crudely diverge from the subtle and illegible text written within.[26] The connection becomes clearer as we recall that Pirandello's Henry IV is permanently interdicted from knowing or being known by his beloved, haunted by madness, undone by his own equivocations as much as by the schemes of his usurping rival, obsessed by his relations with an aging queen (*marchesa*, at least), and convinced that he could be happy bounded in the nutshell of his own fantasy.

Although the intellectual propositions Pirandello so seriously developed are in themselves of limited interest, they function successfully in a dramatic context to project that sense—partly inherited—of the painful, guilty solitude of human life. In the Pirandellesque drama where external appearance is an illusion shifting from observer to observer and even the interior self alters from moment to moment in the flow of time, man lives out his existence in an ultimate isolation where only his torment is immutable. Yearning to escape from flux, he dreams of being reincarnated in a new self that will have the absoluteness of a work of art. But this dream, this longing for a life of perfect fulfillment, can become actual only in death. In life Pirandello's hero must cling to his inner suffering; it is the only real world he will ever know.

Harold Pinter: The Retreat from Power

So striking is Harold Pinter's stylistic originality that on first acquaintance audiences often fail to recognize that his plays deal with familiar materials central to human experience and, inevitably, to literary art. After all, spectators very reasonably want to know what has happened, who the characters are, why they behave so strangely; and they may be pardoned if they are preoccupied by the sense of menace pervading so many of the plays and puzzled by the silences and seemingly inconsequential remarks punctuating the dialogue. But these characteristics, though they help significantly in giving Pinter's plays their special identity, their "unique touch," to borrow a phrase from Stanley in *The Birthday Party,* are essentially expressive devices, means rather than ends.

When Pinter refuses us certain pieces of conventional information as to the characters' identities or actions, he is not merely attempting to intrigue us or to suggest that people and lives are never entirely knowable (though that is part of what he means); rather, he is stripping away some of the concrete surface detail in order to expose the symbolic core. When, for example, Mr. Kidd, the landlord in Pinter's first play, *The Room,* says that he is not certain of the number of floors in his house or if his mother was Jewish, we need not suppose that Pinter is presenting a phenomenally absentminded householder and son, for we may recognize ourselves behind such surface eccentricity. Like Mr. Kidd, many of us are unsure of the dimensions of our part of the world, of how far our responsibility and authority extend; and whatever our mothers' backgrounds, we sense our separateness as congenital, feel ourselves as descended from an alien breed. Pinter, of course, is far from being the only writer to universalize his figures by removing certain particulars from them. Beckett and Kafka, avowed influences, come most quickly to mind, but in fact the origins of such a character as Davies, though probably less glamorous than those of Maeterlinck's Mélisande, are not more obscure.

Just as Pinter focuses on meaning by omitting certain elements in his treatment of character, so his removal of conventional continuity in language directs our attention to otherwise hidden material. Through the "holes" in Pinter's dialogue—the pauses and silences—the submerged fears and aggressions that more coherent speech usually masks become visible. Similarly the rambling stories and repetitive inanities are indicators of concealed emotional activity, often of a struggle for power. Thus, the squabble between Ben and Gus in *The Dumbwaiter* as to whether one should "light the kettle" or "light the gas" is part of the wider battle for authority that is finally settled by Ben's alliance with the ultimate power of the dumbwaiter itself.[27]

But of all the characteristics of Pinter's special style, the sense of menace that haunts so many of his works comes nearest to delineating their content as well. For the ultimate menace in Pinter's plays is not the threat of violence but the threat of meaning. Although the plays are full of hostilities, from the beating that climaxes *The Room* to the verbal duels of *No Man's Land,* the audience's disquiet comes less from the act or anticipation of violence (the ordinary "action" film produces no such feeling) than from the sense that through such occurrences the play is moving from the familiar, comparatively comfortable reality into a symbolic world where painful and frightening meanings are about to be made known. Again, in *The Dumbwaiter,* as the serving chute demands ever more exotic dishes from the fearful gunmen, we realize that Ben's desperate explanations are less and less plausible and that we have entered a world of symbolic fantasy. But paradoxically that world is an all-too-accurate representation of our own where, like Ben and Gus, we attempt with inadequate means to satisfy the irrational and implacable demands made upon us by unknown forces.

The reader or watcher of a Pinter play must be sensitive to these shifts from the realistic mode, for at those moments of symbolic expansion—when the action of the characters moves beyond the psychologically explicable, when the language assumes extra dimensions, when the menace suggests more than physical danger—the concerns of Pinter's work become most apparent. In all of his major plays the central figures have reacted to the threats of existence by retreating, or attempting to retreat to a protected world, to some place of refuge, most commonly a room. From the first, Pinter has portrayed the room as a shelter fiercely yet tenuously maintained against external assaults. Indeed, his initial words as a playwright, in the significantly entitled *The Room,* are a rambling monologue, not only about the safety of a room, but about the dangers beyond it: "No, this room's all right for me, I mean, you know where you are. [. . .] This is a good room. You've got a chance in a place like this." [28] From these first phrases on, this complex theme encompassing motifs of retreat and invasion has run through much of Pinter's work. In *The Birthday Party* Stanley has retreated to the shelter of the boardinghouse only to have Goldberg and McCann pursue him; Aston in *The Caretaker* has largely retired to the room that he will have to defend against Davies; the family world of *The Homecoming* will face the intrusion of Teddy and Ruth; in *Old Times* Deeley and Kate endure Anna's efforts to achieve a position of dominance in their secluded household; and in *No Man's Land* Hirst's alcoholic domain undergoes Spooner's desperate assault. Even in *Betrayal,* Pinter's sole full-length play thus far to shift the focus from the isolated household, the lovers' sheltered flat, the only setting to appear more than once, embodies a dream of fulfillment encroached upon by time and treacherous cruelty, not least their own.

Although the struggle for a room is the central action in Pinter's major plays, that room is only important as a means of delineating a state of mind, a special emotional condition. Those who have withdrawn to the room enter into a state of inaction, of passivity, that to some degree denies other aspects of existence. As a result of fear, incapacity, or trauma, they have ceased to long for any heightened self-realization and have attempted to remove themselves from some vital part of life—family relations, competitive striving, sexuality—and to lead a safe, if limited existence within the confines of their shelter.

If Pinter's rooms are realms of retreat and inaction, of passivity and sexlessness, the powers that intrude upon them come from other worlds that are usually more vital and more sinister, harsher and more potent. In the action that Pinter puts before us, the messenger of these outer worlds, with greatly varying results, rouses the self that has retreated from power into exercising it once again. But that self can no longer aspire to any exalted fulfillment—its dreams are only doubtful reminiscences of happiness or artistic success—and the power that is released is often cruel, always dangerous.

Recognizing the nature of the opposed forces in Pinter's work, one recognizes also a source of its characteristic aura of mystery. For ambiguity is always mysterious, and between such alternatives no clear choice is possible. The disintegrating lassitude that Stanley has lapsed into at the beginning of *The Birthday Party,* for example, is hardly preferable to the bumptious certainties and brutish sentimentality of Goldberg and McCann. To be rescued from apathy is to be destroyed by vitality. Inevitably, the very forces that draw one forth from retreat and safety, from childishness and inaction, are those forces—of hope, of desire, of will to action and power—from which one has hidden. These opposing tendencies are the self's mighty opposites, locked in eternal conflict. In each of his major plays Pinter projects in dramatic form a vision of this central battle between the vital and regressive aspects of the self, never losing sight of the dangers inherent in each.[29]

The Birthday Party is not only Pinter's first full-length play but the first work that conveys the entire range of his subject, characterizing both the impulse of the self to retreat as well as the action of those equally sinister forces that draw it back into the world. The embodiment of this regressive impulse, Stanley Webber, apparently a failed pianist, has taken refuge in the shabby home of Meg and Petey Boles where, treated as an adored though naughty child, he lounges away the days in inaction and safety.

To explain his retreat from artistic fulfillment, Stanley presents himself as the innocent victim of a conspiracy. Claiming to have possessed "a unique touch" as a pianist, he tells Meg that he once gave a concert that was a great success—"At Lower Edmonton." But even this dubious provincial triumph is denied him. "Then after that, you know what they did?" he asks Meg. "They carved me up. Carved me up. It was all arranged, it was all worked out. [. . .] They want me to crawl down on my bended knees." In the midst of his claims of innocence and victimization Stanley lets slip an apparently irrelevant piece of information. "My father nearly came down to hear me. Well, I dropped him a card anyway. But I don't think he could make it. No, I—I lost the address, that was it." Through this moment of doubt and fear, Pinter carefully associates the rejection of the family's central authority figure with the assault that almost destroys Stanley.

Although in the Boles household Stanley has found a surrogate family he need never fear, he has not escaped the cruelty he claims to have fled, for it resides in his own self. Frightened by Meg's casual announcement that two new visitors are coming to stay at the house, Stanley takes refuge in sadistic bullying of the childlike Meg, claiming that "they" are coming in a van with a big wheelbarrow looking for a "certain person." For the most part, however, Stanley's angers are visible only as an impatient tolerance of Meg's tickling, stroking, and hair-ruffling, the only sexuality he seems interested in. When the younger, more attractive Lulu appears, the pointlessness of his abrupt proposal that they go away together is immediately revealed by his tired admission that "there's nowhere to go. So we could just go. It wouldn't matter."

With the appearance of Goldberg and McCann, Stanley's world

of lassitude, petty hostility, and infantile sexuality is abruptly shattered by these embodiments of forces antithetical to his present life. Goldberg's first assurance to his nervous associate—"Do yourself a favour. Learn to relax, McCann, or you'll never get anywhere"—identifies him not only as a purveyor of vulgar commonplaces but as an advocate of the ambition and success Stanley no longer strives for. Even more striking is the contrast between Stanley's desolating and uncertain recollections of his father and Goldberg's assured, crassly sentimental reminiscences of his Uncle Barney:

> After lunch on Shabbus we'd go and sit in a couple of deck chairs. [. . .] golden days, believe me, McCann. *(Reminiscent.)* Uncle Barney. Of course, he was an impeccable dresser. One of the old school. He had a house just outside Basingstoke at the time. Respected by the whole community. Culture? Don't talk to me about culture. He was an all-round man, what do you mean? He was a cosmopolitan.

Besides these clichés of success and family feeling, Goldberg offers those of efficiency and business procedure. "The main issue is a singular issue and quite distinct from your previous work," he tells the questioning McCann. "Certain elements, however, might well approximate in points of procedure to some of your other activities." Not only is Goldberg a successful organization man, in contrast to Stanley, a failed artist, but he is a successful lover who confidently calls Lulu to sit on his lap and the night after the birthday party enters Lulu's room "with a briefcase" and teaches her "things a girl shouldn't know before she's been married at least three times!"

But the passage in which the power of Goldberg and McCann is most openly displayed, and their symbolic identities most directly suggested, is the examination scene in Act II. Standing above the wretched Stanley who crouches in his chair, bombarding him with questions, they become grotesquely inquisitorial presences. In the blurred sequence of questions even the most seemingly trivial ("Why do you pick your nose?") or unanswerable ("Who watered the wicket in Melbourne?") are disturbing and disorienting in their hints of childhood transgressions. Others suggest those areas of life in which we know or presume Stanley has been deficient: "Why did you leave the organization?" [. . .] "Why did you never get married? [. . .] "Do you recognize an external force, responsible for you, suffering for you?" [. . .] "Is the number 846 possible or necessary?" For Stanley in his withdrawal has abrogated any commitments to organized society, to social values and institutions, to religion, to coherent thought and intellectual effort. There is truth in Goldberg's ultimate accusation: "You can't live, you can't think, you can't love. You're dead."

Goldberg and McCann, the living embodiments of all that Stanley has retreated from—religion, patriotism, thought, duty, energy—of worldly life in fact, have come not, like the organizational assassins they appear to be, to remove Stanley from the living but to do no less than raise him from the dead.[30] But to survive in the world of the living to which they wish to restore him one must possess their attributes. That Stanley does so at least latently (he has repressed, not extirpated them) has been hinted in his treatment of Meg and Lulu in Act I and is confirmed at the birthday party in Act II. At the climax of the party, with its vulgarities and threatening hypocrisy, Stanley's repressions break down and he attempts first to strangle Meg and then to rape Lulu. With the lusts and aggressions from which he has hidden now exposed, Stanley is fully vulnerable to the messengers from the world in which the vital, dangerous self is to be actualized rather than concealed.

That world is admittedly a shabby one, its messengers vulnerable to rivalry and insecurities. Even McCann, whose monotonous tearing of the newspaper into neat strips suggests his mechanical (a Pinter pun on his name?) nature, tries to gain power over Goldberg by calling him Simey, a name from his childhood. (Pinter here anticipates Ruth's dominance of Lenny in *The Homecoming* by calling him Leonard, the name his mother used.) And though Goldberg's essential emptiness is revealed when he cannot finish the sentence "Because I believe that the world . . ." except with a series of irrelevant clichés, his adherence to these clichés gives him power in this world. When Stanley finally appears after their ministrations—clean, neatly dressed, but—like the glasses that gave him vision—broken, his speech reduced to gasps—they promise him power, health, and possessions:

GOLDBERG.   You'll be a mensch.
MCCANN.   You'll be a success.
GOLDBERG.   You'll be integrated.
MCCANN.   You'll give orders.
GOLDBERG.   You'll make decisions.
MCCANN.   You'll be a magnate.
GOLDBERG.   A statesman.
MCCANN.   You'll own yachts.
GOLDBERG.   Animals.
MCCANN.   Animals.

But the final repeated term betrays the grossness of their offer. If Monty, the name of the doubtful physician to whom they are taking Stanley, suggests a mounting up from the state of deathly apathy into which he has retreated, it also evokes a sufficiently threatening authority (perhaps to the British ear deriving from Viscount Montgomery, as famous for his vanity as for his military skill) to deter Petey from his well meaning but ineffectual, fatherly attempt to keep Stanley sheltered at home. Petey's last pathetic words to Stanley, "Stan, don't let them tell you what to do!" suggest that whatever the failures and limitations of Stanley's life it was at least an individual attempt to evade a surrounding power.

Another version of an exterior force invading a secluded household and drawing out the inner impulses of its inhabitants appears in the brief *A Slight Ache,* a radio play later televised and staged. Although the old matchseller of *A Slight Ache* never speaks, even after Edward and Flora invite him into their gracious house and garden, his presence enforces Edward's final degeneration and collapse while inducing the vital sexual burgeoning of Flora. When in *The Caretaker* Pinter again took up the figure of the tramp as invader, he also set the old wanderer in relation to two characters partly reminiscent of those in *A Slight Ache,* for one is remote and apathetic, the second full of worldly energy. But here, instead of the tramp's being a mere silent presence, the character is richly expanded, and the two brothers between whom he is placed embody fully the antitheses of the self.

Pinter has epitomized the impulse to retreat from the world of action and aspiration in Aston, who encompasses something of all the sheltered characters of *The Birthday Party*, the rambling incapacity of Meg, the protectiveness and inarticulateness of Petey, the haunting fear of a traumatic past associated with Stanley. To these characteristics is added Aston's Christlike charity. Pinter not only has Aston rescue the downtrodden Davies, give him money, clothes, and if not a garden at least a room to take care of, but he works some suggestive associations into the dialogue. When Aston explains that he is gathering material to build a shed, Davies asks, "Carpenter, eh?" A moment later Aston and Davies look out of the window at the "garden":

> DAVIES. Looks a bit thick.
> ASTON. Overgrown.
> DAVIES. What's that, a pond?
> ASTON. Yes.
> DAVIES. What you got, fish?
> ASTON. No. There isn't anything in there.

But no sooner have the Christian associations of carpenter and fish been established than Pinter adds another symbol, as Davies asks about the statue of Buddha. "Yes," says Aston in identifying it. "I quite like it. Picked it up in a . . . in a shop. Looked quite nice to me. Don't know why." But in this sterile world Christ no longer fishes for souls, and the Buddha is only an unidentified object. There is little fervor in Aston's Christian charity; rather the quiescence and withdrawal of Buddhism characterize him. Obviously Aston *is* in no direct sense either Christ or the Buddha, for Pinter is not allegorizing but by indirection making his characterization carry extra meaning, as he does when near the end of Act I, he makes Aston suddenly interpolate a story about a woman whom he had met casually in a café and who had abruptly asked, "how would you like me to have a look at your body?" But Aston's only comment on the incident is, "Yes. To come out with it just like that [. . . .] Struck me as a bit odd." The anticlimax produces at once a little burst of comic incongruity and a revelation that Aston's retreat is from all sexuality as well as from all coherent striving.

The experience Aston describes to explain his condition, being taken to an asylum and given a kind of brutal electric shock treatment, though it seems at first a very special and personal one, has familiar elements in it. In part it is reminiscent of what happened to Stanley after his concert at Lower Edmonton when "they carved" him up. In both cases there is the frustration of expressive self-fulfillment, for Stanley's pianism is analogous to Aston's speaking in the café or factory about his moments of insight: "everything got very quiet . . . all this . . . quiet . . . and . . . this clear sight." Moreover, in each case the denial of prophetic power is linked with some alienation from parental authority. Stanley's father was not at his concert, for Stanley had lost his address; Aston's mother had signed the release that allowed the authorities to operate on him. Thus, the trauma in Aston's past is not merely a personal horror but something as shadowy and suggestive as the terror of life from which Stanley is fleeing.

That the qualities Aston fears are in himself as well as in the surrounding world, Pinter suggests partly by revealing Aston's own angers and partly by embodying them in the character most intimately linked to Aston, his brother, Mick. As soon as Mick begins to take part in the action, he shows himself as hostile, energetic, argumentative. He torments Davies not only physically but mentally, with a flow of verbiage reminiscent in its power and incoherence of the onrush of questions with which Goldberg and McCann assaulted Stanley. Mick attacks Davies's sense of identity by repeatedly asking his name and insisting that the tramp resembles first the brother of Mick's uncle, then someone else Mick knew, and by entangling each of these personages in an unintelligible blur of events and place names.[31]

> You know, believe it or not, you've got a funny kind of resemblance to a bloke I once knew in Shoreditch. Actually he lived in Aldgate. I was staying with a cousin in Camden Town. This chap, he used to have a pitch in Finsbury Park, just by the bus depot.

The effect of these words is to thrust at Davies the truth of his existence as eternal tramp and wanderer. Moreover, when Mick offers to rent or sell him the apartment on ever more exorbitant terms, Davies's utter inability to cope with a world of contracts and decisions is grotesquely and sadistically emphasized. Indeed, the outpouring of exuberantly incoherent jargon—"down pay-

ments, back payments, family allowances, bonus schemes, re-
mission of term for good behavior, six months lease, yearly
examination of the relevant archives, tea laid on"—suggests that
Mick himself may not have full control of his own fantasy.

Mick, after all, is no more than a tradesman with a van. His
dream vision of a special world—the decorated apartment—in Act
III is only a jumble of details from home furnishings magazines:

> You could put the dining-room across the landing, see? Yes.
> Venetian blinds on the window, cork floor, cork tiles. You
> could have an off-white pile linen rug, a table in . . . in af-
> romosia teak veneer, sideboard with matt black drawers,
> curved chairs with cushioned seats, armchairs in oatmeal
> tweed, a beech frame settee with woven sea-grass seat, white-
> topped heat-resistant coffee table, white tile surround.
> Yes. [. . .]

Enraptured by the picture of this "palace," Davies asks who would
live there. "I would," Mick replies. "My brother and me." For the
vulgar decorator's dream, the crude reward of an imagined worldly
success, is also Mick's vision of a harmony in which the two opposing impulses embodied in the withdrawn passive brother and the
active aggressive one may come together in unity.

But their conjunction, evoked again near the end of the play
when, in Pinter's stage direction, the brothers are seen "smiling
faintly" at each other, is a dangerous one. Mick's aggressive cruelty
and Aston's frigid remoteness ultimately destroy the creature
whose divided nature makes him a prey to the extremes the brothers embody. For Davies is the fulcrum upon which the play is
balanced. As its central characterization, fully and richly developed, he partakes both of Aston's impulse to retreat and of
Mick's shabby and restless ambition. Like Aston, whose former self
has been destroyed in the asylum, Davies's real self has also been
lost, somehow, in the course of his wanderings, left behind among
his "papers" with a man at Sidcup. "They prove who I am! I can't
move without them papers. They tell you who I am." But that past
self is irretrievably gone. When Aston asks him where he was born,
Davies's reply is a helpless stammer: "I was . . . uh . . . oh, it's a bit

hard, like, to set your mind back . . . see what I mean . . . going back . . . a good way . . . lose a bit of track, like . . . you know. . . ." Not only has Davies lost touch with his real identity, but, like Aston also, he has been injured by the institutions of the world. But whereas Aston's story of the asylum is grim and painful, Davies's story of the monastery where he had come to beg for shoes and was told to "piss off," is grotesque and ridiculous. But when, through Aston's charity, he is offered shoes, his querulousness mutes the pathos of his victimization as he finds endless reasons to complain—about the fit, about the lack of laces, about the color of the laces. It is not that Davies is ungrateful, though he is, but that more than shoes he desires the power that the ability to refuse grants him.

Something of Davies's affinity to Mick appears in this desire to exert power, to place himself in the position to choose; but his affinity with the sinister brother is even more apparent in the gift that Davies accepts. When he finds a red velvet smoking jacket in the bag of clothes Aston has brought him, Davies grants that it "ain't a bad piece of cloth," tries it on, even asks for a mirror, and finally admits that he "wouldn't say no to this." Pinter is not only observing that an old tramp may well like something glitteringly useless, but he is also anticipating Davies's attraction to the gaudy vulgarity of Mick's decorating schemes. For both Davies and Mick are susceptible to the desire to possess and to display.

Indeed the aggressive energy that in Mick expresses itself as a nervous ambition ("I got to think about expanding . . . in all directions. [. . .] I'm moving . . . all the time") becomes in Davies a mere nagging hostility and restless self-aggrandizement. Blinded by his conceit, Davies cannot understand the dangers in Mick's offer and, in fact, the dangers in Aston's offer as well. For just as Mick's teasing reflects a cruelty as great as Davies's anger, so Aston's charity masks a rigidity as fierce as Davies's own. Aston refuses to change beds or close the window; and when Davies will not change his sleeping habits, Aston thrusts him out. Offered the alternatives of Mick's brutal vitality and Aston's inhuman kindness, Davies tries to ally himself with Mick, to dominate and take possession. But betrayed by his own greed and weakness, Davies can neither accept the life of withdrawal nor cope with the life of energy and aggressions.

Exactly this second mode of life, however, is what the central figure of *The Homecoming* not only can cope with but must immerse herself in to survive. Like the heroine of the television play *The Lover,* Ruth finds that conventional domesticity cuts her off from a passional life (symbolized in both plays by sexuality) that she takes drastic steps to reestablish for herself. To do so Ruth takes a position at the center of her husband's family; for in *The Homecoming,* as opposed to *The Caretaker,* the intruder succeeds in gaining possession. Although at first this family seems a mere tangle of hostilities, it is in fact a highly patterned symbolic world.

The most immediately noticeable sign of this patterning is found in the semirepetitive names of the male characters, which group them into two units of three persons each; Teddy-Lenny-Joey forming one, Sam-Max-Mac making up the other.[32] Equivalents in each group reveal a further patterning. Mac and Joey are characteristically brutish, violent, more sexually active; Sam and Teddy, on the other hand, tend to be gentle, thoughtful, sexually quiescent. Between stand Max and Lenny, each partaking to some degree of both extremes, each giving his group its essential character. In fact, each of these groups encompasses the range of an individual self fragmented into separate parts that Pinter skillfully sustains both as symbolic entities and as characters. The self of which Max is the center is vital, emotional, a creator and victim of illusions; that with Lenny at its core is ironic, inquiring, more subtle in its aggression. Both, not surprisingly, are profoundly divided in their attitude toward women. For just as each male "person" is fragmented into three parts, so each woman—though embodied in a single presence—plays three different roles: wife, mother, and prostitute. The variety of reactions these differing roles induce in the men is the central concern of the play.

Crucial in expressing the meaning of the work, Ruth's intrusion and the reactions it provokes are as much symbolic as literal occurrences. For the play is not merely about sex or about feminine dominance [33] but, like *The Birthday Party* and *The Caretaker,* about the power of the brutal and passionate elements of the self in men and women—and the ability of these elements to defeat those gentler aspects of the self that attempt to retreat from, or impose some restraining order on, the realm of inner violence.

Although the nature of these elemental forces is revealed in part through Ruth herself, who is their victim as well as their agent, it is most precisely delineated in the male characters—in whom, as we have seen, aspects of the self are broken up into separate entities—and particularly in the younger men, the Teddy-Lenny-Joey group. At the extremes are the Teddy and Joey. The latter, an amateur boxer, is dull, brutish, functioning almost entirely in terms of the physical. Indeed, the emphasis on the body is suggested in the first words that he speaks, "Feel a bit hungry." The seemingly casual line is later picked up and expanded. After the pantomime of sexual intercourse between Joey and Ruth in Act II (though Lenny initiates the sexual contact, it is significantly Joey who consummates it), Ruth rises to her feet and suddenly says, "I'd like somthing to eat. I'd like a drink. [. . .] I want something to eat." At this point Joey's physicality is linked to the powerful and blatant sexuality later seen to be dominant in Ruth. Moreover, the final revelation of that sexuality's force in the open encounter of Joey and Ruth also reveals most explicity the nature of Ruth's husband, Teddy. As he stands holding his wife's coat and impassively watching her and his brother roll from the sofa to the floor still locked in their embrace, Teddy's dissociation from the passionate physical life about him, a dissociation as powerful in its way as Ruth's involvement, is abruptly made clear in an image of striking dramatic power. Up to now Teddy has seemed ambiguous in his attitude toward his family; anxious to see them yet frightened at the prospect. But now he takes refuge from the reality of physical need in a claim that his intellectual achievements put him in a world beyond that of his family. "You wouldn't understand my works," he insists to them:

> You wouldn't have the faintest idea of what they were about. [. . .] I'm the one who can see. That's why I can write my critical works. Might do you good . . . have a look at them [. .] see how certain people can maintain . . . intellectual equilibrium. Intellectual equilibrium. You're just objects. You just . . . move about. I can observe it. I can see what you do. It's the same as I do. But you're lost in it. You won't get me being . . . I won't be lost in it.

This speech confirms that Teddy, doctor of philosophy and college teacher, is the antithesis of his youngest brother. As Joey is the acting physical self, Teddy is the observing—and despairing—intellectual one.

But however much Teddy protests that he "won't be lost in it," he is inevitably connected with Joey's world of passion and physicality through Lenny, the middle brother. In his handling of Teddy and Joey, Pinter sustains a double sense of their existence as both symbolic essences (in the simplest sense, mind and body) and as fully realized characters. In Lenny, however, he develops no such dichotomy, for Lenny as the central personality, the full ego, partakes of both worlds.[34] For example, it is Lenny, as we have noted, who initiates the sexual encounter with Ruth; and Lenny continues caressing Ruth's hair as his younger brother, the physical self, embraces her while Teddy, the contemplative self, stands apart and watches. Yet it is also Lenny, himself intellectual and inquiring, who a few moments earlier has been taunting Teddy with theological and philosophical problems.

From the inability of the intellect to resolve central questions of human life stems the hostility that Lenny, as the full ego self, shows toward Teddy, who has withdrawn to a separate world (academic life in the United States: "the stimulation of it all . . . the Greyhound buses and all that, tons of iced water . . . and all that, on the old campus") or, at any rate, to a world dissociated from the lusts and passions in which Lenny has remained immersed.

But whereas Lenny's angers against Teddy are essentially interior ones directed against his own intellectual self, his angers against his father are directed outward toward a separate personality of a very different order, for Max, like Lenny, is a full ego self. Lenny, as we have seen, is subtle, mordant, thoughtful; Max on the other hand is coarse, blustering, passionate. And from Max's predominant emotionalism comes his tendency to sudden extraordinary contradictions, his disinclination to distinguish between external illusion and internal reality. Almost without transition he leaps from an idealized vision of family happiness ("I remember the boys came down, in their pyjamas, all their hair shining [. . .] and they knelt down at our feet, Jessie's and mine. I tell you it was like Christmas") to an image of domestic horror: "A crippled family, three bastard sons, a slutbitch of a wife." Through such sudden shifts Pinter projects the contrast between the surface world of benign order and the inner, usually concealed psychological world of violence and aggression. In abusing his wife, Jessie, and later Ruth, Max is attempting to negate one aspect of that violent inner world, the brute power of the sexual impulse. "She'll make us all animals," he says of Ruth. By becoming the family cook, he has turned himself into a sort of asexual—and therefore safe—woman. (When Max goes so far as to ask for an apartment in Soho like Ruth's, Lenny refuses, telling him, "You're sexless.") But ultimately Max, too, is in thrall to the power of the animal impulses. It is, after all, he who first suggests that Ruth remain with the family and who begs her to kiss him at the end of the play.[35]

Sam stands in somewhat the same relation to Max as Teddy does to Lenny, suggesting through his gentleness, his distress at the sexual infidelities of Ruth and Jessie, his occupation as a chauffeur—one who controls movement—that he embodies, however ineffectually, some elements of a guiding moral impulse. Mac is his antithesis, Max's unrestrained physical-sexual self. Although Max fondly remembers him as "a big man [. . .] over six foot tall," to Sam he was an "uncouth sodding runt." Yet Sam contradicts his own attempt to diminish Mac in size, and thus significance, when he comes forward, gasps "MacGregor had Jessie in the back of my cab as I drove them along," and collapses. Through this extraordinary symbolic image of the moral self helplessly observing the sensual-physical self debasing an idealized figure, Pinter affirms the inability of the moral self to enforce its demands for order and restraint just as he had asserted the corresponding inability of the intellectual self to come to terms with the passional impulses in the image of Teddy silently contemplating the sexual union of Joey and Ruth. Moreover, by placing Sam's revelation about Jessie at the point of Ruth's final commitment to the family, Pinter reinforces the conception of Jessie and Ruth as parallel wife-mother-prostitute figures.[36]

Re-creating Jessie's role in the next generation, Ruth suggests that its ambiguity is a permanent aspect of the human condition. Even Joey does not view her entirely in sexual terms. His rejection of the animal expression ("you can be happy . . . without going any hog") and his position at the end of the play, kneeling before Ruth with his head in her lap as she strokes his hair (a striking anticipation of Deeley lying across Kate's lap in *Old Times)*, implies that the reverence and affection granted the mother can never be dissociated from the lust aroused by the mistress.

Whereas in America Ruth has been only a wife and mother, in England before her marriage she had been a prostitute, a woman seen almost entirely as a sexual being. The tone of nostalgia as she tells Lenny of revisiting the house where she had been "a model for the body" prefigures her rejection of Teddy's world and acceptance of Lenny's; here though she is to continue as a mother-wife—"do a bit of cooking [. . .] make the beds," "scrub the place out a bit," "keep everyone company," as prostitute, she would also resume the lost sexual identity that is inseparable from the violence and aggressions of her adopted family.

Far from frightening Ruth, the elaborate stories of the beating of two women that accompany Lenny's sexual advances arouse her, for the world of violence and aggressions is also the world of sexual vitality. She quickly dominates Lenny by addressing him, like his mother, as Leonard. When he attempts to reassert himself by taking her glass, she says, "If you take the glass . . . I'll take you." Combining her erotic and maternal power, she invites him to "Have a sip. Go on. Have a sip from my glass. Sit on my lap. Take a long sip."

Although the homecoming of the title is ostensibly Teddy's, it is ultimately Ruth's, for Teddy, who cannot endure his family's world, must return to America; in Ruth the thirst for vitality, for sexuality and violence, having been aroused, can be assuaged only in the passional world of Teddy's family. As Lenny taunts Teddy with theological and philosophical problems, Ruth breaks off the intellectual conflict by suddenly calling attention to her sexuality ("I move my leg. That's all it is. But I wear . . . underwear which moves with me . . .") and then continues:

> I was born quite near here.
> *Pause.*
> Then . . . six years ago, I went to America.
> *Pause.*
> It's all rock. And sand. It stretches . . . so far . . . everywhere you look. And there's lots of insects there.
> *Pause.*
> And there's lots of insects there.

The comfortable America in which Ruth is only wife and mother is to her a dry sterile desert, a wasteland where insects but not human beings thrive. For Teddy, however, America is "so clean," while England resembles "the swimming bath down the road." "You know what it's like?" he asks, "It's like a urinal. A filthy urinal!" If America—the world of intellect and restraint—is to Ruth a desert of rock and insects, England—the world of sexuality and violent intensity of feeling—is to Teddy "a filthy urinal." Teddy cannot endure the aggressions and unrestrained emotions of his family's world; Ruth cannot subsist without them.

The ironic appropriateness of her choice is made apparent in the final scene when we find not only that is she to resume her identity as a prostitute but that Lenny is a procurer. (Their mutual imaginative recollection of the World War II Italian campaign hints at the remnants of an idealized romantic impulse toward self-fulfillment.) Max's protestations of family affection and the formal politeness with which Ruth and Lenny negotiate the terms of her employment contrast with the reality of lust, greed, and hostility dominating the scene, a contrast reinforced by Ruth's name with its biblical evocation of the woman who, after her husband's death, cleaves to his family and accepts their faith. By the end of the play, the non-vital Teddy is returning to the desert world of America; Sam lies unconscious; and Ruth, now embodying the full strength of the sexual impulse, sits relaxed in her chair while Lenny watches as Joey kneels at one side of her and their father at the other. Still desperately desirous, Max moans and sobs and finally cries, "I am not an old man. Do you hear me? Kiss me." Though "sexless," Max is still gripped by the power that Ruth has come to represent, the force not merely of sexuality but of all those blind, brutal, hostile impulses that, sweeping aside the restraints of intellect and morality, make their own claims on the self and offer their own sort of fulfillment.

As Ruth broods over her earlier life in England and feels it drawing her back, this central Ibsenite theme—of the weight of the past—emerges significantly in Pinter's work. But whereas in Ibsen the past is a largely chartered countryside through which one makes a sure, if tormented, journey to some point of illumination, in Pinter the past is a misty wasteland into which one makes sporadic forays, returning with fragments of insight and information that contradict and confuse as much as they enlighten. In the brief, actionless sketches *Landscape* and *Silence* Pinter links this theme to his persistent concern with the opposition between quiescence and vitality. Beth, the heroine of *Landscape*, is poised between memories of her lover on the beach who—whether or not he was her employer, the ambiguous Mr. Sykes—is associated with a gentle quiescence and the coarser, rougher presence of her husband. Similarly Ellen, the central figure of *Silence,* is unable to commit herself to the crude vitality of Bates and is rejected by the sensitive but apathetic Rumsey. In both these plays the characters, as we finally see them, have entered into a condition of actionless withdrawal, their lives dominated by a memory of the past that, however elusive and uncertain, has had a sinister power in shaping the present.

In *Old Times,* where the memory of the past is the central motif, the state of quiescence is associated with Kate, as she appears through most of the play. Not only has Anna described Kate's present condition of life as "a silence," but she says that Kate had always been a dreamer who would literally lose track of what day it was. Deeley, too, says that his wife "hasn't made many friends." He adds accusingly, "She lacks curiosity." And up until almost the end of the play Kate remains uncommunicative, remote, and enigmatic, while Deeley and Anna battle fiercely to possess her.

Even before Anna enters the dialogue, Deeley is aggressive and suspicious. When Kate, reminiscing about the past, mentions that Anna used to steal from her "Bits and pieces. Underwear," Deeley after a pause suddenly asks, "Is that what attracted you to her?" As Deeley and Kate speak, Anna has been standing apart—the past incarnate—visible on stage but not yet realistically recognized by the others, yet almost as soon as she joins the conversation, Deeley attacks her with a characteristic Pinter weapon, words. Pouncing upon Anna's use of the terms "lest" and "gaze," Deeley implies that Anna is affected and snobbish in her speech but suggests that his own is decisive and controlled. Nevertheless, Deeley asserts power by stealing her language. Reminiscing about Kate, Anna had described her as looking around and "flicking her hair." Shortly after, Deeley, talking about his first meetings with Kate, says that she "looked at me [. . .] flicking her hair back."

But his fencing with words is only peripheral skirmishing. The battle is joined seriously when Anna and Deeley vie with each other in singing snatches of old popular songs. The conventional lyrics inevitably become claims on and appeals to Kate:

ANNA. (Singing.) Oh but you're lovely, with your smile
    so warm. . . .
DEELEY. (Singing.) I've got a woman crazy for me. She's
    funny that way.

When this melodious rivalry is inconclusive, Deeley abruptly
launches his major attack. Like Lenny of *The Homecoming,* he tells
stories in which he possesses masculine power and in which women
are degraded or subservient creatures, for he is attempting not only
to fight off Anna but to force Kate to accept her status as his
possession. When Deeley tells us that on a "bloody awful summer
afternoon," he "popped into a fleapit" to see the film *Odd Man Out,*
the phrases denigrate both the time and place at which he met
Kate. Recalling that in the same neighborhood his father had
bought him his first and only tricycle, he at once trivializes Kate,
reducing her to a toy, and exalts her as a sacred possession to be
protected with childish savagery. Deeley's next words suggest the
fierceness of his attack even as they reveal some of the sources of his
doubts: "and there were two usherettes standing in the foyer and
one of them was stroking her breasts and the other one was saying
'dirty bitch' and the one stroking her breasts was saying 'mmnnn'
with a very sensual relish and smiling at her fellow usherette [. . .] ."
Although these surrogates of Kate and Anna are presented in the
lesbian relationship Deeley fears, the atmosphere is squalid and
one is hostile to the other—as if by magical transference Deeley
could make Kate angry with Anna. (There is even a touch of homosexual revenge in Deeley's passionate admiration for the performance of Robert Newton in the film: "And I would commit
murder for him, even now.") But Deeley's major attack comes
when he describes his meeting with Kate. As they were walking out
after the film, his remark about Robert Newton's acting initiated a
conversation:

> [. . .] and I thought Jesus this is it, I've made a catch, this is a
> trueblue pickup, and when we had sat down in the cafe with
> tea she looked into her cup and then up at me and told me she
> thought Robert Newton was remarkable. So it was Robert
> Newton who brought us together and it is only Robert New-
> ton who can tear us apart.

Deeley assumes an air of masculine contempt for the "trueblue pickup" and introduces a grotesque version of the cliché as to what "brought us together;" he nevertheless, ends with a warning to Anna (parodying yet invoking the marriage service) against attempting to "tear us apart."

But Anna's claims are equally intense, and Deeley's weapons are available to her also. She launches her counterassault on Deeley by describing how she arrived home one night, when she and Kate lived together, to find "this man crying in our room" while Kate sat silently on the bed. As Anna undressed, turned out the light, and got into bed, the man continued sobbing, then after a time stopped and came over to her; but, she says, "I would have absolutely nothing to do with him, nothing." The man left, but Anna says that later in the night she woke and saw him with Kate: "He was lying across her lap on her bed."

The story attacks Deeley's claims of masculine power (we accept the man as Deeley even before he performs these acts at the end of the play) by portraying him as abjectly humiliated by some personal or sexual failure. Moreover, it identifies Anna as an aspect of Kate—her vital, sensual self, from which she has retreated in her domestic heterosexual relationship with Deeley. No actual roommate—however possessed of sangfroid—is likely to retire quietly to bed under the circumstances Anna describes. When Anna will have "absolutely nothing to do with" the man who approaches her bed, she embodies Kate's refusal to grant Deeley the passionate arousal he desires and her willingness to accept him only in a submissive, childlike position, "lying across her lap on her bed."

In Pinter's work such symbolic relationships must always be assessed with care and tact. Anna is at once a real character and a symbolic presence. When Deeley, the "odd man out," stands by at the end of Act I and allows his wife to be possessed spiritually by Anna (as the two women drift into the life of the past), the scene, though more subtle theatrically, is only a little less startling than that in *The Homecoming* when Teddy stands by and allows his wife to be possessed physically by his brothers. In both cases the external act becomes symbolic of an internal psychological movement.

The moment in Act I when Anna and Kate are most strikingly identified comes in Anna's description of how they, "almost alone, saw a wonderful film called Odd Man Out." Anna's claim to have been present at the time Deeley and Kate met is not merely a challenge to the truth of Deeley's story by a lesbian rival but an assertion that, as an aspect of Kate's self, she has always been with them, just as she is actually, though not ostensibly, present onstage as the play begins. Indeed, the women's identities are further mingled near the end of Act II when Deeley, again telling a story, explains to Kate that he had met Anna twenty years ago. "She thought she was you," he tells his wife, "said little, so little. Maybe she was you. Maybe it was you, having coffee with me, saying little, so little."

At first this story serves as another of Deeley's attacks on Anna. When he describes her as having been a habitué of a pub called The Wayfarer's Tavern, "the darling of the saloon bar," and as having at a party allowed him to spend the evening gazing up her skirt, he is attempting to force a passive feminine role upon her and through her upon Kate who, he implies, was also at the party. In denigrating language Deeley describes Kate and Anna as having "chatted and chuckled," sitting "squealing and hissing" while he gazed at their thighs and stockings.

But Anna turns the material of the story to her advantage, telling Deeley that she was wearing Kate's underwear at the time Deeley looked up her skirt and that Kate, though she blushed when told, insisted thereafter that Anna sometimes borrow her underwear and then, as the two women sat in the dark, tell her "anything of interest" that occurred while she was wearing it. (Significantly, Deeley and Kate share a tendency toward vicarious sexual experience; Deeley only looks up Anna's skirt; Kate is a kind of voyeur at one remove.) By so adroitly turning the story in a new direction Anna warns Deeley that there is concealed in Kate a powerful sexual presence and hints that she is its embodiment.

However, Anna is not to be reduced to a single allegorical element, for her sinister grace and composure carry a range of suggestions. Not only does she live "on a volcanic island" with its hints of power and latent passion, but she has a villa high on a cliff and sails on a yacht. These evocations of *la dolce vita* are characterized by Deeley, whose speech shows traces of lower-class diction, as "a kind of elegance we know nothing about, a slim-bellied Côte d'Azur thing we know absolutely nothing about, a lobster and lobster sauce ideology we know fuck all about, the longest legs in the world, the most phenomenally soft voices." Anna, then, is at once an independent character, an aspect of Kate's inner self, and an embodiment of an impulse toward a luxurious sophistication, a corrupted ideal that Deeley both aspires to and fears.

But whereas Deeley, with his crude masculinity, is ultimately helpless, Kate, like Ruth, reveals herself at the end of the play as the true possessor of power. Although she has retreated from the urgency and corruption of life to the world of the countryside near the sea where "everything is softer" (indeed, she longs for a further retreat to "somewhere where you can look through the flap of a tent and see sand," a place reminiscent of Ruth's sterile desert in *The Homecoming*), nevertheless, when sufficiently threatened, she can assert herself. As the coveted sexual object she, too, has power over those who desire her, though Ruth's power lies in the promise of sexuality, Kate's in the denial. Kate has, in fact, the power to kill them; that is, by denying herself to them, she negates the life they would have through possession of her.

When the struggle between Deeley and Anna reaches its climax, Kate suddenly rouses herself and turns to Anna, saying, "I remember you dead." The line is in part her revenge on Anna, who had spoken of Kate as if she were dead in Act I, but it is essentially a reminder that Kate can deny Anna's existence, can withdraw from the life of passion she embodies. Kate continues:

> I remember you lying dead. You didn't know I was watching you. I leaned over you. Your face was dirty. You lay dead, your face scrawled with dirt, all kinds of earnest inscriptions, but unblotted, so that they had run, all over your face, down to your throat. [. . .] When you woke my eyes were above you, staring down at you. You tried to do my little trick, one of my tricks you had borrowed, my little slow smile [. . .] but it didn't work, the grin only split the dirt at the sides of your mouth and stuck. You stuck in your grin. [. . .] Your bones were breaking through your face. But all was serene. There was no suffering. It had all happened elsewhere.

Like Deeley and Anna, Kate is telling a story that gives her power. She has killed her vital but corrupt self and rejected its passionate appeals, its "earnest inscriptions." Despite Anna's attempt to maintain her identity with Kate through the "little trick," Kate affirms her psychic withdrawal. But Kate also uses a "little trick" to suggest equally her remoteness from Deeley's conventional heterosexual demands. By attempting to plaster his face with dirt she affirms that he, too, is dead to her. Although she accepted Deeley's proposal of a wedding and a "change of environment," "neither mattered." These figures remain forever as we see them in the moment of illumination—literal and metaphorical—at the end of the play: Kate, maintaining her equilibrium by living withdrawn in a psychic blur where nothing has shape or form; Anna, the passionate self, lying on her divan, dead and yet eternally latent within; and Deeley, humiliated and in despair—like Davies poised between intolerable opposites and unable to cope with either.

Old Times, with its subtlety and understatement (it is not less sinister than *The Birthday Party* or *The Homecoming,* only less violent), offers its particular variation on Pinter's themes and techniques—as indeed do other plays. *The Collection,* for example, anticipates *The Homecoming* in its study of the power of feminine sexuality and of an intruder's disturbing effect on a male household. *No Man's Land* echoes the latter motif and develops further the idea of a struggle for dominance conducted through stories of sexual power that began in *The Homecoming* and expanded to become a central action in *Old Times.* But the four plays considered here in detail give in their interrelationships a full sense of Pinter's concerns. Just as Anna—with her associations of passion, indulgence, and worldly power—is an ally of Goldberg and Mick, so Kate echoes the emotive withdrawal of Stanley, Aston, and Teddy. Confronting these two women, Deeley evokes the psychic state of Davies confronting the two brothers: one remote and withdrawn, the other full of worldly energy and visions of luxury. Moreover, like Mick and Aston, as well as other Pinter figures, Anna and Kate maintain a double existence both as genuinely personalized dramatic characters and as symbolic entities. If Mick and Aston, linked like Teddy and Joey by their relationship as brothers, suggest opposing aspects of the self, Anna and Kate, liked by their assumed relationship as lesbian lovers, embody the impulses of the self toward and away from sensual freedom and vitality that have always been at the center of Pinter's work.

Pinter, the romantic artist, knows the lures and threats of the liberated self. His plays embody the destructive as well as the gratifying elements in the urge to self-fulfillment through dominance, luxury, action, possession, sensual gratification. Davies of *The Caretaker* may be as near as Pinter has come to drawing a portrait of archetypal man; and though one pities Davies because he is weak, ignorant, lost on an endless journey, subject to age and death, one knows that the unbounded self-aggrandizement of so vain and dangerous a creature cannot go unchecked. Yet so pressed are Pinter's characters by the overweening demands of the self that they can only escape by withdrawing to some room—a world where they will be sheltered.

The theme of a sheltered place reminds us of the quest for a realm of innocence in the work of Tennessee Williams, but the greater modern playwrights have always confronted guilt more directly. And indeed Pinter's doubtfully protected room where aspects of the self struggle for dominance recalls Pirandello's prison of the inner self where bestiality lurks and which hostile intrusion threatens. If Pinter shares with Pirandello a sense of the self as profoundly vulnerable, as having retreated to its own confines, he shares with Ibsen a recognition that the menacing forces stem from within. The dream, so powerful in Ibsen, of fulfilling the self through some exalted ideal is hardly visible in Pinter. (Its sad remnants are discernible only in the unexpected vocations of Pinter's heroes: Stanley is a pianist, Aston a prophet, Teddy a philosopher, Deeley a filmmaker, Spooner and Hirst writers.) But the opposite tendency in Ibsen, to aggrandizement of the self through gratification, appears in Pinter as that impulse to dominance, sensuality, and power from which so many of Pinter's heroes are impelled to retreat. Such confluences in the work of writers apparently so disparate remind us again of the underlying unity in the drama of our age.

Afterword

The Doctor performs the experiment . . . and transforms the dying man into a thing of beauty. . . . Peeling the scalp away neatly. Carving out the stickiness and placing cool summer breezes inside. In place of the hair goes a grassy field with a few dandelions falling toward the back.

The Doctor is torn by desires that cut through his brain as he leads the hysterical mob on the trail of the beast he once loved. . . . The mob is confused and frightened without the Doctor. They become enraged and set the forest on fire. Doc . . . finds a narrow stream . . . and slowly submerges under the surface. He swims along easily . . . moving through flowing green plants and yellow goldfish. . . .

They've crossed the river and picked up his trail. Doc pries loose a boulder and lets it crash down the side. His beautiful hands are bleeding from clawing. . . . He squeezes in between cracks in the rock as bullets ring out and torches flare in the sides of his eyes. He uses his mouth to pull himself up, and his diamond teeth blind the mob with their flash. Doc must get there first and escape with the beast.

This hallucinatory passage from the conclusion of Sam Shepard's *La Turista,* however wrenched from the text as it appears here (I have condensed, ignored differing speakers, accompanying dialogue, and typography), nevertheless offers a glimpse of our subject in a different guise. Working with materials from popular films—the mad scientist and his monster from a Frankenstein movie, the pursuing posse from a Western—the most gifted of recent American playwrights evokes precisely the motifs we have been considering: the self transformed, the flight from a hostile reality, and the achieving of a visionary fulfillment, here through an archetypally romantic union with a beneficent nature. Moreover, the theme of the divided self that we have traced in plays from Wilde through Pinter is sounded once again, as the rational, scientific, "American" Doc becomes absorbed by the vital energy of the beautiful beast he has created. Having put "cool summer breezes" in the beast's head in place of intellectual "stickiness," Doc himself is drawn into a vegetative state, submerging "under the surface" into a world of "flowing green plants." But the ultimate vision of escape in the play is not this verbalized image but something more dramatically daring and more fragile: just before the final curtain, the hero, Kent, leaps through the back wall of the set, leaving the remaining characters to gape at his cut-out silhouette.

As the curtain descends upon Kent's disequilibrating departure to a realm beyond theatrical "reality," his release suggests a self no longer bounded by the humanly predictable. The various realizations of such special and separate realms in the modern drama have been a primary subject of this study. From J. M. Synge's evocations of Irish myth as a world of beauty to Pirandello's presentation of history as a world of stasis for his nameless hero in *Henry IV,* these realms have functioned as possible refuges for the self from the flux and pain of existence. Indeed, when these realms are at their most attractive and the self at its most exuberant, an ultimate fulfillment can at least be glimpsed. At other times, however, these worlds are sought in the flight from more devastating threats, the hostilities of external reality or, even worse, the destructive impulses within. Both of these aspects, of flight and pleasure, appear in the passage from Shepard where Doc/Kent flees the mob's anger and achieves, for a moment, a paradisical immersion in the natural world. This union with nature, startling in a play so contemporary in its style and concerns, is a clue to the ancestry of this world, for it derives, in part at least, from those fairylands, at once alluring and evanescent, that appear so often in nineteenth-century poetry. Heine, for example, in *Das lyrische Intermezzo* suggests this lure of an otherworldly place of birds and flowers: "Out of the old folk tales signals the pale hand, / singing and ringing come / from a magic land":

> Aus alten Märchen winkt es
> hervor mit weisser Hand,
> da singt es und da klingt es
> von einem Zauberland; . . .

But having glimpsed the land where the trees themselves sing the most ancient melodies, at the climax of his song the poet admits, though with his own characteristic wryness, that in effect, "the fancy cannot cheat so well / As she is famed to do." His has been an insubstantial vision: "Ah, that land of bliss, / I often see it in dreams, / but as the morning sun comes up, / it melts like empty foam."

> Ach! jenes Land der Wonne,
> das seh' ich oft im Traum,
> doch kommt die Morgensonne,
> zerfliesst's wie eitel Schaum.

Just so, almost a century and a half later, Shepard's hero finds only a momentary immersion in his world of water plants; then reality pursues him, and he must leap forth beyond the confines of the stage to another quest. However distinctive the tone and manner of this contemporary figure, escape and transcendence beckon him still.

J. M. Synge's Irish countryside, with its natural scenery and its peasants and kings, is hardly more than a step removed from

Heine's German fairyland. Almost as tenuously poised, it offers a refuge in beauty from the sense of mortality that haunted Synge's imagination. Similarly, Oscar Wilde's exquisite urban fairyland, the realm of dandyism, shelters the self from the threats of Victorian morality by its magical transformation of ethical into aesthetic values. Other longed-for realms appear in richer, more complex contexts. In Chekhov a future beyond the melancholy entrapments of the present may bring fulfillment; in Shaw it is to found in an exalted heaven of contemplation; in Giraudoux, whose *Ondine* returns us literally to the land of the *alten Märchen,* the self is poised ambiguously before a supramortal realm, at once alluring and disquieting. Although in all these writers the vision is directed outward, the sense of shelter or fulfillment associated with those realms illumines their symbolic function as aspects of the inner life—as states of the psyche. In Tennessee Williams and Arthur Miller, as the emphasis on psychic reality is intensified, the self desires to find or shape a world in which it is recognized as innocent. But for those dramatists who deal profoundly with guilt, the quest into the inner world is more problematic. Ibsen's heroes, drawn toward some realm of icy aspiration, are tormented by contradictory impulses to self-gratification; Pirandello's characters feel agonizingly the impossibility of making coincident the worlds of inner solitude and of external demands; in Pinter the inner self is populated by "animals"—beasts in Pirandello's term, trolls in Ibsen's—but here the central figures no longer aspire to idealism as in Ibsen or to be known as in Pirandello. The pale hand beckons the Pinter hero to a sheltered room, a desert of apathy and withdrawal, where he will be only dubiously safe from the forces raging in the self.

Resuming thus the material of this book, one sees how consistently, if with diminishing anticipation, modern playwrights have pursued the image of the "magic land," the visionary realm where the self might find, if not fulfillment, at least shelter from the assaults of existence. The variety of temperaments and styles observed here testifies to the richness of our century's drama, but equally notable is the commitment to an overarching concept. Heine's *Zauberland* has been many times transformed, from Wilde's elegant world of social artifice to Pinter's shabby rooms, as has the poet's romantic longing, from Shaw's resolve to ascend to the Life

Force's heaven of contemplation to Pirandello's will to control the image that the inner self presents to the outer world. Nevertheless, as the concluding leap in Shepard's play suggests, the realm on the further side of reality and the desire to attain it are still part of our dramatic imagination.

Notes

Introduction

1. I have used the term "romantic" both here and in the essays that follow with the knowledge that it is always ambiguous and sometimes disputed. In his celebrated essay "On the Discrimination of Romanticisms," A. O. Lovejoy argued that there was no single phenomenon properly called romanticism but only "various historic episodes or movements to which different historians of our own or other periods have, for one reason or another, given the name." Most students of romanticism, however, would probably accept René Wellek's judgment that there is in fact "a closely coherent body of thought and feeling" that the term identifies. That many of them would not agree on a comprehensive definition is not to the point, at least not here, for the characteristics I refer to as romantic are so regularly associated with the term as ot to be in dispute. That the self is essentially innocent, that the inner life is at least as significant as the outer, that self-fulfillment is to be desired, that progress is possible—these ideas, their wider implications, and the disillusion that followed the optimism they first engendered are essential aspects of romanticism and, as these studies will suggest, of the modern drama as well. Lovejoy's essay, originally published in *PMLA,* is reprinted in his *Essays in the History of Ideas* (New York: George Braziller, 1955); Professor Wellek's comment will be found in his study "Romanticism Re-examined" in *Romanticism*

220

Reconsidered: Selected Papers from the English Institute, ed. Northrop Frye (New York: Columbia University Press, 1963).

Chapter 1

OSCAR WILDE

1. Quotations from Wilde are taken from the *Complete Plays* (London: Collins, 1961).
2. Arthur Symons, *A Study of Oscar Wilde* (London: Charles F. Sawyer, 1930), p. 73. William Archer, *The Theatrical World of 1895* (London: Walter Scott, 1896), p. 57. This critical attitude is summed up most gracefully by W. H. Auden in his description of *The Importance of Being Earnest* as "perhaps the only pure verbal opera in English." Auden is on the verge of a further perception when he adds that in *The Importance* Wilde chose to "subordinate every other dramatic element to dialogue for its own sake and create a verbal universe in which the characters are determined by the kinds of things they say, and the plot is nothing but a succession of opportunities to say them." Unfortunately, he seems to assume here that Wilde's verbal art had achieved "the condition of music" (to adapt a phrase of Pater's that Wilde was especially fond of) and become entirely abstract. He does not consider the significance of a "verbal universe" as opposed to the other sort, or note that the "kinds of things" the characters say are startling and specific in their meaning.
3. Otto Reinert, "Satiric Strategy in *The Importance of Being Earnest,*" *College English,* 18 (October 1956): 16, 17.
4. In his review of the original production of *The Importance* Shaw noted the superficial resemblances to Gilbert, especially in the quarrel scene between Gwendolen and Cecily in Act II, as part of his complaint that he had not been "moved to laughter" by Wilde's play. What is curious here is not merely that Shaw was voicing a point so often to be raised about his own plays but that he and Wilde stood in precisely the same relationship to Gilbert: whereas a motive force in the English librettist is often an impulse of cruelty toward those who deviate from society's norm, a generative emotional element in both Anglo-Irish playwrights is their sense of social and psychological exile.
5. Although Matthew Arnold used the term "Philistine" (in *Culture and Anarchy*) to suggest primarily the narrow chauvinism and vulgar admiration of its own wealth and power in the English middle class of the late nineteenth century, I have taken it not only to refer primarily to the antipathy to beauty and culture that Arnold intended as well but to the moral, and especially the sexual, prudishness of the age, to which Arnold, whatever his sympathies, was not specifically referring. Moreover, I have extended the term beyond the middle class, to include the aristocracy.
6. Our first impulse is to admire the charm and wit of Wilde's dandies but to

insist that although the shabby mechanisms of his well-made plots might have been suitable for our grandfathers, they will not pass muster with us. In justice to late Victorian literary taste, it should be pointed out that this attitude was precisely that of our grandfathers. William Archer thought he had discerned an English Ibsen in the author of *A Woman of No Importance,* and even Shaw felt that Sir Robert Chiltern of *An Ideal Husband* had struck "the modern note" in defending his wrongdoing, but these examples are exceptional. Most of the Victorian critics grudgingly admired Wilde's wit and pointed out that his plots were compounds of various well-worn devices. (Wilde found the plays of Dumas *fils* a particularly useful sourcebook, borrowing Mrs. Erlynne's second act entrance in *Lady Windermere's Fan* from *L'Etrangère,* the situation of *A Woman of No Importance* from *Le Fils naturel,* and the misunderstood letter at the end of *An Ideal Husband* from *L'Ami des femmes.* Significantly, Wilde's borrowings appear in the Philistine parts of his plays but not in the dandiacal.) What was said about the society comedies when they first appeared is, for the most part, what has been said about them since.

7. *Oscar Wilde: Appréciation d'une oeuvre et d'une destinée* (Rennes: Imprimeries réunies, 1948), p. 355.

8. Of all Wilde's plays, probably the one that derives most immediately from his sexual life is the one that seems most remote from the modern age, *Salome.* Although Wilde might escape from Victorian London, he could not evade his self. A play in which the protagonist is destroyed for perversely desiring to kiss the lips of a beautiful, delicate male figure obviously derives from Wilde's own psychological circumstances. In fact, not only does *Salome* offer a figure, the sinner who is punished, remiscent of some in the society comedies, but in its gaudy embroidery of "poetic" language it has something analogous to, if less admirable than, the glittering wit of the plays of London life. In each case the language attempts to translate something morally dubious into the realm of art where it will be preserved from ethical judgments. An ingenious reading of *Salome,* also centering on the problem of ethical judgments, is presented by Richard Ellmann in his essay "Ouvertures to *Salome,*" originally published in *Yearbook of Comparative and General Literature,* no. 17 (1968, pp. 17-28, and reprinted in his *Oscar Wilde: A Collection of Critical Essays* (Englewood Cliffs, N.J.: Prentice-Hall, Inc., 1969), pp. 73-91. Here Ellmann suggests that two central influences on Wilde, his teachers at Oxford, Ruskin and Pater, are obliquely present in the play, the puritanical morality of Ruskin embodied in Iokanaan and the contemplative sensuality of Pater in Salome, with the doubts and fluctuations of Wilde himself reflected in the tormented figure of the Tetrarch Herod. Ellmann, too, finds a link between *Salome* and the comedies, observing that "In *The Importance of Being Earnest* sins which are presented as accursed in *Salome* and *unnameable* in *Dorian Gray* are translated into a different key, and appear as Algernon's inordinate and selfish craving for cucumber sandwiches." "Introduction: The Critic as Artist as Wilde," *The Artist as Critic: Critical Writings of Oscar Wilde* (New York: Random House, 1968, 1969), p. xxvii.

9. For a discussion of Wilde's admiration for Disraeli, see J. Joseph Renaud, "Oscar Wilde et son oeuvre," *La Grande revue,* 30-34 (1905): 403.

10. See Barbey's *Oeuvres complètes,* vol. 11 (Paris: Bernouard, 1927), and Baudelaire's "Le Dandy," in *Le Peintre de la vie môderne,* a section of *L'Art romantique* (Paris: Garnier, 1931).

11. The fact that all these dandies are titled is by no means coincidental. Since he should possess social as well as intellectual superiority in order to dominate his society, the Wildean dandy tends to inhabit the upper reaches of the peerage.

12. Writing a few years after my first comments on this subject, Ian Gregor also recognizes the difficulties in fitting the figure of the dandy into the comparatively realistic world of the society comedies. "Only in a *world* of dandies," Gregor writes, "will his [the dandy's] voice and actions become harmonious: a world where the categories of serious and frivolous will no longer apply. . . . The dandy can exist fully only in a world of idyll, or pure play." Though Gregor does not recognize the sinister element in dandyism or the explicit meaning in Wilde's wit, he does point out the essentially aesthetic nature of the world of dandyism. "Comedy and Oscar Wilde," *Sewanee Review* 74 (1966): 512. For my own studies on Wilde and dandyism, see "The Divided Self in the Society Comedies of Oscar Wilde," *Modern Drama* 3 (1960): 16-23, and "The Meaning of *The Importance of Being Earnest,*" *Modern Drama* 6 (1963): 42-52.

JOHN MILLINGTON SYNGE

13. A combination of prudery and thwarted patriotism led Synge's attackers very near to suggesting that somehow the depiction in *In the Shadow of the Glen* of a peasant girl discontented with a crass, cold, miserly husband or the mention in *Playboy* of a woman's undergarment could subvert the institution of marriage or demonstrate that the Irish people were unfit for home rule. The best accounts of the attacks on these plays are contained in *J. M. Synge* by David H. Greene and Edward M. Stephens (New York: Macmillan, 1959), pp. 143-49, 234-50.

14. It has been asserted that Synge's plays are not actually true to Irish life and language. A defense against this charge is presented in Alan Price's *Synge and Anglo-Irish Drama* (London: Methuen, 1961), pp. 28-51. But in any case, Synge's plays create through language a self-sustaining world of thought and feeling; whether or not the pattern of life and speech portrayed in them is precisely coincident with that of the Irish peasantry at the turn of the century is irrelevant to critical analysis or judgment.

15. W. B. Yeats, "Preface to the First Edition of *The Well of the Saints,*" *Essays and Introductions* (New York: Macmillan, 1961), p. 299.

16. Quotations from Synge are taken from *The Complete Works of John M. Synge* (New York: Random House, n.d.).

17. *The Well of the Saints,* though revelatory of the processes of Synge's mind (again the hero and heroine accept exile—indeed, even blindness—to retain

their vision of beauty), is the only one of his plays that is without artistic interest. If *In the Shadow of the Glen* is almost too concentrated, *The Well of the Saints* is too mechanical and too thin to stretch over three acts.

18. *Playboy* is full of references to the power of language. In *Synge and Anglo-Irish Drama,* pp. 176-77, Alan Price has assiduously collected a large number of them. Although he recognizes that Christy, Martin Doul, and the Tramp are artist figures, Price does not observe that the concern with art is central to Synge's work.

19. *The Poet in the Theatre* (New York: Hill and Wang, 1960), p. 111. Peacock, too, has observed the ironic quality in the dialogue of *Playboy* and the fact that art is the major concern of the play.

20. Maurice Bourgeois, *John Millington Synge and the Irish Theatre* (London: Constable, 1913), p. 228. Daniel Corkery, *Synge and Anglo-Irish Literature* (Dublin: Cork University Press, 1931), pp. 87-90, 95-96.

Chapter 2

ANTON CHEKHOV

1. *Chekhov the Dramatist* (New York, Hill and Wang: 1960), pp. 159-287 passim.
2. "Chekhov as Playwright," *Kenyon Review* 11 (1949): 226-50.
3. *Chekhov the Dramatist,* p. 42.
4. Ibid., pp. 272-73.
5. Daniel C. Gerould, *"The Cherry Orchard* as a Comedy," *Journal of General Education* 11 (1958): 109-22; Jacqueline E. M. Latham, *"The Cherry Orchard* as Comedy," *Educational Theatre Journal* 10 (1958): 21-29; Norman Silverstein, "Chekhov's Comic Spirit and the Cherry Orchard," *Modern Drama* 1 (1958): 91-100.
6. Introduction, *Six Plays of Chekhov* (New York: Holt, Rinehart, 1962), p. xx. In this essay all quotations from Chekhov are from this volume.
7. *Chekhov the Dramatist,* p. 168.
8. Philip Bordinat, "Dramatic Structure in Chekhov's *Uncle Vanya,"* *Slavic and East European Journal* 16 (1958): 195-210.
9. *Selected Letters of Anton Chekhov,* ed. Lillian Hellman (New York: Farrar, Straus, 1955), p. 315.

BERNARD SHAW

10. Edmund Wilson, "Bernard Shaw at Eighty," *The Triple Thinkers* (New York: Oxford University Press, 1948), p. 189.
11. Ludwig Lewisohn, "Shaw Among the Mystics," in *George Bernard Shaw: A Critical Survey,* ed. Louis Kronenberger (New York: World Publishing Co., 1953), p. 113.
12. Robert Brustein, who well understands the dichotomy in Shaw's work, maintains that his "socio-political-philosophical" aspirations impose "crucial restrictions on his art" by blocking the expression of its negative aspects. This study suggests, rather, that Shaw's art is made up precisely of the conflict

between these elements and that it draws its strength, as well as its weakness, from the tension they generate. See *The Theatre of Revolt* (Boston: Atlantic-Little, Brown, 1964), p. 209.

13. All quotations from Shaw's plays are drawn from the *Complete Plays with Prefaces*, 6 vols. (New York: Dodd Mead, 1962).

14. As he points out to Vivie that scholarships are established out of such money, he is—in the jargon of a later day—saying that the military-industrial complex has taken over the universities.

15. "Fool that I was not to make him a playwright instead of an architect!" Shaw exclaims in whimsical rage at the corruption of taste and judgment by the popular theater. ("The Author's Apology" to *Mrs. Warren's Profession*).

16. "The Making of a Dramatist (1892-1903)," Foreword to *Plays by George Bernard Shaw* (New York: New American Library, 1960), p. xxvii.

17. "Ibid., p. xxii.

18. *Collected Letters 1898-1910*, ed. Dan H. Laurence (London: Max Reinhardt, 1972), p. 415. Shaw often referred to Candida in his correspondence, always explaining that the ending represented the triumph of Marchbanks's maturity. But one of his letters, to a "disciple," Eva Christy, is particularly suggestive of his own divided feelings on the nature of that maturity. Although he begins by claiming that "To the poet the night means the transfiguration of the sordid noonday world by the veiling shadows of magical starlight into a poet's world," the dreamy indulgence of this Wagnerian vision of escape and tranquility gives way in the very next paragraph to the assertion that Marchbanks has achieved a kind of vigorous stoicism: "Eugene has realized . . . that life at its noblest leaves mere happiness far behind; and indeed cannot endure it. . . . Happiness is not the object of life: life has no object; and courage consists in the readiness to sacrifice happiness for an intenser quality of life." *(Letters 1898-1910,* p. 203.) A hint of Shaw's personal identification with Marchbanks's retreat into the poet's night appears in a letter written to Charlotte Payne-Townshend before their marriage and complaining, at once jokingly and seriously, of her possessiveness. Near the end of the letter comes a teasing but suggestive flourish: "It is close to midnight: I must stalk off into the path round the park, to embrace my true mistress the Night." *(Letters 1898-1910,* p. 25.) Ultimately, Shaw's marriage to Charlotte achieved something of the comfort of Morell's domesticity and the remoteness of Marchbanks's "heaven."

19. "Letter of 13 March 1897," *Bernard Shaw: Collected Letters 1874-1897*, p. 734.

20. Shaw's difficulty in achieving such a resolution is suggested by his very choice of historical personages in which to embody the qualities of the superman. In his major plays these figures of supreme vigor and competence meet, or are destined for, tragic ends: Burgoyne is defeated; Caesar is to be murdered; Joan is burned at the stake.

21. The most striking illustration of the Shavian self divided into disparate parts occurs in *John Bull's Other Island,* the play that followed *Man and Superman.* Although the play is too careless and discursive to be of aesthetic interest, it is extremely informative, and less about Ireland than about Shaw. In the

foolish and jovial Broadbent, who will marry Nora Reilly and organize efficient enterprises, is the activist; in the mysterious and saintly Father Keegan
is the thinker; and in Larry Doyle, who would like to find a country "where
the facts are not brutal and the dreams not unreal," is the sensitive, troubled
Shaw who is committed to working in the world but feels the futility of the
work.

22. *The Doctor's Dilemma,* which comes at this point in the chronology of Shaw's
work, leads to some medical byways that it is not appropriate to explore here
(they are well mapped by Roger Boxill in *Shaw and the Doctors* [New York:
Basic Books, 1969]), but it also offers us a variation on Shaw's great theme,
the choice between the common world and the higher Shavian one, appearing here—in highly theatrical form—as a medical choice between saving a
good man to work in the world or a good painter to offer a more beautiful
vision of it. Indeed, as the painter Dubedat dies, we hear again those characteristic suggestions of escape and ascent that we have often heard before: "I
don't want to live. I've escaped from myself. I'm in heaven, immortal in the
heart of my beautiful Jennifer."

23. One man in the play is sensitive to Hesione's charms and yet immune to
them. Mazzini Dunn's marriage was, like Shaw's, a "safety match" (as Hesione calls it in a pun that Shaw should have resisted), a release from serious
attentions of other women. Their flirtation is one of the most genuinely
gracious passages in the play:

> MAZZINI. . . . I have never been a favorite with gorgeous women like you.
> They always frighten me.
> MRS. HUSHABYE [*pleased*] Am I a gorgeous woman, Mazzini? I shall fall in
> love with you presently.
> MAZZINI [*with placid gallantry*] No you won't, Hesione. But you would be
> quite safe. . . .

An intriguing illumination, possibly of this relationship and certainly of the
play, is provided by the concluding paragraph of a letter written by Shaw to
Virginia Woolf in 1940 when Shaw was eighty-four and quoted by Leonard
Woolf in his autobiography:

> There is a play of mine called Heartbreak House which I always
> connect with you because I conceived it in that house somewhere in
> Sussex where I first met you and, of course, fell in love with you. I
> suppose every man did.

> always yours, consequently
> G. Bernard Shaw

The temptation to suppose that the endearing relationship of Mazzini and
Hesione owes something to that of Shaw and Virginia Woolf is so alluring

that no one need endeavor to resist it. See *Beginning Again: An Autobiography of the Years 1911 to 1918* (New York: Harcourt, Brace & World, 1963), p. 126.

24. Another hint about Hector's ultimate desire to transcend this world comes when Mangan threatens to rush out of the house and Hector teasingly says, "Let us all go out into the night and leave everything behind us." The echo of Marchbanks's "out then into the night with me" is suggestive, especially as it is reinforced a few moments later when Hesione leads Mangan out, saying, "Come, Alfred. There is a moon: it's like the night in Tristan and Isolde." Shaw himself had, as we have noted, called the night into which Marchbanks went, disdaining human happiness, "Tristan's holy night."

JEAN GIRAUDOUX

25. Giraudoux draws his subjects from so wide a variety of sources—contemporary life, classical legend, folklore, the Bible—that the variety of material, coupled with the ambiguity of the writer's attitude, tends to mask the regularity of theme. Jacques Guicharnaud suggests this apparent diversity in describing Giraudoux's plays as great debates "between war and peace in *La Guerre de Troie,* the love of a young man and an old man in *Cantique des cantiques,* the human and the supernatural in *Ondine* and *Intermezzo,* English morality and natural amorality in *Le Supplément au voyage de Cook,* sensual love and saintliness in *Judith,* man and woman in *Sodome et Gomorrhe.*" *Modern French Theatre* (New Haven, Conn: Yale University Press, 1961), p. 20. But behind these antitheses (and others, sacred and profane love in *Pour Lucrèce,* e.g.) stand Giraudoux's persistent opposites of which these are aspects.

26. In the Introduction to his volume of adaptations of Giraudoux, *Four Plays* (New York: Hill and Wang, 1958), Maurice Valency notes the conflict of ideal and real in some of the plays, though he seems to suggest that it is largely a metaphor for the condition of marriage. He does not point out that in Giraudoux the ideal is dangerous as well as alluring and that to see it is to look down as well as up.

27. This ambiguity is reflected in Giraudoux's celebrated style, the elegant whimsicalities of which are not ornamental but essential to his meaning. The typical Giraudoux witticism depends on the incongruous juxtaposition of the commonplace and the exotic. Thus, in *Ondine,* Hans, the knight errant who has been searching for giants in an enchanted forest, enters and at once complains that the rain has been running down his neck and getting into his armor. When we laugh, we are recognizing the disparity between the romantic, visionary world toward which one aspires and the pedestrian world to which one is confined.

28. Since many English translations of Giraudoux are either adaptations or extremely free versions, I have made translations following the text of the Edition Bernard Grasset, *Théâtre,* 4 vols. (Paris, 1958).

29. *La Guerre de Troie* dates from 1935. As a member of the French diplomatic corps with a special interest in Germany, Giraudoux was in a position to understand the coming catastrophe with particular lucidity.

30. A very different view of this play is presented by René Marill Albérès in his exhaustive study, *Esthétique et morale chez Jean Giraudoux*. Citing Giraudoux's admiration for Tolstoy, Albérès writes: "the war is fatal not so much because of its anecdotal pretext, the rape of Helen by Paris, but because it is inscribed in the economic and social conditions of the human world, which are not to be separated from the general march of the universe. This idea is that of Tolstoy in *War and Peace*." (Paris: Librairie Nizet, 1967), p. 396. When generalizing about Giraudoux's work as a whole, Albérès seems to recognize its central theme and the ambiguous attitude evoked (see, e.g., such comments as those on pp. 329 and 416-17), but when dealing with individual plays, he tends to make each a special case, as here, and to lose the sense of continuity.

31. An intriguing sidelight is cast on this moment of Electra's self-realization by Jean-Paul Sartre in his study of Giraudoux's novel *Choix des Elues*. Describing Giraudoux's world as "the world of Aristotle," one in which things exist in a series of absolute states independent of exterior determinism, Sartre says that in this world man "is at the origin of first beginnings: his acts emanate only from himself. Is this freedom? It is at least a *certain kind* of freedom. It seems, moreover, that Mr. Giraudoux confers another kind of freedom on his creatures: man spontaneously *realizes* his essence." "M. Jean Giraudoux et la philosophie d'Artistote," *Nouvelle Revue Française* 54 (March 1940): 351. It is doubtful that Sartre's view is very generally applicable to the plays, but certainly Electra's instant of spontaneous self-realization is by far the most existential moment in them.

32. Not only do four years pass between the production in 1939 of *Ondine*, with its wit, its pathos, its rich development of the characteristic Giraudoux fantasy, and the presentation in 1943 of *Sodom and Gomorrah*, with its darkness, its astringency, its harsh focus on a perverse destructiveness, but in Giraudoux's life, and the life of the world around him, major events occur. Giraudoux himself becomes minister of information in the Daladier government, and his beloved France is defeated and occupied. Under such circumstances Giraudoux's work, perhaps inevitably, lost the strength and richness that had marked it previously. (Even his postwar comedy, *The Madwoman of Chaillot*, owes something of its popularity to its comparative simplicity and sentimentality.)

33. See Agnes G. Raymond, *Jean Giraudoux: The Theatre of Victory and Defeat* (Amherst: Univ. of Massachusetts Press, 1966), pp. 99-121, for a discussion of the play as a political allegory.

34. One critic suggests that we may consider Lucile, Judith, and Electra "as moral figures, tragic for being excessive, and their dramas as moralities teaching moderation." To do so, however, is to limit Giraudoux's scope of perception and ambiguity of feeling. See Laurent Le Sage, *Jean Giraudoux: His Life and Works* (University Park: Pennsylvania State Univ. Press, 1959), p. 162.

Chapter 3

TENNESSEE WILLIAMS

1. All quotations from Williams's works are taken from the editions published by New Directions.

2. John Gassner, with whom Williams studied briefly at the New School in New York, sees social forces, such as the decline in her family fortunes, as central in Blanche's case and her marriage as gratuitous: "But Williams, unsatisfied with normal motivations, adds the causative factor of marriage to a homosexual which has not been established as inevitable." Yet such a view reverses the actual order of significance; the sense of social decay hovering over Blanche only echoes and symbolically enlarges her moral failure. See Gassner's "*A Streetcar Named Desire:* A Study in Ambiguity," in *Modern Drama: Essays in Criticism,* ed. Travis Bogard and William I. Oliver (New York: Oxford, 1965), p. 377.

3. Esther Merle Jackson suggests, perhaps a trifle grandiloquently, the wider implications in this shift in Alma's nature: "We watch her transformed, on the stage, from a Corneillian heroine, devoted to love, duty, honor, and chastity, to a Racinian woman, torn by insatiable desires and inner longings. Williams illustrates, in her personal disintegration, the crisis of modern civilization: its inability to choose, finally, between the lofty ideals of the humanistic tradition and the materialistic values given systematic explication by the great nineteenth-century determinists." One may doubt that this rather slight play embodies quite so momentous a cultural crisis, but there is no doubt that Williams wishes to suggest antithetical forces in conflict as well as particular personalities. See *The Broken World of Tennessee Williams* (Madison: Univ. of Wisconsin Press, 1966), pp. 137-38.

4. The handling of Big Daddy is of special, though peripheral interest. In her comments on the prevalence of the word "disgust" in the dialogue, Ruby Cohn also notes that "Big Daddy proclaims a sexual aversion to Big Mama, as Brick does to Maggie. As Brick voices his disgust, Big Daddy voices *his* disgust." Observing that Big Daddy has nevertheless fathered his two sons while Brick "will not touch his wife," she points to the contrast between "Big Daddy's acceptance and Brick's rejection of the lies that are life." See *Dialogue in American Drama* (Bloomington: Indiana Univ. Press, 1971), p. 114. But passing beyond even this aspect of the relationship between father and son, we may recognize a private fantasy—of the playwright's. Since Big Daddy almost certainly derives from Williams's own virile, overbearing father, the writer creates an imaginative circumstance in which he is loved by such a figure (who forgives him and perhaps even secretly shares his predilections) but in which he can simultaneously revenge himself for neglect and contempt by killing that figure.

5. Gilbert Debusscher provides an excellent summary of the homoerotic implications in the hero's linkage to his namesake, St. Sebastian. See "Ten-

nessee Williams' Lives of the Saints: A Playwright's Obliquity," in *Tennessee Williams: A Collection of Critical Essays* (Twentieth Century Views), ed. Stephen S. Stanton (Englewood Cliffs, N.J.: Prentice-Hall, Inc. 1977), pp. 150-53.

ARTHUR MILLER

6. Quotations from *The Misfits* and Miller's plays are all drawn from the editions published by The Viking Press. Citations of *All My Sons, Death of a Salesman, The Crucible,* and *A View from the Bridge* are from *The Collected Plays;* others, from the individually published volumes.

7. But there is every reason to suppose that Miller was trying to achieve something personal in developing this characterization. In *After the Fall* Maggie, whom Miller based on Marilyn Monroe, attempts desperately to combat her guilt by believing that she is "all love." This notion of transcendent innocence, though a rationalization for Maggie, remains central throughout Miller's work.

8. Denis Welland, arguing that Willy is the victim of his past rather than capitalism, points out that Howard's "ingenuous pride in his children" makes him indifferent to Willy as Willy's pride in his sons has blinded him to the virtues of Bernard. The equivalence is well observed, but Howard is also peevish and insensitive with his family as he is cruel and insensitive with Willy who, in the context of this scene, remains a victim. See *Arthur Miller* (New York: Grove Press, 1961), p. 54.

9. These psychological and thematic simplicities and inconsistencies may be instructively compared with the rich complexity of *The Wild Duck* (probably, in part at least, an unconscious source), which also deals with a businessman accused by his son of maneuvering his partner into bearing the blame for his own misdeeds.

10. Raymond Williams, more sympathetic to Miller's linkage of social and personal concerns, observes thoughtfully that "this establishment of significance after breakdown, through death, was the pattern" not only of Eddie Carbone but of Joe Keller, Willy Loman, John Proctor, and even of Gus in *A Memory of Two Mondays.* Calling this action "the heart . . . of Miller's dramatic pattern," he argues that it carries a social meaning: "the heroes of these plays, because, however perversely, they are still attached to life, still moved by irresistible desires for a name, a significance, a vital meaning, break out and destroy themselves, leaving their own comment on the half-life they have experienced." Unfortunately, the nature of that comment and why their life was not whole remain obscure. See Williams's "The Realism of Arthur Miller," in *Arthur Miller: A Collection of Critical Essays* (Twentieth Century Views), ed. Robert W. Corrigan (Englewood Cliffs, N.J.: Prentice-Hall, Inc., 1969), pp. 78-79.

11. Benjamin Nelson justly observes that although Victor acts out once again the crucial commitment of his life, the old furniture dealer, with his courage and vitality, is quite the opposite of Victor's actual father. Gregory Solomon has also paid the price for his life and recognized his own failure and even his

guilt. See *Arthur Miller: Portrait of a Playwright* (New York: David McKay, 1970), pp. 309-10.

Chapter 4

HENRIK IBSEN

1. Halvdan Koht, *The Life of Ibsen,* trans. Ruth L. McMahon and Hanna A. Larsen (New York: The American-Scandinavian Foundation, W. W. Norton, 1931), vol. 1, p. 24. Not only the tone of this comment but the circumstances under which it was made reflect the romantic style, for it was uttered on the top of a mountain. Ibsen had climbed to a summit near Skien accompanied by his sister Hedvig, the only member of his family aside from his mother for whom he seems to have had any genuine affection and whose name he afterward gave to the pathetic child of *The Wild Duck.*

2. All quotations from Ibsen's plays are taken from *The Oxford Ibsen,* ed. James Walter McFarlane, published by Oxford University Press. When in 1875 Ibsen published a second edition of *Catiline,* he wrote in the Preface that the play anticipated much in his later work, "the contradiction between ability and desire, between will and possibility, the intermingled tragedy and comedy in humanity and in the individual." The later works that Ibsen referred to included at that time only *Brand* and *Peer Gynt* of the plays that have made him a figure in European literature, but so coherently did Ibsen's mind and art develop that his comment remains applicable to the realistic plays still to come.

3. *The League of Youth* (1869) interrupts this chronology, but though differing in style, it is essentially a pendant to *Peer Gynt.* Indeed, Stensgaard, the orator who deceives himself and others, has been called Peer Gynt in politics. (Koht, vol. 2, p. 60.)

4. G. Wilson Knight, however, suggests that the hawk is Brand's fierce pride. *Henrik Ibsen* (New York: Grove Press, 1963), p. 22.

5. Other alternatives, as catalogued by F. L. Lucas, seem decidedly unlikely. *Ibsen and Strindberg* (London: Cassell, 1962), pp. 66-67. Brand's strivings, his determination to live by the demand of All or Nothing, have often been related to Kierkegaard's "Either/Or." A convenient discussion of this relationship will be found in Maurice Valency's *The Flower and the Castle* (New York: Macmillan, 1963), pp. 126-33. Brian Downs's *Ibsen: The Intellectual Background,* contains a fuller, more general commentary on Ibsen and Kierkegaard. (Cambridge: Cambridge Univ. Press, 1948), pp. 79-93.

6. From *Pillars of Society* (1877) to his last play, *When We Dead Awaken* (1899), Ibsen produced a play almost every two years. The exceptions are *An Enemy of the People,* on which he spent one year, and *When We Dead Awaken,* which took him three.

7. Essentially a social drama about commercial morality, its subject is by no means dated, but Ibsen's treatment of it is simplistic. Moreover his plot, Scribean and melodramatic, culminates in a psychologically dubious regeneration of the central character that is, as McFarlane and others have

pointed out, somewhat equivocal. (See the Introduction to vol. 5 of *The Oxford Ibsen,* p. 3.) The play's other theme, of stultifying provinciality, also remains valid but is hardly sufficient to make the work genuinely viable.

8. Rosmer's view is clearly meant to be received sympathetically, for it is Ibsen's own, appearing first in his jottings for *The Wild Duck* and then in his speech to the workers of Trondheim. See *The Oxford Ibsen,* vol. 6, pp. 431, 447.

9. The best-known discussion of Rebecca's sexual history is that of Freud, who develops Ibsen's hints of Rebecca's relations with her father and concludes that in driving Beata to suicide she had been reenacting her earlier life, in which she had displaced her mother and unknowingly become her father's mistress. "She stood under the domination of the Oedipus complex," Freud wrote, "even though she did not know that this universal phantasy had in her case become a reality. When she came to Rosmersholm, the inner force of this first experience drove her into bringing about, by vigorous action, the same situation which had been realized in the original instance through no doing of hers—into getting rid of the wife and mother, so that she might take her place with the husband and father." Freud shows awareness that the play is more than a dramatized case history, but he limits his discussion to the aspect of it relevant to his own work. The passage on *Rosmersholm* is in Section II, "Those Wrecked by Success" (the first part of this section deals with *Macbeth)* of the essay "Some Character-Types Met with in Psycho-Analytic Work." *The Complete Psychological Works of Sigmund Freud,* trans. James Strachey (London: The Hogarth Press, 1957), vol. 3, pp. 324-31.

10. F. L. Lucas's suggestion that Rosmer's appeal to Rebecca to commit suicide with him is not credible because "no gentleman would ever do such a thing" is an endearing instance of the humaneness of that distinguished scholar.

11. *The Oxford Ibsen,* vol. 6, p. 434.

12. *Hedda Gabler* also has a remarkable series of connections with *A Doll's House,* Hedda's vision of Lövborg being, to some extent, parallel to Nora's idealization of Torvald. I have commented in detail on these and other linkages in "Miracle and Vine Leaves: An Ibsen Play Rewrought," *PMLA* 94 (1979): 9-21.

13. See, for example, the strained attempt of Hermann J. Weigand (often a perceptive analyst) to equate the fire that destroys Aline's home with the Prusso-Danish War of 1864 in *The Modern Ibsen* (New York: Dutton, 1960), pp. 299-309. Readers interested in the biographical background of Ibsen's plays will find a full account in Michael Meyer's *Ibsen: A Biography* (Garden City, N.Y.: Doubleday, 1971). See especially pp. 403-23 ff. for a description of Ibsen's relations with Emelie Bardach, the probable original of Hilde Wangel.

14. Benedetto Croce, *European Literature in the Nineteenth Century* (London: Chapman and Hall, 1924), p. 336.

LUIGI PIRANDELLO

15. Domenico Vittorini. *The Drama of Luigi Pirandello* (New York: Dover, 1957), p. 368.

16. Compare the similar conclusions reached by Eric Bentley at the end of a different route in the Introduction to *Naked Masks* (New York: Dutton, 1958), p. xxvi.

17. The extraordinary influence of *Six Characters in Search of an Author* on the developing antirealist drama, especially in its first Paris production by Georges Pitoëff in 1923, obscures the fact that of Pirandello's forty-four plays only *Six Characters* and the other plays of the "trilogy of the theatre" *(Each in His Own Way* and *Tonight We Improvise)* go beyond the standard devices of the realistic theatre, and even these plays do not involve symbolic or nonrepresentational staging.

18. *The Theatre of Revolt* (Boston: Atlantic-Little, Brown, 1964), p. 285.

19. Adriano Tilgher, one of the most influential of Pirandello's critics, argues that the conflict between life and form is "the fundamental motif underlying all of Pirandello's work." For Tilgher the "crystallized Forms" of life, "the concepts and ideals of our spirit, the conventions, mores, traditions, and laws of society," are in perpetual conflict with "blind, dumb Life . . . darkly flowing in eternal restlessness through each moment's renewals." Although Pirandello was himself influenced by Tilgher's formulation (Tilgher's *Studi sul teatro contemporaneo* first appeared in 1923), it is doubtful that the notion of "life versus form" is an adequate summation of his work. Pirandello was certainly committed to the romantic vision of existence as a vast, indeterminate flux, but the sense of man as lost and isolated in that flux is nearer to his central concerns as a writer. The translation of passages from Tilgher's chapter on Pirandello quoted above is from *Pirandello: A Collection of Critical Essays,* ed. Glauco Cambon (Englewood Cliffs, N.J.: Prentice-Hall, Inc., 1967). Some discussion of Pirandello's relation to the intellectual and political forces in the Italy of his day will be found in the first chapter of Oscar Büdel's *Pirandello* (London: Bowes and Bowes, 1966).

20. Pirandello's collected plays are published in two volumes (vols. 4 and 5 of the six-volume edition of the complete works) by Mondadori of Milan (1958), but there is no complete edition in English, and about ten of the forty-four plays have apparently not been translated at all. Those available are scattered in various collections and in a few individual volumes published primarily by Dutton and Samuel French. The following contain the versions of major plays cited in this study:
Naked Masks: Five Plays by Luigi Pirandello, ed. Eric Bentley (New York: Dutton, 1958). [*Maschere Nude* is Pirandello's own title for collections of his plays; it is used also for the Mondadori edition.]

To Clothe the Naked and Two Other Plays, trans. William Murray (New York: Dutton, 1962).

Tonight We Improvise, trans. Samuel Putnam (New York: Dutton, 1932).

As You Desire Me, trans. Samuel Putnam (New York: Dutton, 1931).

A translation of *Man, Beast and Virtue* is available on microfilm in the Columbia University Library.

The Outcast, trans. Leo Ongley (New York: Dutton, 1935).

21. Between the writing of these plays Pirandello had made from one of his short stories a one-act comedy called *The License (La patente)* in which role playing is successful in a far grimmer way. Rosario Chiarchiaro, accused by his fellow townsmen of having the Evil Eye, finds himself so ostracized and impoverished that he can survive only by assuming the role of the malignant bearer of bad luck and forcing people to pay for his absence. But though the role brings him money, he is so trapped and isolated in the grotesque persona he had been forced to assume that he even comes to believe in it himself.

22. Although the usual English title is appropriate to the play, the original Italian one emphasizes more strongly the element of deliberate impersonation. *Il giuoco delle parti* means literally "the game of the roles." Like the nameless hero of *Henry IV,* the central figure of *The Rules of the Game* chooses to play a part in order to control his life and bridge the gap between the inner and outer worlds, but the chosen role takes command of his existence and traps him forever in his unendurable identity.

23. The "abstracting" of oneself from the flux of existence and committing oneself to a particular role—Pirandello is here a kind of primitive, protoexistentialist—makes dramatically, and especially theatrically, visible that discontinuity between inner and outer worlds that represents the general circumstance of human life as Pirandello sees it.

24. In his remarkable study of *Six Characters,* Eric Bentley, pointing out that Pirandello removed this speech from editions of the play after the first, says that it "links the Old Testament shame at the sight of parental nakedness with the Pascalian sense of hopeless isolation in an alien universe." Although Bentley suggests that the speech was deleted because of "Pirandello's wish to hide this scene" of the father as lover, he argues that nevertheless the family relationships in the play are fantasies of psychological guilt and that in asking the Director to embody him in a play the Father (for Bentley, the crucial figure) is seeking a release from an intolerable psychological condition. "Father's Day," *The Drama Review* 13 (1968): 57-72. Unquestionably, the material of *Six Characters* lies close to certain traumas in Pirandello's life. That the Father sends his wife away and almost has sexual relations with his stepdaughter reminds us that in 1919, two years before writing *Six Characters* (which had, however, been forming in his mind for several years), Pirandello finally institutionalized his mentally ill wife, one of whose jealous fantasies was that he was having an affair with their daughter. See Gaspare Giudice, *Pirandello* (London: Oxford, 1975), pp. 98-101.

25. Pirandello uses the image of the beast to represent the unconstrained inner self at least as early as 1908 in his monograph *Humor (L'umorismo)* in which he speaks of "the instinctive soul which is like a wild beast hidden deep in

everybody." (A translation by Teresa Novel of part of the last chapter of this work will be found in the *Tulane Drama Review* 10 [1966]: 46-59.) See the near surreal one-act play, *The Festival of Our Lord of the Ship (Sagra del Signore della nave)*, for Pirandello's most extreme presentation, in dramatic terms, of man as an essentially bestial creature.

26. *The Artist's Journey into the Interior and Other Essays* (New York: Random House, 1965), pp. 145, 143-44.

HAROLD PINTER

27. A detailed discussion of Pinter's language will be found in the chapter "Language & Silence," in Martin Esslin's *The Peopled Wound: The Work of Harold Pinter* (New York: Doubleday Anchor Books, 1970), pp. 207-242.

28. Quotations are from the Grove Press editions of Pinter's plays. Because Pinter often uses dots to suggest pauses, square brackets are here placed around dots that indicate omissions from the texts.

29. Here opposing aspects of the inner self in Pinter's vision (as in Ibsen's) are related to but not identical with the id and the superego. The vital self in Pinter is more than the unconstrained, emotive id, the regressive self less than the rational, moral superego.

30. In her early study of Pinter, "The World of Harold Pinter," *Tulane Drama Review* 6, no. 3 (1962): 55-68, Ruby Cohn pointed out that Goldberg and McCann were representatives of "The System."

31. Martin Esslin *(The Peopled Wound,* pp. 110 ff.) suggests that an uncle's brother who is not designated as another uncle ("But I never called him uncle," Mick says, "As a matter of fact I called him Sid. My mother called him Sid too. It was a funny business") is evidently the father and that part of *The Caretaker's* suggestive power comes from its evocation of "the battle between the sons and the father." Esslin's suggestion, though arguable and even defensible, seems peripheral. These hints are so obscure and, more important, Davies has so little emotional weight as a parental figure that the play's primary symbolic power must stem from other sources.

32. Mac and Jessie, though they do not appear onstage, are significant characters and integral parts of Pinter's conception. There is in fact another group of three male characters, the sons of Teddy and Ruth, who do not appear but who suggest the continuation, and thus the universality, of the psychological pattern that Pinter is delineating.

33. Even so perceptive a reader of the play as Bernard F. Dukore sees it essentially as a depiction of the triumph of masterful woman over "sexually ambivalent" men. "A Woman's Place," *Quarterly Journal of Speech,* 52 (1966): 237-41.

34. Davies and the two brothers of *The Caretaker* form a related, though by no means identical triad, with Davies as the connecting link between the two extremes.

35. See Dukore, passim, for interesting comments on the "sexual impoverishment" of the men in *The Homecoming.*

36. The very division of the male figures into separate entities increases the range of reactions to the feminine figures. To Mac, Jessie appears to have been no more than an object for sexual gratification. To Sam, despite his knowledge of her sexual nature, she remains an admired figure. To Max, who partakes of both these selves, Jessie is alternately the moral basis of his family and a moment later "a slutbitch of a wife."

Index